The Politics of Urban Water

CHANGING
WATERSCAPES
IN AMSTERDAM

Kimberley Kinder

The University of Georgia Press
ATHENS AND LONDON

© 2015 by the University of Georgia Press
Athens, Georgia 30602
www.ugapress.org
All rights reserved
Designed by Kaelin Broaddus
Set in 9.5/13 Scala by Graphic Composition, Inc.

Most University of Georgia Press titles are
available from popular e-book vendors.

Printed digitally

Library of Congress Cataloging-in-Publication Data

Kinder, Kimberley.
 The politics of urban water : changing waterscapes in
Amsterdam / Kimberley Kinder.
  pages cm
 Includes bibliographical references and index.
 ISBN 978-0-8203-4794-3 (hardback)   ISBN 978-0-8203-4795-0
(paperback) — ISBN 978-0-8203-4836-0 (ebook) 1. Urban renewal—
Netherlands—Amsterdam—Citizen participation—History—20th
century. 2. Urban renewal—Political aspects—Netherlands—
Amsterdam. 3. Urban renewal—Social aspects—Netherlands—
Amsterdam. 4. Waterfronts—Netherlands—Amsterdam. 5. Sociology,
Urban—Netherlands—Amsterdam. I. Title.
 HT178.N42A456 2015
 307.3'41609492352—dc23
                                                            2014036311

British Library Cataloging-in-Publication Data available

To my mother

Contents

Acknowledgments ix

Introduction The Politics of Urban Water 1

Chapter 1 Hippies on Houseboats 16

Chapter 2 Queers on Parade 35

Chapter 3 Heritage Buffs on Canals 54

Chapter 4 Planners on Harbors 74

Chapter 5 Ecologists on Islands 94

Chapter 6 Investors on Floodplains 117

Conclusion The Everyday Politics of Urban Water 139

Notes 149

Bibliography 167

Index 195

Acknowledgments

Several institutions provided financial support for the research and writing of this book, including the National Science Foundation (Grant No. 0903073), the Geography Department at the University of California, Berkeley, and the University of Michigan Society of Fellows.

This book would not have been possible without the interviewees in Amsterdam. Their advice and insights profoundly shaped the research trajectory as it unfolded.

The faculty at the University of California, Berkeley, provided invaluable support and guidance during the research and early write-up phases for this book. Michael Watts, Richard Walker, Teresa Caldeira, and Jake Kosek contributed most heavily to this work. Other influential mentors included Gill Hart, Paul Groth, Donald Moore, and Daniel Buck.

My special thanks go to Mick Gusinde-Duffy and the rest of the editorial staff at the University of Georgia Press, as well as to their anonymous reviewers, whose comments and advice elevated the level of analysis throughout the book. Similarly, at the University of Michigan, I owe a debt of gratitude to Rebecca Sestili for her sage publishing advice and to the members of the informal Michigan Society of Fellows Humanities Writing Group.

A small portion of this book appeared as a freestanding article in *Environment and Planning A*. The anonymous reviewers for that article provided valuable feedback that strengthened the project as a whole.

I presented portions of this book to several academic audiences between 2010 and 2012. The comments and questions I received from those audiences influenced the book's development. Conference audiences included attendees at several Annual Meetings of the Association of American Geographers, the American Society for Environmental History Conference on History and Sustainability, the Mini-Conference on Critical Geography, and the Biennial Conference of the Urban History Association. Additional audiences at the University of Michigan included the Michigan Society of Fellows, the Urban and Regional Planning Program, and the School of Natural Resources and Environment.

This book would not have happened without the intellectual and emotional support of my Berkeley cohort. Most notably, Jen, Greta, Sapna Alex, and Sarah: thank you.

At the most personal level, thank you to Ross, who was there through it all, Charlie, who arrived partway through, and Cora, who came in at the end.

INTRODUCTION

The Politics of Urban Water

The face of urban water has changed dramatically since the mid-twentieth century. During the transition from industrial production to service-oriented economies, waterfronts emerged as prime redevelopment sites across Europe and North America. City builders transformed defunct factories and harbors into festival marketplaces and mixed-use neighborhoods. These changes marked an important paradigm shift in the economic functionality of shorelines. On paper, this paradigm shift appeared swift and decisive, dominated by large-scale infrastructural redevelopment that integrated brownfield sites into the changing economy by creating new motifs of water-oriented living and leisure. In practice, however, reimagining water was a slow, winding process, punctuated by several small shifts and provisional appropriations that reworked the meaning of wet urban spaces. Moreover, new uses of water have continued to emerge, signaling that the spatial forms and political valence of urban water remain decidedly open-ended.

The stereotypical narrative of urban waterfront transformation crystallized in the early 2000s. Industrial-era economic growth involved the dramatic re-engineering of hydrological landscapes for shipping and manufacturing. Subsequent deindustrialization after World War II drained waterfronts of capital and labor power, leaving abandoned brownfields in their wake. By the century's end, real estate investors working through public-private partnerships had built new, ostentatious cultural centers and mixed-use neighborhoods in scores of cities, including, for example, Baltimore, Sydney, Toronto, and London.[1] These shorelines attracted elite workers and shoppers, and they gave older cities a new global face in the competition for future economic growth.

Case histories and architectural profiles of these spatial transformations generally read as top-down affairs with investors capitalizing on self-evident rent gaps in supposedly derelict spaces. Recent scholarship describing informal occupancy and provisional uses of these spaces prior to their redevelopment has successfully dispelled notions of waterfronts as tabula rasa sites.[2] These insights underscore the need for greater attentiveness to the formative role of cultural practices and regulatory structures—alongside market pressure—in processes of waterfront reinvention. The history of water in Amsterdam shows that shoreline sites of disinvestment only appeared as "rent-gap" spaces once alternative uses of those spaces became thinkable. Cultural movements and everyday practices that connected water to countercultural activism, heritage preservation, and ecological resiliency transformed the meaning of water and redirected the modes of waterfront development.

Amsterdam was an especially apt location to study these changes for several reasons. Amsterdam is famous as a water city. Its historic canals are a major international tourism attraction, and many prominent cultural institutions and elite neighborhoods face canals, harbors, or other water surfaces. Additionally, large-scale waterfront reconstruction in Amsterdam was proceeding rapidly during the early 2000s at the same moment that, internationally, architects and planners were heralding the imagined climax of the postindustrial water-oriented real estate development model. The ubiquity of water in the local landscape created heightened conditions of possibility for water to have especially deep and diverse cultural meanings and, by extension, for these cultural connotations to influence large-scale processes of waterfront transformation.

Using Amsterdam as an example, this book unsettles the master narrative of urban waterfront revitalization on three fronts. Beginning with a focus on the past, the book exhumes a genealogy of praxis that analyzes the most widely discussed social movements making provisional use of the city's shorelines in the decades preceding the formal, capital-intensive, infrastructural reconstruction underway in the early 2000s.[3] Next, the project foregrounds the social narratives of water that connected past cultural practices to subsequent waterfront investments, underscoring the influence of these narratives in enabling, derailing, and reorienting the process of waterfront transformation. Then the book evaluates future-oriented narratives that, since the early 2000s, have begun connecting water with a shifting set of political impulses that are replacing the site-specific focus of brownfield projects with a more generalized discourse of water-based urban growth involving larger geographic footprints and a wider range of political stakeholders.

Tracing this trajectory of Amsterdam water required looking beyond high-profile case studies of infrastructural reinvestment to foreground the diverse interaction of culture, water, and place making as it occurred in many locations, at many scales, and at many moments in time. Qualitative evidence of these entanglements came primarily from three Dutch-language data sources: local and national newspapers circulating in Amsterdam between 1960 and 2010; government-generated and government-commissioned reports from several administrative levels, branches, and affiliates involved in water-related decision making; and self-published pamphlets, letters, magazines, and booklets from the cultural groups informally mobilizing waterscapes during that fifty-year period. Additionally, secondary publications and a few interviews with select academics, politicians, and social advocates with special ties to Amsterdam waterscapes functioned as supplemental data, helping to clarify motives, histories, and spaces of interest.

Using these sources, this book explains how people bring urban waterscapes to life. Between 1960 and 2010, ex-hippy squatters and queer-rights advocates built makeshift homes and organized celebratory parades on water. Amateur historians and professional architects mobilized water in campaigns to define national identity and sell real estate. Environmental activists and government officials connected water to ecological resiliency and disaster capitalism. These actions put water to cultural and economic use, inspiring innovative forms of waterside living.

This rereading of water across time, space, and purposes underscored the pivotal importance of everyday social activism on a wide range of cultural fronts in enabling and shaping the transformation of urban waterscapes. The interwoven history of Amsterdam water recounted in the chapters that follow traces water's piecemeal ascent from a residual industrial space into a prime investment site through its association with alternative countercultures, heritage identities, and environmental innovations. Far from a swift, monolithic transition, the resulting water assemblage coalesced incrementally, skipping from place to place and from group to group in tangled processes of cultural activism and city building.[4] The slow interweaving of old practices turned to new ends generated friction, both among cultural subgroups and between cultural actors and real estate interests. Throughout this history, water remained decidedly multivalent, leading to unexpected conflicts that productively expanded the physical forms and cultural import of water in processes of urban transformation.

The Urban Water Paradigm Shift

In the early 1980s, Austrian philosopher Ivan Illich opened his now-classic treatise *H₂O and the Waters of Forgetfulness* with the story of an urban development controversy over whether to construct a small lake in Dallas, Texas. Illich supported the project. In his eyes, during the industrial revolution cities across the Western world and the waterscapes that once traversed them were "man-proofed."[5] This man-proofing occurred on an intellectual level, through the creation of scientific discourses that demarcated urban planning and hydrological engineering as the exclusive purview of professional experts. It also occurred on a physical level, through the construction of fixed steel and concrete city forms. City building experts buried streams and drained marshes to "tame" nature and increase buildable land area. Simultaneously, regional and national governing bodies paid engineers to straighten, wall, and dredge large bodies of water, such as major rivers and estuaries. These interventions enabled large-scale shipping and manufacturing, often at the expense of other informal uses or ecological functions.[6] The result, Illich lamented, was a dehumanized urban waterscape of engineering equations and subterranean tubes that ordinary residents could neither access nor alter. Illich's hope was that restoring shorelines, such as by constructing a small lake near the center of Dallas, could begin to undo the industrial infrastructure that had left water and cities so sterile.[7]

Illich's wish came true, at least in part. Scores of city building projects implemented since the 1980s have smashed the concrete walls and roads that once divorced residents from waterscapes. In cities across Europe and North America, streams have been excavated, marshes restored, and harbors revitalized. By the early 2000s, architectural and planning commentators were heralding water's supposed metamorphosis from its former isolation in sewers and shipyards into the celebrated centerpiece of countless festival marketplaces. The figural form of the redeveloped industrial port held an especially prominent place in the international city-building literature. Luxury retail centers, flashy entertainment venues, and elite-oriented live-work districts photographed against the backdrop of glittering coastlines became icons of the imagined completion of an economic and cultural paradigm shift that brought accessible waterscapes back into city centers.

The dramatic physical changes accompanying these projects, however, concealed a significant continuity between industrial and postindustrial waterscapes. The rehydrated cityscapes remained "man-proofed," at least in part. The financial cost of demolishing concrete embankments, remediating industrial pollution, and rebuilding the so-called naturalized shorelines and accessible promenades meant that investors with significant financial resources often monopolized redevelopment agendas. Excavated shorelines were locked in place, and their edges were lined with luxury shops and surveillance cameras. Only profitable plants and tadpoles were incorporated into development schemes, and children could only play in designated areas and in predefined ways. Environmental and civil society groups engaging with these processes often found their interests thoroughly subordinated to market-based profitability models.[8] Although these redeveloped shorelines made water "accessible" in that recreational boaters and strolling pedestrians could see, touch, and smell the water, market dictates, rather than everyday use, environmental concerns, or creative play, structured the modes of permissible human-water interaction and contained its possible reappropriation.

While recognizing that the expense of building large-scale infrastructure constrains waterfront investment goals during peak construction periods, stories from Amsterdam demonstrate that these processes, while important, constitute only one moment within an ongoing process of waterscape metamorphosis. Similarly, these narratives show that cultural actors have historically exerted significant influence over the timing, shape, and meaning of urban waterside living and that evolving water associations continue to emerge today. This interpretation builds on recent work in the field of urban political ecology that unsettles the dominant master narrative of urban waterfront revitalization by shifting attention from large-scale port redevelopments to smaller-scale, community-instigated initiatives.[9] These accounts recognize the heavy-handedness of market constraints, yet they also provisionally create room to see the cultural mediations that give water meaning. Using Amsterdam as an example, this book builds on these themes, analyzing the political plurality of water to illuminate the underlying kaleidoscopic interplay among culture, water, and real estate that has given rise to pluralized and unfinished postindustrial urban forms.

Learning from Amsterdam

Amsterdam, for several reasons, emerged as an especially potent location to observe the unplanned influence of everyday cultural practices on urban waterfront transformations. The ubiquity of water in Amsterdam was one important factor. Water in that city was never so thoroughly "man-proofed" as it was in other contexts. Dutch city builders attempted to modernize Amsterdam using many of the same water elimination techniques at work elsewhere in Europe and North America. Between 1828 and 1970, municipal officials filled seventy-eight canals in older sections of the city. Simultaneously, as the city's footprint expanded, builders used new technologies, such as hidden pumps and subterranean pipes, to reduce the need for surface drainage systems. Those practices reduced the city's land-to-water ratio compared to its preindustrial form. However, unlike in the United States, where most urban water disappeared behind concrete walls and into subterranean sewers, in the Netherlands, the regional preponderance of water, combined with the country's more limited economic resources, meant that water remained prominent in the everyday surface topography of Dutch cities. Canals, ponds, and small harbors never dipped below 24 percent of Amsterdam's total surface area, resulting in an astoundingly wet cityscape by mid-twentieth-century international standards.[10]

Waterfront housing, terraces, houseboats, and pleasure boats in Amsterdam, ca. 2013. ©iStock.com/badahos.

The ubiquity of water in Amsterdam amplified opportunities for people to have everyday encounters with waterscapes. In contrast to other cities where streams and coastlines had to be physically exhumed from their concrete tubes and embankment walls using capital-intensive demolition and reconstruction methods, interacting with water in Amsterdam only required a boat, a set of eyes, the ability to swim, or a moment of inattention when a driver or cyclist might accidentally fall in. Moreover, water was a privileged, if also commercialized, element in local folklore and artistic traditions. This physical arrangement, combined with the cultural circulation of water-based symbolism, reduced barriers to entry. Anyone wishing to interact with water could do so—at least to some degree—without having to physically transform infrastructure in deference to market pressures.

These encounters increased opportunities for cultural actors to make provisional uses of wet city spaces and turn them to new ends. Squatters made water habitable. Queers made it performative. Historians added narrative content. Architects encased it in iconic edging. Environmentalists naturalized its flows, and governments popularized its climate-related functions. These engagements added complexity to urban water debates while simultaneously revealing the lingering influence of earlier socio-spatial frameworks. Water was not a neutral surface. Amsterdam's canals, harbors, and lakes were enmeshed within an array of long-standing regulatory structures, social policies, and environmental attitudes that did not easily relinquish their hold on wet city spaces either to cultural actors or to real estate interests. Even so, provisional mobilizations loosened water both from its iconic industrial forms and from the emerging postindustrial paradigm shift by inviting onlookers to rethink the identity, significance, and potential of shorelines.[11] This lengthy and unscripted process, involving many digressions and spanning several decades, functioned as a rich period of agonistic reinvention with many social groups mobilizing water in pursuit of cultural agendas that diversified water as a cultural landscape and put it to new uses.

Another advantage of studying water in Amsterdam was that the prevalence of water and its diversity of physical forms created opportunities to examine its cultural plurality at several locations around the city. In other places, a single large-scale port reconstruction could monopolize that city's waterfront discourse. By contrast, any such spatial, temporal, and formal singularity was impossible in Amsterdam, where scores of planned and improvised waterscape mobilizations occurred on a cluster of sites distributed citywide. These sites included canals, lakes, and floodplains, and these forms became visible in public imaginaries at different historical moments. Given their geographic proximity within the same city, as well as the continuity of jurisdictional structures and development agencies across these sites, reshaping water in Amsterdam involved sustained back-and-forth engagements across a wide array of cultural groups and waterscape typologies. These negotiations amplified opportunities for the cultural experimentation occurring in one part of the city to influence subsequent transformations occurring elsewhere.

Importantly, although Amsterdam's preponderance of accessible water allowed observers to perceive the interplay among culture, water, and real estate in a magnified form, the notion of an inherently pluralized waterscape can productively inform scholars' readings of the urban waterscape transformations occurring in many other European and North American contexts. First, the creative mobilization of waterscapes, rather than the prevalence of water itself, gave meaning to Amsterdam water. Although opportunities for provisional appropriations may have been especially prolific in Amsterdam, they were by no means wholly absent in cities like Los Angeles, San Francisco, Toronto, and Berlin, where other scholars have tentatively begun studying similar reappropriation techniques.[12] Second, although the diversity of water-land interfaces within the single municipality of Amsterdam enriched local discussions of the many potential faces of urban water, similar if less spatially consolidated discourses connect waterfront transformations across cities internationally, bringing insights and adaptations from early mover cities to bear on later interventions elsewhere. This book, in highlighting the diverse modes, sites, and phases of urban waterscape transformation, creates opportunities to recognize the plurality of water in general, not just in Amsterdam. The book also pushes planners, architects, and investors to recognize plurality in urban water not only as an inevitable feature but also as a desirable attribute that enhances the cultural richness and market potential of redeveloped shores.

Enabling Capital Reaccumulation

Rethinking the master narrative of urban waterfront transformation through the lens of Amsterdam creates opportunities to reevaluate the circuitous—rather than direct—influence of cultural practices on political economic processes. Within the field of urban political economy, an important and unresolved tension exists between rent-gap theories of cyclical reinvestment and cultural explanations of those same practices. On the rent-gap side, Neil Smith's foundational research on urban gentrification in New York City provides invaluable evidence of the overwhelming importance of property values and market-based logics in driving spatial cycles of devaluation and reinvestment. During these processes, disinvestment in roads and buildings that allows them to deteriorate is a rational economic practice since, once infrastructure has lost sufficient value, its total destruction and replacement with a wholly new urban form no longer registers as a capital loss. Moreover, Smith's data showed a sharp geographic line demarcating the frontlines of reinvestment, which reinforced the importance of systemic real estate values, rather than idiosyncratic cultural activities, in urban regeneration processes.[13]

On the cultural side, four years after the publication of Smith's rent-gap theory, a lesser-known study by Christopher Mele offered a counterpoint by asserting that symbols of place were central to reinvestment undertakings. Like Smith, Mele's research also focused on gentrification in New York City. Mele acknowledged the importance of real estate values and market-oriented investments, especially compared to the difficulties that passionate but otherwise ineffectual artists and countercultural groups faced when trying to make their self-generated symbols and spatial representations stimulate neighborhood-wide revitalization. However, these symbols, which had little structural consequence in the hands of local actors, gained crucial significance when real estate interests selectively mobilized them in coordinated efforts to devalue some neighborhoods and revalue others. In sum, cultural factors helped investors conceive of "better" uses for spaces, as well as to sell their redevelopment ideas to consumers.[14]

The relative importance of land values versus cultural practices in cycles of reinvestment remains unresolved. Recent studies from U.S. cities generally build on both legacies, teasing out the political economic processes associated with advertising and gentrification that are neither reducible to blunt accounts of economic determinism nor simplified into idealized models of consumer sovereignty.[15] In my reading, cultural interests often figure as placeholders building a neighborhood buzz and absorbing the greatest risks while testing possible redevelopment frameworks on a variety of disinvested sites. The cultural practices that gain market traction then generate conditions of possibility for rent gaps to emerge, helping some reinvestment plans advance while other equally devalued spaces continue to languish. Large real estate investors with significant financial resources and systemic working methods then selectively mobilize cultural tropes to advance the frontline of spatial reaccumulation as quickly and profitably as possible.

Despite these insights into the importance of cultural symbols in gentrification processes, rent-gap theories continue to dominate most accounts of waterfront transformation, especially those occurring in central urban cores. The history of Baltimore's HarborPlace—a quintessential embodiment of the urban water paradigm shift—provides a case in point. Redevelopment narratives emphasized a seemingly invisible market hand guiding deindustrialization that transformed the port into an insolated, derelict brownfield. Investors then filled that imagined spatial void with a newly constructed boardwalk, convention center, aquarium, marketplace, concert pavilion, theme park, and sports stadium. The revitalized harbor appeared on the cover of *Time* magazine in 1981, and it became the first and still most popular poster child for rent-gap waterscape redevelopment.[16] This type of narrative—chronicling industrial decline leading to "underutilized" infrastructure then superseded by new "higher" uses—has become a ubiquitous storyline that analysts use to make sense of—and promote—shoreline reinvestment in cities across the North Atlantic. Devaluation can take the form of regional industrial decline, as in the case of Baltimore, where port activity relocated to other cities, or it can emerge from hyper-investment, as in the case of Vancouver, where the construction of a consolidated, offshore container port rendered smaller inland facilities redundant.[17] In either context, analysts all too easily conflate devaluation with an imagined rent gap premised on the assumption that alternative economic uses are readily apparent.

Although the existence of a rent gap may appear self-evident in hindsight, a genealogy of urban water in Amsterdam emphasizes the ambiguity characterizing these processes in practice. Amsterdam investors did not simply awake one day and decide that the rent gap for disused harbors and ports had reached a tipping point that justified reinvestment. Moreover, even once city builders embarked on harbor revitalization projects, investors expressed considerable anxiety about the marketability of postindustrial city spaces and the value of water in redevelopment schemes. In other words, although devaluation was evident, the potential for revaluation remained deeply uncertain. Instead, a genealogy of praxis revealed that cultural groups making provisional, low-value use of water and water-related infrastructure generated a diverse array of symbols and practices that made a wide range of unexpected replacement uses thinkable. These cultural practices influenced the timing, form, and profitability of subsequent port revitalizations while also helping beyond-the-port models of waterside urbanism gain traction.

The Amsterdam experience, in highlighting the productive tensions that emerged among cultural actors making creative uses of waterscapes, sheds light on the role of cultural experimentation and symbolism in enabling capital accumulation. Alongside real estate investors and their engineering and planning partners, the spectrum of water-related agents in Amsterdam included hippy houseboaters, queer partiers, heritage enthusiasts, experimental artists, foreign tourists, media reporters, urban ecologists, and national cabinet officials. These groups' engagements with waterscapes over a fifty-year period brought a diverse array of cultural agendas into messy association with real estate development. When cultural actors directly challenged infrastructure investment processes at the precise, capital-intensive moment of their construction, market interests generally prevailed. However, subsequent investments bore the imprints of these cultural challenges and innovations, illustrating the influence of everyday practices in shaping shoreline living downstream. Cultural appropriations gestured toward unanticipated, unconsolidated, potential investment pathways, and these gestures enabled, redirected, and contained the investment decision making that followed. These agonisms and the generative tensions among cultural groups and market interests modulated city building processes. The resulting urban spaces bore the indelible imprint of cultural actors and created new material landscapes for ongoing, exploratory mobilization.

Putting Waterscapes to Work

In conventional accounts of urban waterfront transformations, the material medium of water gets little attention. Investors use water as a spectacle vista for outdoor terraces, fireworks displays, and marina traffic. However, real estate–centered narratives generally emphasize changes in land use and land values, saying preciously little about the changing forms and meanings of water. The few accounts that mention water directly usually emphasize technical issues, such as pollution remediation or shoreline stabilization techniques, rather than engaging in political speculations about the substantive contribution of water to urban regeneration. As such, in discussions of urban waterscapes, the political potential of water remains largely invisible.

Rethinking redevelopment through the lens of Amsterdam water presents opportunities to connect knowledge about culture and real estate with discussions about the political ecology of waterscapes more broadly. Alongside the tension between economic and cultural explanations of cyclical investment, a similar tension exists within the field of urban political ecology over the nature of agency in material objects and infrastructure. Philosopher Bruno Latour has indelibly influenced these debates with his assertion that any human action is, in reality, distributed among a variety of human and nonhuman entities that, acting in concert, shape and modify the state of affairs.[18] In other words, investors produce natural-social worlds that stabilize economic processes, but, at the same time, the capacities inherent within the natural-social world infuse and constrain the spaces that investors can produce.

Among political ecologists adhering to this line of thought, scholars disagree over the relative determinacy of material forms. On the one hand, some experts insist that the material composition of artifacts predisposes them to enable select political ends. For instance, rail lines increase long-distance trade; tractors reduce peasant labor; and sidewalk curb ramps increase universal access to city spaces.[19] These arguments suggest that artifacts, landscapes, and objects will inherently push social practices in specific directions. On the other hand, other scholars emphasize the malleability of social processes giving landscapes their material form and associated significance. For example, the capacity for state officials to use street grids to govern commercial activity and topographic maps to coordinate urban administration is contingent on the things people do to bring grids and maps to life and, therefore, is not inherent in the essence of the material trace.[20]

During the late twentieth and early twenty-first centuries, water in Amsterdam was not politically neutral, but neither was its political valence set in stone. Legal frames, landscape paintings, building projects, and scientific discourses from the past gave water shape and meaning. Filtered through these lenses, water as a material medium flowed, reflected, and buoyed in particular ways. However, those practices were only part of the story. Cultural actors with concerns about commodification, homophobia, heritage, and environmentalism mobilized water's natural-social properties for a variety of sometimes competing purposes. Water became real estate; lake vistas became history channels; and newly built undercurrents supported ecological diversity. These appropriations harnessed the capacities for action that past social practices had built into waterscapes while turning those capacities to new, unanticipated ends.

These mobilizations left indelible imprints on the shape and symbolism of water and, by extension, on the material form of newly emerging shorelines. These cultural imprints outlived the individual cultural movements themselves. Houseboaters came and went, historians shifted tactics, and environmentalists moved on to other locations. The waterscapes they left behind partially preserved the modifications these groups made to water's physical footprint, regulatory status, symbolic importance, and customary use. That modified water then became fodder for subsequent rounds of selective, pluralistic appropriation that left the assemblage of water, and not just of land, thoroughly modified.

Water as a Plural Cultural Landscape

Alongside these political economy and political ecology debates, the story of water in Amsterdam presents an invaluable opportunity to rethink the utility of pluralized cultural landscapes. These sorts of landscapes exert influence together with their more hegemonic counterparts. Some landscapes acquire hegemonic forms at certain historical moments when they come to embody, naturalize, and reproduce a narrow set of social hierarchies and behavioral norms. For instance, formal gardens in seventeenth-century France replicated in miniature the practices of fortification, transportation, standardization, and decorum that legitimated imperial rule at the birth of the modern French nation state. Similarly, against the backdrop of pastoral village greens and rolling hills in mid-twentieth-century England, Boy Scouts and farmhands figured as the legitimate faces of British citizenry while nonwhite residents and laboring women appeared out of place.[21] These cultural landscapes were hegemonic in that seemingly natural and distinctive physical topographies became deeply interwoven with judgments about morality and belonging. The conflation of physical form with social order made malleable spaces and societies appear fixed, inevitable, and natural.

The history of water in Amsterdam resonates with this cultural landscape tradition, but without generating expectations of a fixed or totalizing emergent topography. Unlike hegemonic landscapes, water in Amsterdam presented a nebulous case of seeping influence, rather than concrete resolve. Water lore has deep roots in Dutch history; Amsterdam is renowned as a quintessential water city; and residents are keenly aware of these circulating discourses. Nevertheless, despite the temptation to read waterscapes as a singular, essentializing terrain at the core of local Dutch culture, the history of postindustrial water transformations instead revealed water to be an overtly acknowledged, shape-shifting element with inconclusive political valences.[22]

Instead of generating a direct, absolute reality effect, cultural waterscapes exerted lateral influence in two senses. First, social groups pursuing interests that, on the surface, seemed to have little to do with water nonetheless mobilized water to advance their causes.[23] Squatters resisting commodified housing turned boats into dwelling units. Queers concerned about hate crimes used water to visualize their rights to public space. History enthusiasts told stories of water to naturalize neighborhood identity claims. Environmentalists concerned about birds redesigned currents to increase avian habitat. Architects used climate-related flooding to appropriate rural farms for urban expansion. In these types of practices, actors used water in oblique ways to advance other, non-aquatic interests.

Second, city builders incorporated aspects of these cultural waterscape reinterpretations into subsequent investment processes. Public-private partnerships added floating homes, performance venues, heritage themes, and ecological functions into their visions of waterfront living. Their selective mobilization of cultural symbols in modified forms lent credibility to urban expansion agendas. In these ways, cultural practices from previous decades and certain neighborhoods influenced but did not wholly define investment practices in other times and places.

The utility of water in advancing social causes and development discourses stemmed from its embodied association with regulatory apparatuses, identity symbols, and biophysical processes. These associations—some long-standing and others newly invented—imbued water with its form and content, which coalesced into an inherently unstable fodder available for selective mobilization. Many actors tugged at these strands—for instance, by bringing water's historical life and environmental significance to the fore. The strands never emerged cleanly, entwined as they were with other aspects of water's identity. Moreover, when released, the manhandled waterscape retained some deformation from its previous strain, all while other actors were simultaneously tugging at strands and adding new threads of their own. Water, as a cultural assemblage, existed in an agonistic nexus that united otherwise disconnected cultural movements into a landscape of strange bedfellows and ongoing innovation.

The malleability of water as a multivalent political actor explained its widespread utility as a culturally distinct landscape that was used to advance many causes and that resisted ossification into a singular hegemonic terrain. Mobilizations of water carried a charge that had limited but still real connotations. As a pluralized entity, water functioned as a witness that could indirectly—although never cleanly or conclusively—naturalize many, even contradictory, agendas. This plurality undermined water's emergence as a hegemonic topography and instead contributed to its flexible, playful, and popular significance during a wide range of city building moments.

Organization of the Book

The case material and stories included in this book were chosen because they provided useful insights into the mechanics of waterfront redevelopment and the influence of cultural mobilizations of waterscapes in those iterative processes. In telling the history of water through a cluster of sites located within one city, I realize that I risk implying that Amsterdam's decidedly wet environment is somehow an exceptional case. However, the goal of telling the waterfront story by skipping from site to site and year to year within a consistent municipal frame is to underscore the inherently diffuse, evolving, and contingent process of building shorelines and cities. The narrative that follows is about how cultural practices mobilize water in concert with other spaces and symbols for many purposes. These practices push other actors and investors to reevaluate spatial opportunities in unexpected ways. When these practices gesture toward potentially profitable reinvestment strategies, they indirectly influence subsequent urban development patterns and help bring new city spaces and shoreline meanings to life.

Chapter 1 offers a description of water in the 1960s and 1970s when, in the wake of deindustrialization, water emerged as a residual space available for informal reappropriation. It was at this moment that squatters built homes on outdated industrial barges and, turning regulatory structures to new ends, transformed mooring spaces into residential addresses. These early, provisional experiments, which crystallized in the figural persona of the houseboat hippy, helped establish a new romance associated with self-built, countercultural, water-top aesthetics.

Chapter 2 explores the conversion of water into a performance stage for demonstrations of group identity. Like houseboat hippies, queer partiers used water to visualize their rights to the city, using water to enable performance strategies that were not possible on land. These practices foreshadowed the rapid emergence of several other cultural events that, in the 1990s, connected water with distinctly nationalistic cultural identities. These events changed the political valence of water, transforming the act of going to the canals into a supposedly quintessential Dutch experience, which reinforced latent associations between water, nationalism, and heritage.

Chapter 3 offers a close look at a sustained effort by heritage enthusiasts to capitalize on the growing popular interest in central city canals by displacing supposedly inauthentic houseboats and parades from the waterways and by restoring lost seventeenth-century waterscapes. Enthusiasts realized that heritage interests alone might not garner sufficient public support for their cause, and so they framed preservation as a real estate development opportunity. This economic rationality proved a double-edged sword when working-class residents fearing displacement delayed, and ultimately defeated, the canal restoration campaigns even as heritage-related discourses became mainstream.

The book then shifts focus in chapter 4 from central city canals to industrial harbors where city builders, after a sustained struggle, eventually incorporated heritage discourses into official redevelopment agendas. With squatters, tourists, architects, and reporters lauding the cultural value of nautical history, planners decided that mining history—rather than trying to ignore it—could be financially advantageous. This fundamental reassessment of the value of aging ports not as blank slates but as history sites helped elevate waterfront redevelopment into a key economic growth strategy for the metropolitan region.

Chapter 5 explores the shift from waterfront redevelopment to the creation of entirely new urban shorelines through a modern variant of land reclamation. City planners built new islands adjacent to the redeveloped harbors, and environmentalists seeking resources for habitat restoration pushed planners to use island infrastructure to stimulate ecological resiliency. This nature-making agenda legitimated the reversal of a long-standing moratorium prohibiting urban encroachment into protected lake areas, creating new opportunities for investors to capitalize on water's romantic, celebratory, and heritage associations in Amsterdam.

Alongside new island construction, city builders also expanded urban shorelines by flooding greenfield sites and building floating cities on top of them. Chapter 6 explores these experimental technologies connecting water and city building with global warming and disaster capitalism. In this process, invocations of a nationally shared Dutch identity evidenced in part through local customs of houseboating, canal parading, heritage preservation, and ecological sensitivity helped investors overcome popular resistance to land use reforms.

As this material demonstrates, urban waterside living in Amsterdam has evolved, and continues to evolve, through winding, contingent, socio-spatial processes. Cultural actors making opportunistic uses of water incrementally shift the types of waterscapes that investors produce and the methods they use to build them. Born out of agonistic tensions, postindustrial urban water transformations partially aligned with the paradigmatic icon of harbor revitalization in the early 2000s. Water discourses then quickly pushed past that model in an ongoing process of social activism and technological innovation. Far from constituting a top-down, rapidly constructed, and instantly iconic model, new modes of waterside living are emerging through entangled cultural agendas and market interests that facilitate reinvestments in all sorts of urban waterscapes within a storyline that remains productively open-ended.

CHAPTER ONE

Hippies on Houseboats

During the mid-twentieth century, industrial restructuring in European and North American cities fundamentally transformed the economic functionality of waterfronts. Ports consolidated, manufacturers outsourced factory work, and air and highway travel expanded. In Amsterdam, these changes meant that the city's smaller harbors and inland canals—along with their warehouses, workshops, and barges—entered a marked phase of economic devaluation. Over the following fifty years, a wide range of cultural and economic groups would make use of those shorelines, reconfiguring them to once again become a central territory of profit, this time in Amsterdam's emerging real estate and service economy. This transformation, far from following a simple rent-gap development model of disinvestment and reconstruction, emerged through the tangled nexus of social movements, regulatory restructuring, and market cooptation beginning in the 1960s and 1970s with squatting skippers and houseboat hippies.

The history of houseboats in Amsterdam constituted an early phase in this multipronged, multiphased, and multisited process of water's metamorphosis. At a time when city planners hoped to replace canals and canal-fronting workshops with plazas and office buildings, new social groups actively appropriated those spaces for alternative purposes—for instance, by squatting in warehouses and converting derelict barges into informal floating homes. Although squatters lost their hold on most central city buildings in the mid-1980s, longstanding policy frames that treated water as though it were distinct from the streets and housing around it unexpectedly protected squatting skippers and houseboat hippies from municipal crackdowns, at least for a few decades. The persistence of informal houseboats domesticated the waterways and articulated a new type of romance with water-based lifestyles, both of which influenced public perception about the identity, value, and architectural character of Amsterdam water.

The emergence of houseboat politics in the 1960s and 1970s involved the material construction of new floating objects and, even more importantly, a shift in the social practices bringing water to life. Squatting skippers and houseboat hippies renovated barges, challenged lifestyle norms, and exploited regulatory loopholes, giving the waterscape assemblage a new political thrust. These processes loosened the canals from their industrial transportation associations, and they strengthened notions that water could instead become a self-expressive living space. This loosening effect, while lasting several decades, was temporary. Efforts to assimilate houseboats into the regulated and commodified cityscape since the 1990s pushed the Amsterdam public to reinterpret houseboat politics yet again, this time by aesthetically distancing houseboats from their anarchist roots and financially connecting them with market-based measures of value.

Houseboaters' mobilizations of water as a countercultural living space demonstrated the importance of embodied action and social regulations in defining the public identity of water. Physical infrastructure and small retrofits to boats and mooring spaces were crucial to the development of houseboat living. Even so, living on boats demonstrated the versatility of water as a political entity. It inscribed water with new functions and meanings in an incremental way that did not require a full physical redevelopment of the landscape. The mechanism of hippy houseboats transformed the central city canals from an industrial space into a romanticized countercultural zone and, tentatively by 2010, into an emerging territory of profit. This metamorphosis and the political debates it prompted subsequently inflected the public perception of water in other locations citywide.

The history of Amsterdam houseboats and their domestication of Amsterdam water was preserved in written newspaper, government, and civil society archives. Local and national newspaper coverage of the changing financial and legal face of houseboat living during the past twenty years included extensive personal commentaries from houseboaters, their supporters, and their detractors about the nature and purpose of houseboat living. Even more revealing were the self-published manuscripts from leading houseboat advocacy groups, such as the National Houseboat Organization (Landelijke Woonboten Organisatie) and the Amsterdam Boat Committee (Amsterdams Boten Comité), as well as from their opponents with groups like the Friends of the Amsterdam Inner City (De Vereniging Vrienden van de Amsterdamse Binnenstad). Secondary sources describing Amsterdam's economic history and new social movements put these sources in a historical context, and municipal reports from the Amsterdam City Council illustrate the more recent market and policy changes giving houseboat living a new role in city life in the 2000s.

Using these sources, this chapter traces the emergence of houseboat living in the 1960s and the 1970s beginning with a general overview of central city activism and a description of the methods that new social movement activists used to make the transition from buildings to houseboats. In this history, the evolving policy frames governing water were crucial in explaining the persistence of provisional domestic uses of water over time. The proliferation of houseboats led to the creation of an official zone of exemption where informal houseboaters could build their own homes in an affordable, expressive form. This regulatory borderland was not permanent, as evidenced by legal changes and gentrification processes during the 1990s and 2000s. Even so, these activities imbued water with a residential identity and, tentatively, suggested new ways to invest in real estate along shorelines.

New Social Movements on the Amsterdam Canals

Geert Mak, a popular Dutch historian, described the new social movements occurring in Amsterdam between 1964 and 1985 as "The Twenty Year Civil War."[1] Similar protests on a larger and more violent scale occurred in Paris, London, Rome, and West Berlin during this same period. In Amsterdam, secondary history sources chronicle a period of sustained political activism on a constellation of issues, such as market consumerism, nuclear weapons, land speculation, factory closures, environmental degradation, and gender inequity.[2] Concomitant with these new social movements, several shifts in Amsterdam's political economy simultaneously reconfigured the functionality of water. One set of factors stemmed from decolonization and industrial restructuring. A second set centered on municipal housing and urban renewal policies. These social movements and economic factors collided on many fronts, giving rise to Amsterdam's potent and internationally renowned squatting movement, including one splinter group of activists who used boats to squat on water.

Amsterdam residents after World War II faced a significant housing shortage. Wartime damage contributed to the problem, but social transformations perpetuated it in the long term. Extended kinship living arrangements were becoming less popular, especially among young people who were marrying later, having children later, and enjoying the privilege of independent living. Simultaneously, agricultural mechanization pushed many people into the cities in search of employment and educational opportunities. These social trends meant that Amsterdam's housing shortage persisted for several decades despite the rapid construction of new housing high-rises and suburbs.[3] This housing shortage, when combined with the political economic transformations occurring in the 1970s, became a central rallying point for new social movement activists of many stripes.

During this same postwar period, Amsterdam's economic base narrowed considerably, beginning with the collapse of long-standing colonial trading institutions. Amsterdam's port was not large, especially compared to the Port of Rotterdam, which surpassed Amsterdam in size in the late nineteenth century and which has been the largest European port since 1962. However, while Rotterdam specialized in bulk river trade with Germany, Amsterdam specialized in the long-distance sea trade of high-value specialty items from the Dutch East Indies. The formal independence process, which began for present-day Indonesia in 1949, had little economic impact on the Netherlands overall, but it significantly affected Amsterdam and greatly reduced the quantity of goods and money circulating through its waterways.[4]

Concurrent with decolonization, the Dutch government invested heavily in infrastructure expansion nationwide, which enhanced the Netherlands' overall competitiveness at the expense of the small-scale industries connected with Amsterdam's waterways. During the 1950s and 1960s, the Port of Rotterdam was enlarged, and major industrial-scale canals opened that allowed large ships to pass directly from the North Sea into Europe's major river valleys without requiring transshipment in Amsterdam. Simultaneously, regional and national governments invested heavily in freeways, tunnels, and airports. With fewer ships and commodities passing through Amsterdam, the city's internal waterways experienced significant reductions in cargo traffic, which undermined the warehouse and business activities that the cargo industry once sustained.[5]

These shipping-related reconfigurations occurred alongside industrial restructuring at the global scale. For a time, postwar rebuilding in Europe fueled industrial activity in Amsterdam, a boom that helped explain the city's low unemployment rate of 5 percent in the 1950s and early 1960s. Then, with the effects of decolonization and infrastructure consolidation, combined with the rise of industrialization in Southeast Asia and the onset of the 1973 international economic recession, Amsterdam's industrial base contracted sharply. The whole country was affected, but Amsterdam was especially hard hit, with unemployment rising to 25 percent between 1979 and 1983 and lingering for several years after the rest of the Netherlands had begun to recover.[6]

The municipal government responded with an urban renewal agenda that, no matter the good intentions, sparked widespread opposition. Under mayoral guidance, the Amsterdam Physical Planning Department had been building large roads and high-rise apartment complexes in outlying areas since the 1950s to alleviate the city's postwar housing shortage. In the early 1960s, planners turned their attention from these fringe locations to the central city, unveiling plans to demolish underused warehouses—and the low-value, working-class housing around them—to consolidate land for new office construction.[7] This apparent betrayal of local housing interests in the context of major economic restructuring and rising blue-collar unemployment collided with Amsterdam's already burgeoning new social movements. Urban renewal became a central rallying point uniting several strands of these anticapitalist and antiauthoritarian opposition groups into a loose yet politically potent coalition of squatting protestors.

Amsterdam's formidable squatting movement played a leading role in the city's physical and social transformation between 1964 and 1985. Protestors, students, and struggling families seized abandoned factories and boarded apartment buildings on the grounds that it was unethical for private owners and speculators to let their buildings stand empty when so many people needed a place to live. Squatting activity was especially prolific in the formerly light-industrial areas of the canal belt, the same area where municipal officials hoped to demolish several city blocks in their quest to replace so-called working-class slums with international office towers. Popular resistance to urban renewal, which peaked in the late 1970s and early 1980s, involved several high-profile confrontations between squatters and the hired thugs and riot police sent to harass and evict them.[8] These confrontations eventually rallied public support to stop demolition and to expand the city's already extensive social housing infrastructure. In the meantime, the squatting movement also generated a splinter group of activists who shifted their focus from buildings to canals and began to squat directly on the water.

Squatting Skippers and the Canal Regulations That Protected Them

Jan was one such squatter-turned-houseboater whose personal memoir of the experience was preserved alongside other similar accounts in the archived diaries and self-published treatises connected with local and national houseboat advocacy groups (such as Amsterdams Boten Comité and Landelijke Woonboten Organisatie). In Jan's account, he vividly described how desperate he felt in 1967 searching for housing in Amsterdam. "We were suffocated, couldn't find any housing. Yeah, a cellar room without windows for an outrageous price. [. . .] Acquisition costs, sinister housing agencies, it made you sick." To paraphrase from his account, for a time Jan lived in the cramped linen closet of a collectively squatted central city building with a roommate whose own home had recently been demolished. A friend then introduced Jan to an anarchist boater who helped him buy an old coal barge. Jan gutted and rebuilt the barge by hand, carting away the debris on his bicycle and using scrounged materials to make a home. Looking back, he described the project as a natural extension of his earlier squatting convictions. "Houses were squatted, and we squatted on water. And we felt strong as house-skippers."[9]

Among the subset of squatters making similar moves from land to water, most people, like Jan, mobilized the spaces and objects associated with the declining shipping industry. Their innovation was to apply squatting mentalities to decommissioned cargo vessels and empty mooring spaces. Harbor mechanization, cargo containerization, and the general decline of canal-based industry made smaller skiffs redundant. People with limited resources could buy these skiffs cheaply, anchor them in desirable neighborhoods, build a shell on top, and then sleep aboard the boat.[10] This process stretched the limits of permissible stay, turning long-term parking into short-term housing.

Amsterdam was unique among its peer cities in Europe and North America in that, in the mid-twentieth century, surface water channels continued to weave through many neighborhoods, including the mixed industrial and residential areas slated for urban renewal. This physical accessibility, combined with the loosening of the shipping industry's hold on canal functionality, enabled the squatters' reappropriation of this landscape form.

Physical accessibility and industrial disuse did not imply that the canals were an unfettered space free for the taking. Instead, as the memories and memoirs of these early houseboaters demonstrated, surface water existed within a regulatory framework that stipulated its legal conditions of use. In Jan's words, "Everyone was a little fearful of the harbormaster's talk."[11] Although the nautical fairways were not intended as living spaces, and despite ongoing threats that the harbormaster would impound the boats, the preexisting policy frames that differentiated water from land quickly emerged as the most important factor enabling the proliferation and persistence of low-cost informal houseboating during this period.

In Amsterdam, as in most western cities, a bureaucratic divide separated the governing entities with authority on land and those controlling activity on water. On land, the Physical Planning Department (Dienst Ruimtelijke Ordening) was the strong arm of the municipal government with considerable top-down authority over land use and public space. This agency established development agendas and wrote building codes. It held a near monopoly over new home construction during this period, acting as the primary landowner, financier, and contractor for most urban development projects.[12] The planning department also maintained the city's public open spaces—its parks, streets, and squares—and regulated the types of social behaviors permitted in those spaces.

Despite the extensive, centralized authority of the Physical Planning Department, its authority did not extend to water. Instead, the Port of Amsterdam (Gemeentelijk Havenbedrijf Amsterdam) had authority over the industrial-scale waterways connecting the port with the North Sea and the German river valleys. Authority over the smaller interior canals threading through the rest of the city resided initially with the Department of Locks, Bridges, and Harbor Dues (Sluis Brug en Havengelddienst) and then, from the 1990s until the early 2010s, with the Department of Inland Waterway Management (Dienst Binnenwaterbeheer). These regulatory entities coordinated shipping, allocated permits, collected fees, and established rules about boat sizes, speeds, and mooring arrangements. These agencies' missions were to maintain shipping infrastructure and coordinate nautical transportation. Their regulations contained no direct language about the use of canals as a living space.

This type of jurisdictional division between land and water was, and remains, standard practice in most European and North American cities. However, unlike Amsterdam, in places like Chicago or San Francisco, lakes and oceans lay firmly to one side of an engineered, hard-edged coastline. In these dumbbell-style arrangements, water was adjacent to the city, but it rarely extended inland. In other cities like London and Los Angeles where prominent, navigable rivers bisected the urban core, hydrological engineering projects that locked river channels in place behind solid concrete levees meant that the rhythms of daily life on land and the barges passing through the city on water rarely intersected in meaningful ways. In Amsterdam, by contrast, a more zebra-striped geographical pattern emerged. Small-scale waterways were prolific. Streets, squares, and houses literally sandwiched those canals, creating a densely interlaced jurisdictional map of wet spaces and dry ones, and people could move between streets and waterways with relative ease.

Importantly, despite this geographic interweaving and permeability, Amsterdam's land and water regulatory agencies have historically operated independently of each other, and over time their codes of conduct diverged in important ways. For instance, the Physical Planning Department enforced a law that prohibited people from sleeping in public spaces. Residents weren't allowed to nap on a park bench, pitch a tent in a plaza, or live in a car parked on the street. However, the nautical regulatory agencies had no such rules. The canals, as transportation spaces, included expectations that skippers would moor their vessels against the bulkheads along the street while awaiting shipments, loading cargo, or making repairs. Skippers and other shipping-related workmen routinely slept aboard their freighters during these periods, and they had done so in Amsterdam at least since the sixteenth century.[13] As such, nautical authorities voiced comparatively few objections when squatting skippers began sleeping aboard boats that were essentially parallel-parked in the canals immediately adjacent to streets where sleeping in parked cars was expressly prohibited.

These traits—the decline of local shipping industries, the physical accessibility of surface water, the pressure to find alternative housing arrangements, and the jurisdictional division of authority—combined in the 1960s in unexpected ways. It was at this moment that a splinter group of squatters took to the canals and began building new homes using the cast-off objects associated with industrial decline, a move that set Amsterdam's late twentieth-century tradition of houseboat living in motion.

The Rise of Romanticized Houseboat Hippies

"Amsterdam is famous for its houseboats."[14] This sentiment, which the self-publications of houseboat enthusiasts promoted, echoed the romanticization of houseboat lifestyles common in the tourism brochures and editorial pages circulating through Amsterdam by 2010. Despite houseboats' present-day popularity, the initial rise of squatting skippers in the 1960s and 1970s was a controversial affair. As documents from the Physical Planning Department and houseboat advocacy groups recount, municipal officials in the 1960s initially tried to displace informal houseboaters just as they worked to evict squatters. However, due to the legal differences between land and water, these entities instead eventually formalized the practice of houseboat living by creating a legal zone of exception, which remained in place until the 1990s when gentrification processes on land were largely complete and investors began looking for new ways to capitalize on water.

Central city houseboat purchased by owner in the mid-1970s, ca. 2005. Image courtesy of Paul Spoek, Amsterdams Boten Comité.

Paul, a spokesperson for Amsterdam's Boats Committee advocacy group, was one such houseboater who benefited from this historical zone of exception. When I interviewed Paul in 2010, he was one of 4,400 houseboaters living on Amsterdam's 2,256 houseboats, about half of which were moored in the central city.[15] To paraphrase Paul's story, he moved to Amsterdam as a university student in 1974 and had difficulty finding a satisfactory place to live within his price range. He initially stayed in a crowded apartment block on the outskirts of the city where "twelve units shared one kitchen, and it was the same on several stories stacked." At the time, his sister was living in a subdivided canal house in the city center, and she noticed an empty, rundown houseboat anchored in front of her building. Eager to have his own living space in a central neighborhood, Paul found the boat's owner and convinced him to sell. Paul then made the obligatory rounds to several governing authorities requesting permission to purchase the boat "as a houseboat." One by one, he said, he convinced "the city voting office," "harbor services," "police special laws," and so on, to review and approve his application. Paul considered himself lucky. His boat was already registered as a houseboat when he bought it, which made his uphill struggle to acquire the mooring permit a little less steep. Paul then dropped out of college and began working at the airport and harbor to earn the money he needed to make his new home habitable.[16]

Paul's experience, and the experiences of others preserved in the written archives that he and other activist volunteers saved over the years, illustrated that sleeping on boats provided access to otherwise inaccessible central city spaces. Since people sleeping on boats ostensibly slept in transportation vehicles and not in permanent buildings, they did not pay landlords or property taxes. They were also exempt from residential permitting processes, building codes, and zoning laws. Houseboat advocacy groups looking back on this period from the mid-2000s agreed that, for flower-power anarchist squatters, this nonmarketized mode of living promised a "nonconformist, free and easy, adventurous lifestyle, with minimum costs and maximum freedom," where residents "did their own thing and created their own individual living environment."[17] Houseboaters prided themselves on their industriousness in reclaiming derelict barges in industrial areas of Amsterdam. "Out of these undignified circumstances, they stopped up mud, banged out risers, laid out paths, fought for a school bus for their kids, a phone booth, a street light."[18]

This combination of affordability, sweat equity, and self-expression fueled their popularity. According to houseboat advocacy groups, about 400 houseboats were moored in Amsterdam in 1933. This number fell to fewer than 100 boats during World War II and then rose again to about 350 boats in 1950. The prevalence of houseboats then grew substantially over the following three decades. The number of houseboats grew to 1,222 in 1960 in response to the postwar housing shortage. More explicitly politicized squatters then pushed the number to 1,780 boats in 1972 and up to 2,250 boats in 1980. The houseboat count peaked at 2,600 boats in 1988, by which time the squatting movement had entered a sharp decline and the persona of the houseboat hippy had come to the fore.[19]

This proliferation in houseboat activity in the 1950s and 1960s occurred despite municipal efforts to prevent its rise. In response, beginning in the early 1970s, city officials changed their tactics. With the squatting movement raging, instead of trying to expel houseboats outright, officials in the mayor's office with influential connections in the water management agencies pressured those groups to incrementally absorb houseboats into their institutionalized management policies. While outright displacement was politically unpopular, officials could use health and safety rhetoric to eliminate the so-called worst offenders—for instance, by impounding houseboats that were impeding ship traffic or whose occupants were stealing electricity. Simultaneously, at the mayor's request, city planners pressured their nautical management peers to grant the remaining houseboats "official" status. At the time, only about 60 of Amsterdam's then nearly 1,800 houseboats were legally authorized dwellings. By expanding this circle, the newly "officialized" houseboaters received short-term protections from police harassment and displacement. However, to qualify, boats had to meet certain standards, such as not obstructing views of historic bridges and not slowing the flow of nautical traffic.[20]

Importantly, officialization was not the same as legalization, and the legal categories developed during this period were hardly black-and-white. Beginning in 1974, houseboats were divided into four categories: legal (*legale*), tolerated (*gedoogde* or *officieuze*), illegal (*illegale*), and super-illegal (*super-illegale*). A boat's classification depended on its location, its physical condition, and its inspection and registration status.[21] The designation of most houseboats as "official" created a legal shade of gray. This category tolerated some forms of houseboat living for a time, which kept housing protestors at bay. However, it also imposed boundaries on boaters' permissible transgressions and stopped short of guaranteeing the long-term mooring rights that municipal planners continued to oppose. With most "official" houseboats neither legal nor illegal, these residents lived for nearly three decades in an institutionalized zone of ambiguity outside the usual property laws and housing regulations governing the rest of Amsterdam.

Although the increase in houseboats was fueled by the burgeoning squatter movement, over time the meaning of the houseboat as an architectural prototype evolved and acquired its own symbolic connotations. Living on a houseboat was a labor-intensive undertaking, and for the most outspoken houseboaters, that undertaking was a labor of love. Paul, for example, said he spent nearly all his free time for over thirty years sawing, sanding, and painting his boat by hand. He used repair and maintenance tasks as an opportunity to "make a study" of his boat—for instance, by marking and logging every rivet holding the boat together.[22] The scores of new houseboaters who joined him on the canals in the 1970s and 1980s engaged in similar practices as they self-built their homes from scratch. In this largely unregulated context where the usual building codes did not apply, as one architectural historian phrased it, "anyone could construct a houseboat according to their own design," and many do-it-yourselfers cobbled together custom homes using whatever materials they could scrounge and whatever skills they could muster.[23]

By the 1980s, the squatting movement and the houseboat movement, which shared a common origin, had firmly diverged and began moving along separate paths. For the squatters, the mid-1980s brought a decisive end to their political influence, as well as to their presence in central Amsterdam. With the supply of newly constructed housing finally meeting pent-up demand, public sympathy for squatters lost momentum. Then, under the banner of preexisting private property rights, city officials comprehensively displaced most squatters from the city center. In the decades that followed, squats were generally confined to more isolated districts on the outskirts of Amsterdam.

Houseboats experienced a different fate. Houseboaters had limited protections from idiosyncratic evictions, but no private property laws existed on the water, so city officials had no grounds for systematic displacement. Informal houseboaters were able to remain in central areas for a few decades longer, even after squatters in buildings were removed.

From the 1960s through the 1980s, Amsterdam's new social movement activists transformed a residual industrial waterscape into an alternative living space. These actions benefited from jurisdictional specializations that inadvertently helped houseboating persist over time. People seeking alternative housing looked to the canals because the legal framework surrounding water permitted the possibility of informal, low-cost, central city living that was not possible in buildings. Without existing legal precedent to displace boat residents, municipal officials instead created a zone of exemption that partially constrained houseboat activity and that also unintentionally gave boaters time to develop a distinctive, do-it-yourself cultural identity that popularized the romantic image of water-top living. This zone of exemption persisted after the squatters in canal-fronting buildings were gone, and it only began to close in the 1990s and 2000s once urban renewal and gentrification on land was complete.

Renewed Controversy on the Water

The persistence of houseboats in the central city after the squatters in buildings were gone generated renewed controversy in the 1990s and 2000s. The voices of houseboaters captured in newspapers—oftentimes during moments of strife—illuminated the tensions. Adjacent private property owners often criticized houseboats, but tourists adored them, all while houseboaters themselves voiced growing frustration with the growing popularity of canal-related activities. These mild but sustained conflicts emerged as the gentrification of central city neighborhoods reached a plateau. This slowing rate of real estate appreciation generated pressure to find new strategies to keep markets growing, in part by finding ways to incorporate houseboats into formal real estate markets.

Following the late 1970s defeat of the municipal urban renewal agenda premised on demolition and redevelopment, the Physical Planning Department began advocating a "build for the neighborhood" approach to upgrade infrastructure and amenities in situ without requiring direct displacement.[24] Urban political economist Neil Smith explored these in-place gentrification processes in detail. Gentrification in Amsterdam initially emerged in the 1970s in the housing sector with state-subsidized residential upgrading. By the early 1990s, gentrification had become an institutionalized citywide policy intended to expand Amsterdam's wealthy residential base. Spatially, these processes of neighborhood investment and upgrading were initially concentrated along certain major avenues and the central city canals, most notably taking the form of converted warehouse lofts and renovated canal houses. By the 1990s, central city gentrification was nearly complete, and the pressure was mounting to find new ways to keep local property markets growing.[25]

Simultaneously, the rising international popularity of waterside living, combined with new investments in Amsterdam's central city spaces, gave canal-fronting housing a new cache. This shift heightened tensions between residents on land and their neighbors afloat. Some canal house residents complained that houseboats blocked their physical access to the waterfront. Houseboats, they said, occupied the spaces where other residents wanted to moor pleasure boats, and they reduced entry points for children trying to ice-skate on the canals in the wintertime. Residents also complained that houseboats obstructed resident views of the canals and bridges and that they reduced the ambient light reflected into their windows, both of which purportedly undercut the market value of canal-fronting property. The more scathing critiques denounced houseboats as ugly floating eyesores and dangerous fire hazards that sheltered people who were illegally occupying public spaces and consuming neighborhood services without paying into the public coffers.[26] These critiques emanated primarily from central city areas where international interest in historic waterways was the greatest and where private homeownership, rather than price-controlled social housing, predominated.[27]

The growing importance of pleasure boating and water-oriented tourism, a topic discussed at length in the following chapter, added to the problems from the houseboaters' perspectives. As early as 1992 and continuing through the mid-2000s, houseboaters publicly voiced their frustration over the growing popularity of high-speed pleasure boating. The waves from passing motorists caused dishes to rattle, boats to shake, occupants to fall, and water to slosh in through open windows.[28] The occupants aboard these vessels could be disconcerting as well, especially with the popularity of canal tourism rising. Some houseboaters, for instance, described enjoying peaceful mornings at their breakfast tables only to have the sudden arrival of a tour boat interrupt the quiet moment. As one resident described in a newspaper editorial, "Twenty pairs of eyes and 60 cameras and camcorders focus on our croissants and breakfast buns. I'm picking my ear. Two dozen cameras click."[29] The rising popularity of canal concerts added to these tensions. Although some houseboaters enjoyed these spectator events, others expressed irritation over the noise and waves from throngs of pleasure boaters and the disruption it caused when these boaters moored for several hours at a time eight or ten rows deep across the width of the canals.[30]

Water-based regulatory agencies initially responded to these houseboater complaints with a decidedly dismissive air. In their eyes, canals were transportation spaces intended for movement. People who chose to live on water outside of legal housing channels had to accept that motoring vessels had priority. This lack of regulatory support explained the tendency for some houseboaters to respond aggressively to passing pleasure boats. A newspaper article from 2005, for instance, profiled a houseboater who stood on his rooftop shouting profanities at tour boats. Another houseboater, who could recite tour boat sightseeing scripts in four languages, said the words haunted his dreams. A third houseboater described angry neighbors who threw water balloons at her when she decided to join the throng of pleasure boaters attending a floating concert.[31] These frustrations reflected the changing nature of the canals. Houseboaters in the 1970s had built homes on underused industrial sites. By the 1990s, however, with the character of water changing around them, houseboaters faced heightened opposition to their presence and greater disruption in their living spaces.

Although the late twentieth-century houseboat scene owed much to early squatting skippers, after so many decades of living on boats, many houseboaters felt entitled to greater stability in their mooring spaces. These residents acknowledged that they lived in indeterminate areas that were not really intended for housing, but they emphasized that ambiguity and criminality were not the same thing.[32] On the contrary, by the 1990s, "official" houseboaters could produce two decades' worth of municipal paperwork documenting their prompt and reliable payment of mooring permit taxes and fees. Even if the designation of their boats as "legal" was never formally granted, residents felt that the paper trail of approval slips and tax receipts should protect them from being treated as second-class citizens or from being displaced from their mooring sites.

With central city urban redevelopment slowing in the 2000s, forming new water connections was one of the few low-cost strategies available to continue stimulating real estate value and commercial activity. These practices put houseboat-mooring spaces in jeopardy. One houseboat spokesperson, a freelance journalist turned city alderman, felt painfully aware of houseboaters' continued vulnerability in their traffic-oriented regulatory environment. Until the mid-2000s, he wrote, "a mooring permit was person-specific, boat-specific, spot-specific, had to be renewed every three years, and offered the boat resident absolutely no guarantee that he could remain in his spot."[33] Through the 1990s, with official and legal mooring spaces filled to capacity, and with new permits difficult to acquire, many arriving or displaced houseboaters simply anchored their boats illegally wherever they could. Although these houseboaters often stayed in that location for many years, the threat of impoundment was ongoing.[34] Even residents living in legal boats with official permits were easily displaced. For instance, museums and other public institutions interested in increasing the connectivity between their facilities and the growing pleasure boating traffic could have houseboaters' mooring permits permanently revoked with thirty days' notice to clear spaces for short-term mooring risers catering to pleasure boating patrons.[35] These tensions, and the public debate they prompted, created opportunities for municipal officials to reregulate the waterways and bring houseboat living in line with housing policies on land.

New Regulations and Market Penetration on the Water

The late 1990s and early 2000s saw renewed tensions among residents, houseboaters, and pleasure boaters in a context of rising market attention to urban water and tourism interest in houseboat romance. These intersecting trajectories emerged as the backdrop for a period of regulatory reforms. Documents from the planning department, houseboat advocacy groups, and real estate sector chronicle the enactment of new regulations that appropriated houseboat hippy legacies in favor of pro-market water-top living.

Central city gentrification, combined with the rising international popularity of waterside living in the 1990s and 2000s, increased the attractiveness of houseboats among white-collar residents unable to afford rental prices in the gentrified central city. Dutch- and English-language media sources have reported on this transition. For instance, a *New York Times* article profiled a middle-aged graphic artist who bought a canal freighter in 2005 and converted it into a residence. The artist described himself as "a very boat-minded person," but cost was clearly a factor. He sublet a room to paying guests to reduce his housing expenses, and he emphasized that living on a boat was cheaper than renting an apartment, which, in his seventeenth-century neighborhood, cost nearly double what he paid for his renovated houseboat.[36] A similar Dutch-language example profiled a middle-aged British hippy turned website designer whose unofficial houseboat home protected him from gentrification. His street, he said, had been transformed during the 1990s and 2000s into "a lovely shopping street. The middle class has returned to this neighborhood, and the City Council restored the houses around me."[37] While concerns over displacement were rife on land, this houseboater felt safe from the changes because his water-top home was exempt from dominant real estate investment circuits. These examples illustrated the growing popularity of houseboats among artistically inclined, white-collar residents using water to evade gentrification on land.

Despite the lingering value gap between boats and apartments, these types of accounts also demonstrated that this gap had narrowed significantly between the 1970s and the 2000s. Rising consumer demand for a limited supply of mooring permits increased their informal transfer costs.[38] New boat regulations designed to take the unpredictability out of living on water played an even greater role in enabling this market penetration. In 2005, for instance, the municipal city council issued street addresses to houseboats. This standardization measure, which assigned mooring locations a fixed position, size, and numerical referent, integrated slips into citywide property management databases.[39] Another municipal mandate passed two years later required houseboaters to connect to wastewater utility lines by 2017, an infrastructural investment that they estimated would cost houseboaters up to €20,000 each.[40] Then, in 2009, the Physical Planning Department received permission to adapt its building safety and aesthetic codes to apply to floating structures as well. For houseboater Paul, whom I interviewed shortly after this change was announced, this new regulation meant that he might have to replace his synthetic skylights with glass panes and substitute artificial insulation for the potted plants on his roof, both of which would add cost and weight to his boat while decreasing the versatility of the boat's design.[41]

Cumulatively, these sorts of regulations meant that residents could no longer rely on scrounged materials and sweat equity to build homes and instead had to construct their housing in accordance with stringent, professionalized, higher-priced building standards. In exchange for compliance, houseboaters gained long-term legal protections against displacement, easier access to bank mortgage resources, and increased opportunities to accrue equity in their mooring spaces. However, houseboat advocacy groups and their allies asserted that these rules reduced the affordability and design freedoms that gave houseboat living its characteristic romance.[42] From the perspective of houseboaters, the renewed municipal push to "tame" the waterways read as an assault on a space that popular historian Geert Mak dubbed "the last piece of administrative wilderness in the Netherlands."[43] Houseboaters complained that new rules undermined houseboaters' freewheeling lifestyles and hodge-podge homes. In the words of one resident speaking publicly, "I enjoy some liveliness. [. . .] In my opinion, the people who complain bought a house for a lot of money and get annoyed at anything that is not neat and tidy. It bothers me that these yuppies get to determine the rules in Amsterdam."[44]

Some sense of freedom has persisted despite these changes. One woman, for instance, built a cardboard scale model of her dream home in the early 2000s, sent the model to a commercial boat builder, and then waited for her custom abode to come sailing across the lake to her mooring spot. "Within the maximum dimensions," she said, "you can do whatever you want."[45] Unlike her previous bungalow-style houseboat, which she bought years earlier to live cheaply, her new two-story home, with its big terrace, spacious interior, and the evocative name *Versailles*, "barely reminds one of a boat. [. . .] It could just as easily be a villa *on* the water, rather than *in* the water."[46] Similarly, another resident, a personnel executive, commissioned an architect to design a split-level home on a dilapidated boat he bought from "an elderly German who came to Holland during the flower power days." He envisioned a high-style, convenience-packed house. "I wanted people to say, 'O.K.!' Maybe even a little over the top."[47]

In a city where large-scale, government-managed, speculative construction dominated nearly 100 percent of the housing market, being able to design a custom home in this way carried significant emotional weight. Moreover, the specialty homes still carried an air of romance in the eyes of their occupants. As the personnel executive explained, while acknowledging that houseboats had become "a yuppie market," he added, "sometimes, though, I still feel like a gypsy, but I have a big mortgage."[48] Even so, this kind of design freedom and water-top romance with commercial builders and high price tags was very different from the self-built, anticapitalist squatter and hippy houseboats that emerged in the 1960s and 1970s.

With housing tenure increasingly connected to market transactions in the 2000s, houseboat living lost much of its initial political impetus. According to architectural historian Marijke Beek, in contrast to the "original" low-income, flower-power houseboaters "who have fought for many years for their attainments and still do," the moneyed "newcomers" were apathetic.[49] To paraphrase her analysis, these higher-income buyers felt secure that their financial investment alone was enough to guarantee them all the expected property rights and protections they would have enjoyed had they lived on land. Their self-proclaimed identity as homeowners with good jobs and high incomes in a city seeking to expand its white-collar residential base justified their claims to space at the expense of lower-income houseboaters resisting rising taxes and maintenance expenses.

By 2010, the consolidation of houseboats into a territory of profit had begun turning boats into sites of consumer-oriented wealth and prosperity. The institutionalization of new regulations and building codes enabled these processes. These changes came at a time when market demand for water-oriented real estate was rising. The growing government commitment to uphold long-term mooring rights made it practical to invest larger sums of money into houseboats and to calculate returns over a longer time horizon. These changes made higher boat prices possible, and they contributed to the growing tendency to replace hippy houseboats with custom-commissioned floating homes.[50]

Longtime houseboaters watching the expanding regulations and rising prices have tried to resist these changes. Among their strategies, these activists have self-published leaflets and booklets celebrating the diversity of Amsterdam houseboats and the resourcefulness of their occupants in efforts to garner public support for their cause. In a typical and especially popular example, a small book filled with high-quality photographs of houseboat hippy homes profiled residents who devoted decades of ingenuity and sweat equity to converting derelict concrete hulls and cargo vessels into prized custom housing.[51] These celebrations of "free spirits with little money but handy hands" cast government regulation and market integration as a poison pill to aesthetic diversity and owner independence.[52] As houseboater Jan phrased it in his memoir, "here, it isn't about project developers and powerful interest organizations" exploiting unprotected renters and instead is "about a handful of people, mostly of modest means, who have the house they want. Leave them be."[53] These types of advocacy efforts sought to preserve residents' autonomy from government oversight and market co-optation. For houseboater Paul, speaking to me in 2010, "it is still continuing, the fights for the last free bits of town."[54]

The Institutionalization of Water Romance

By the early 2000s, Amsterdam's houseboaters were living in the remnants of a self-made borderland that once skirted government authority and market integration. Squatting skippers in the 1960s built homes using the cast-off material associated with the local decline of shipping activity and small, canal-based industries. Preexisting jurisdictional specializations inadvertently enabled the persistence of these informal living arrangements. Water-top squats conformed to regulatory laws mandating a minimum degree of transience in a designated transportation zone even as they incorporated new dwelling functions into those spaces. For a time, the legal shades of gray that emerged surrounding these homes created an officially sanctioned zone of nonconformity exempt from conventional building ordinances and market processes. The lingering hesitancy to polarize houseboats into one of two categories—either legal or illicit—allowed informal houseboats to persist over time, further popularizing the romantic image of houseboat hippies.

This border effect was not permanent, as the successive officialization measures show, but the temporal grace period created opportunities for a distinctive, romanticized houseboat lifestyle to emerge. When turning water to domestic ends, squatter skippers and hippy houseboaters made profound statements about their desire for affordable housing and creative self-expression. Over time, the pride and delight residents felt for their boats was evident in the detailed foliage and vivid paint treatments adorning doorways, rooftops, walls, walkways, lampposts, and railings. This romantic imagery persisted as the central city gentrified. Tourists paid extra to sleep in informal houseboat hotels, visitors returned home with copious photographs of houseboats, and white-collar professionals began paying high prices for the opportunity to live on a central city houseboat. By the 1990s and 2000s, these romantic associations overshadowed the previous generation's political calls for low-cost housing. Instead, the rise of houseboat living inadvertently contributed to the figurative reinvention of the waterways from a castoff industrial space into a romanticized and increasingly commodified domestic waterscape.

From these activist roots reinterpreted in an era of central city gentrification, ongoing rounds of regulatory reform began enabling greater market penetration into houseboat living. The adoption of building requirements and longer-term mooring guarantees implied that mooring spaces could theoretically be managed according to the same real estate laws governing housing on land.

In the otherwise fully revitalized city center, the creation of untapped housing sites with direct waterfront access could soon make mooring spaces exceptionally valuable to the point where, some fear, affluent homeowners may gain a monopoly on this once-insurgent residential typology.

These emerging houseboat practices domesticated water, transforming it from a residual industrial space into a living space. These domestication impulses reinforced the romantic symbolism and market potential of living afloat. As the subsequent chapters explain, other activist groups and real estate interests then mobilized these domesticated landscapes both in public discussions about the identity of Amsterdam water and in efforts to refine the architectural typology of nascent floating homes.

CHAPTER TWO

Queers on Parade

After the emergence of houseboat hippies, Amsterdam water entered another distinct phase of social reimagining during the 1990s. Central city gentrification was slowing, and international interest in the spectacle of urban shorelines was rising. During this period, alongside the nascent pressure to strengthen connections between water and real estate, several cultural groups began mobilizing water as an informal gathering space for public parties and festivals. These provisional activities transformed the canals from a postindustrial landscape where houseboat hippies had once hoped to live in relative obscurity into a highly visible stage for cultural events and city boosterism. Queer pride advocates played an especially significant role in this transformation, alongside the holiday partiers and classical music fans who followed them. By the late 2000s, their water-top events crystallized popular perceptions that water could be a public space—and not just a transportation zone or domestic space—and that canals were deeply symbolic of national identity and cultural enrichment.

In the United States, spectacle attractions became a standard ingredient in postindustrial waterfront transformation during the 1980s and 1990s. Business groups mounted fireworks displays, installed shoreline loudspeakers, and organized river cultural tours to attract visitors who, while attending those events, also spent money in stores and restaurants. Some designs emphasized private control over consumer-oriented shorelines, while other designs included parks and outdoor amphitheaters that doubled as publicly accessible open spaces when not being used for an organized event.[1] Investors mounting spectacle events in these locations expected that the novelty of water enhanced the performances and, therefore, that water and shorelines should be focal points where business interests staged their consumer-oriented attractions.

Water did not simply become visible of its own accord, either in the United States or in the Netherlands. Rather, water was made visible through the social practices that brought water to life. In the United States, market-oriented infrastructure redevelopment and promotional tactics gave urban waterscapes heightened visibility. In Amsterdam, with its abundant and accessible water surfaces, the mechanisms of making water visible as a public gathering space emerged more haphazardly as cultural groups, in the aftermath of the hippy houseboater ascent, mobilized water for new purposes. Once this heightened visibility was established, market interests began redirecting water festivities to more directly profitable ends. This market co-optation shifted, but did not erase, the specific group identities and politics that gave rise to water as a space for public events and spectacles. Instead, this history continued to imbue Amsterdam water with notions of group identity and cultural performativity.

Like the houseboat experiments from earlier decades, these cultural explorations beginning in the 1990s initially involved minimal cash outlays and few market considerations. Queer parade participants sought heightened visibility; holiday pleasure boaters wanted unrestrained frivolity; and classical music fans wanted cultural edification. Market considerations influenced these groups as they experimented with events on the canals, but these cultural practices were not primarily concerned with finding new economic uses for canals. It was not until the late 2000s, after several years of cultural innovation had transformed public expectations about the symbolic importance and functional role of the waterways, that water—and especially water beyond the central city canal belt—began to appear as a rent-gap space potentially useful in citywide boosterism.

The physical characteristics of water and the canals deeply influenced cultural groups' capacities to mobilize these landscapes in meaningful ways. Water as an enabling element generated certain capacities to act that contributed to the sense of visibility, novelty, and political neutrality in the public events that people staged afloat. However, these capacities embedded within water were not inherent to water and, instead, owed much to the regulatory apparatuses and customary uses inscribing water with social meaning. Amsterdam's postindustrial canals were devalued in the 1950s, then partially domesticated from the 1960s through the 1980s, and subsequently appropriated in the 1990s as de facto public spaces for gathering, celebrating, and cultivating group identity. The physicality of water was central in all these processes, yet these reconfigurations initially involved minimal infrastructure redevelopment and instead owed much to the daily practices that gave water new functionalities. Canals did not direct people toward a singular political end. Instead, people mobilized water in pursuit of many different agendas.

The cultural mobilization of the canals as a space for promenades and festivals transformed water into a stage for the public display of social identities. The growing importance of these activities in international exhibitions of national culture by the late 2000s significantly increased the symbolic weight of water as a marker of Dutch identity. However, while foreign audiences may see canals primarily through these televised and photographed performances, for local residents living with water every day, the canals cannot be fully reduced to these seemingly hegemonic moments of national identity and, instead, continue to fulfill other transportation, housing, and countercultural functions on most days of the year. Events and spectacles have generated a strong narrative of water's symbolic import, but the canals as a stage host a wide range of performances, including some that challenge the imagined coherence of a unified national identity or that push spectators to adjust their expectations about which types of people and behaviors belong within those boundaries. As such, water as a cultural landscape became more strongly connected to symbols of nationhood even as the social content of that symbolism remained contested.

This transformation of urban water into a de facto public space and identity stage began informally as people sought alternatives to the conventional and increasingly sanitized public streets and plazas elsewhere in Amsterdam. In the 1990s and 2000s, many cultural groups set this metamorphosis in motion largely by happenstance. Queer partiers, holiday revelers, and music aficionados, among others, hosted one-off celebrations on the canals to make social statements, stage spectacles, or just to have a little unfettered fun. They situated their events on the canals because, through trial, error, and coincidence, these cultural actors found innovative ways to use water's physical novelties to attract attention and to use its jurisdictional attributes to challenge social conventions. When repeated annually, these improvisations encouraged other residents, visitors, and investors to reimagine nautical thoroughfares as de facto public spaces or as places to go to stage demonstrations and experience culture. As this notion gained traction, municipal officials and city boosters organized to bring these disparate festivities together and to incorporate them into city advertising campaigns.

This story of reinvention took shape through the rise of the three largest annual festivals held on the central city canals in the late 2000s, all of which emerged in the mid-1990s. The Gay Pride Parade was especially noteworthy since it was among the first organized events in several decades if not centuries to systematically use water as a civic space.[2] Parade organizers played a pioneering—albeit unintended—role in the canals' metamorphosis into a prominent gathering space. A second event, Queen's Day (Koninginnedag), is a national holiday dating from the late nineteenth century that, in the 1990s, became widely associated with leisure boating in Amsterdam. The third event, the Canal Festival (Grachtenfestival), was the most consumer oriented of these events from its inception and, by the late 2000s, involved a multiday collection of musical and cultural events centered around Amsterdam water. These three festivals were the largest of twenty-five floating events hosted on Amsterdam's canals in 2007, and they were consistently among the top five most popular festivals citywide in the mid- and late 2000s.[3]

An extensive written record from organizers, participants, spectators, commentators, and regulators has preserved the history of these events' emergence and evolution. These festivals were explicitly public in their orientation, and the experiments and controversies surrounding their mobilization of waterscapes figured prominently in the cultural and editorial pages of newspapers, as well as in the promotional documents and municipal reports advertising and regulating these activities. A small handful of supplementary interviews with the 2009 organizers of Gay Pride Amsterdam, the chief editor of Amsterdam's leading cultural magazine, *Ons Amsterdam*, and select local academic experts on history and water further clarified these archival sources.

By tracing the emergence of these events, the motives and strategies involved, and their shifting character over time, this chapter underscores the significance of cultural experimentation and spatial opportunism in the creation of new public spaces and symbolic meanings associated with urban shorelines. The reinvention of water as a de facto public space did not negate the previous domestication of the canals by squatting skippers and houseboat hippies. Rather, these evolving mobilizations added new political dimensions into the mix. The increased visibility of canals and their emerging role as a national stage strengthened the iconic status of houseboats as a locally authentic mode of waterside living. Similarly, the emerging associations of water with performances, nationalism, and city marketing also became fodder for heritage preservationists, architectural critics, and government regulators envisioning their own water forms and city building projects in later years and in other neighborhoods.

Water as a Forgotten Gathering Space

Prior to the 1990s, it was not intuitively obvious that postindustrial water would become a prominent public gathering space. For most of the twentieth century, Amsterdam's canal network functioned as a transportation space that, after World War II, fell into increasing disuse. Informal houseboaters partially transformed this residual landscape into semi-legal residential spaces, but those activities recast the canals as private and domestic spaces, not as collective demonstration sites. When paraders, partiers, and performers began using water as a public open space, historians, cultural analysts, and city officials writing newspaper editorials, magazine pieces, and planning documents emphasized the novelty of this spatial rescripting. The use of water as a public gathering space had historic precursors, but those practices were not a routine part of the waterways' policy frames or customary uses during the twentieth century. Instead, until the mid-1990s, public space legally, culturally, and symbolically stopped at the water's edge.

In previous centuries, the water, walls, and bridges comprising Amsterdam's canalscape and harbor often functioned as a public space. For instance, political leaders in the sixteenth and seventeenth centuries organized elaborate water-top spectacles to entertain visiting political dignitaries. When the founder of the Dutch nation-state, William of Orange, visited Amsterdam, his welcome included a grand floating fireworks display and a nautical reenactment of his military victory against Spain. Similar theatrics of boats sailing in formation commemorated a visit from Russian czar Peter the Great.[4] Alongside these grand performances, water also functioned as a meeting ground in more quotidian contexts. In the nineteenth century, for example, rival neighborhood teams organized "eel pulls" where, in a tug-of-war fashion, the teams standing on opposing sides of a canal won by pulling their opponents over the edge and into the water.[5] Similarly, ice-skating on the frozen canals was a popular nineteenth-century pastime that functioned as a rare opportunity for people of different social classes to mix and mingle.[6]

Despite this range of activities from previous centuries, few public events occurred on water during the twentieth century. This general disuse included a few notable exceptions: the Beatles gave a floating concert in Amsterdam in 1964; a local pianist performed for hotel guests on a rented barge in 1981; and the city's soccer team paraded through the canals after returning home from winning the European Soccer Championship in 1988.[7] Despite these idiosyncratic activities, new social movement activists overwhelmingly preferred to gather, protest, and riot in the city's streets and squares.[8] It was not until the mid-1990s that people began consistently and systematically using water as a public open space.

Twentieth-century zoning designations reinforced the conceptual divide between water and public space. Municipal land use documents from that era categorized streets and squares as public open spaces (*openbare ruimte*) and parks as public open greens (*openbare groen*). Within these official public spaces, the Physical Planning Department set rules to regulate activities, coordinate events, and control demonstrations. Water, however, was not classified as public and instead received a separate classification as a waterway (*waterweg*) or canal (*gracht*). These spaces, like streets, were open to anyone engaged in shipping and transportation. Moreover, like the Physical Planning Department, the nautical regulatory agency, the Department of Inland Waterway Management, had rules about permissible boat lengths, driver's license requirements, and speed limits. These nautical managers tolerated other activities, such as houseboats, floating gardens, and pleasure boats, but only so long as commercial traffic remained unimpeded.[9] Beyond these transportation-oriented rules, no public space regulations applied to the water surface.

Squatting skippers and houseboat hippies made use of this jurisdictional difference between water and land in the 1960s and 1970s, and during the 1990s other cultural groups followed suit. Within the nautical constraints mandating that commercial traffic remain uninterrupted, partiers in the 1990s were entitled to float on the water and motor through the canals as they pleased. Large gatherings that would have required event permits or venue coordination on land had carte blanche on the water, so long as traffic kept flowing. Moreover, the lack of rigorous behavioral constraints, combined with the canals' physical characteristics, enabled a subset of event typologies to flourish on water that could not easily have succeeded on streets, parks, and plazas. These cultural mobilizations of water, which generated tension between partiers and residents along the canals, and which inspired new city marketing tactics, prompted renewed public discussions about the role of water in city life and the meaning of water as a cultural landscape.

Cultural Events Emerge on the Water

Cultural groups began to stage recurring floating events on the Amsterdam canals in the 1990s. Economic considerations played a small role, but activities involving minimal cash outlays and pursued for nonfinancial purposes dominated the process in the early years. Three activities that emerged during this period—the Gay Pride Parade, Queen's Day pleasure boating, and the Canal Festival—subsequently grew into annual events of national importance. These events' growing size and publicity played a critical role in the transformation of water into something it was not before: a de facto space for public gathering and celebrations.

Early organizers of the Gay Pride Parade became the first of many social groups to systematically use water as a de facto public open space. A precursor to this festival occurred as a one-time event in 1994 when Amsterdam hosted EuroPride and routed the international floats through the central city canals. Two years later, an association of queer organizations and businesses began hosting the parade as an annual event. Commercial interests played an important but limited role. In the words of a parade organizer speaking publicly in 1997, "every big city in Europe has a queer parade with floats. But Amsterdam had nothing. We needed this [event] to keep from falling behind."[10] Amsterdam at the time had a strong queer tourism market. Queer visitors in the 1990s and early 2000s spent 30 percent more on average per day than straight tourists, and those exchanges bolstered the queer-owned local businesses catering to that market.[11] More importantly for parade organizers, this niche market facilitated social exchanges among an emerging international LGBT community and concentrated some of those interactions in Amsterdam. For these reasons, maintaining the image of a queer-friendly atmosphere was central both to local sensibilities of social tolerance and to hotel and restaurant business interests.

Alongside these financial and social exchanges, the parade was, first and foremost, a celebratory performance. Promoters of the EuroPride Parade in 1994 advertised it as an opportunity to display "the Dutch Way of Gay" to other nations.[12] Since then, although most floats over the years have featured choreographed dancers in elaborate costumes, some participants used their performances to send political messages to other countries. For instance, boaters satirized Pope John Paul II's homophobic public statements in 2000; they commemorated Iranian youth executed for their sexuality in 2005; and, in 2009, paraders conducted floating marriage ceremonies for Dutch-American couples denied marriage rights in the United States.[13] According to parade organizers speaking with me in 2009, even the more lighthearted displays of dancing and cheering were intended to give hope to grassroots activists in other countries. As for domestic audiences, organizers said, "the Amsterdam City Council likes the event because it's not just a party in the summer. It expresses ideas of how we want Amsterdam to be."[14]

In just over a decade, the pride parade grew from about 10,000 spectators in its initial 1996 installment to an estimated 560,000 onlookers in 2009. With this audience count, the pride parade was the largest public event in Amsterdam that year.[15] Drag queens on party boats and dance troupes on barges snaked in procession through the picturesque canals. Parents hoisted young children onto their shoulders to get a better look at the dazzling scene gliding past on the water below. Queer and straight, young and old, people came in droves to witness the spectacle and show their support.[16] By the late 2000s, the parade had become a celebrated Amsterdam institution, receiving awards and honorable mentions from local cultural and business cooperatives, national folk culture institutions, and international cable television stations.[17] Additionally, as the president of the 2009 organizing committee told me, that year his organization successfully lobbied the Amsterdam City Council to "pass a resolution that says Gay Pride is one of the most important events in the city. Now, we'll see if they put their money where their mouth is."[18]

During the same period that the floating pride parade was gaining popularity, municipal officials and cultural commentators began publicly discussing the growing use of the canals as a general place for assembling, celebrating, and advertising. As the chief editor of a local culture magazine told me, and as a local history professor echoed, "the use of the canals as 'just fun' has grown since the '80s and '90s."[19] People began buying boats explicitly for pleasure instead of for hauling freight, a seemingly illogical act a few decades earlier. Around the same time, newspaper commentators began speaking of boating as an emerging national hobby. This rise in pleasure boating was uneven in its distribution. Even by the late 2000s, after a decade of consistent pleasure boating growth, on most days the canals saw little traffic beyond guided tour boats, a few small pleasure craft, and the occasional eccentric "old man in a cap" in an aging or self-built dinghy.[20] In sharp contrast, on a few dozen special holidays, festival days, and rare sunny afternoons, pleasure boaters filled the canals. On those days, according to Amsterdam's Physical Planning Department, water became "an essential part of the public space in the central city."[21]

The most significant annual spike in pleasure boating activity occurred every April 30 on Queen's Day, which tourism guides described as "by far the most widely celebrated holiday in the Netherlands."[22] Commentators characterized the holiday for North American audiences as a cross between the U.S. Fourth of July and the New Orleans Mardi Gras. The long-standing holiday tradition prior to the 1990s had no relationship with water. Instead, elementary school children celebrated the so-called national hobby of free trade by impersonating merchants. These children built makeshift stalls in parks, streets, and sidewalks where they sold games, performed tricks, or charged passersby a few cents to look inside their homemade dioramas.[23]

By the mid-2000s, however, the event had become a holiday for adults, and water had become the main attraction. Hundreds of thousands of partiers began taking daytrips to Amsterdam, where they wandered through vendor-packed streets wearing orange-colored shirts, hats, wigs, capes, feather boas, and face paint. Among these revelers, many began renting, building, buying, or borrowing boats for pleasure rides on the water. Newspaper reporters covering the event since the mid-1990s have consistently reported the same trend: "Everything that can float and carry cases of beer is queued up on the water to make a tour through the canal scene."[24] In groups of ten, twenty, or thirty people, partiers went drinking, singing, and shouting through the central city waterways. The canals, which were nearly empty only a few days earlier, suddenly became so congested that motorists had to bob rather than drive. On those days, the canals emerged as a de facto public space of national resonance.

Alongside Gay Pride and Queen's Day activities, a third and more commercial water tradition emerged in the form of the annual late-summer Canal Festival. This event ostensibly began in 1981 when managers with the Pulitzer Hotel and the Cristofori piano house jointly hired a solo pianist to perform for guests atop a so-called shabby barge that they rented from the municipal sanitation department.[25] However, it took another fifteen years before this periodically recurring performance coalesced into a large, annual festival. After the Gay Pride Parade and the Queen's Day pleasure boating traditions had gained a solid following, the envisioned Canal Festival began growing as well. According to newspaper reports, by the late 1990s the five-day gala involved several dozen classical music concerts performed afloat in Amsterdam's seventeenth-century canal belt. By 2001, the festival had developed a trademark finale involving a "singing crowd" of twenty thousand people "on small boats, the bulkheads, and a VIP-pontoon" who joined a floating brass ensemble in a rendition of "the traditional ode 'On the Amsterdam Canals.'"[26] The nine-day festival in 2007 grew larger still, with seventy thousand visitors attending over 160 music, architecture, literature, and history events citywide. Many of the smaller activities were free to the public, and nearly all events took place "on floating stages, canal-side terraces, or the banks of the IJ River."[27]

The Canal Festival, which was an explicitly tourist-oriented and media-centered event, catered to local participants but was staged for international audiences. The promotional documents and speaking events were exclusively in Dutch, not English, which reflected the expectation that attendees were primarily residents living in the Netherlands and visiting from outside Amsterdam. Nevertheless, the Canal Festival was elaborately staged, frequently televised, and extensively photographed for guidebooks, travel channels, postcards, and other tourism promotional documents. The focus on water reinforced the already strong international association that, for foreigners, the beauty of Amsterdam resided in its canals.[28] The emerging Canal Festival reinforced those trends. Its performances and their pictorial reproductions taught spectators to read water—and especially the central city canals—as the quintessential place of Dutch history, government, and culture.

These three cultural events, which by the late 2000s had become among the largest public events citywide, initially emerged as small-scale, group-specific searches for tolerance, relaxation, and cultural enrichment. Economics were relevant, but the events were not mercenary, and only the Canal Festival was explicitly commercial in its origins. These practices added complexity to Amsterdam water, transforming canals into public spaces in everything but name.

Mobilizing Water as a Stage

There were good reasons cultural groups in the 1990s used water to stage these emerging festivities. Water had jurisdictional associations, customary uses, and material properties that differed from streets, parks, and plazas. Event participants mobilized those differences to escape the physical limitations and social conventions associated with official public spaces on land, using water to heighten visibility and add novelty, as well as to downplay select political implications associated with collective action. Through these mobilizations, using central city canals as framing devices, water was transformed into a stage for political life and, later, as a repurposed icon of national identity.[29]

The potential to use water to enhance visibility was central to the evolution of the floating Gay Pride Parade. Prior to 1994, when Amsterdam hosted EuroPride, this traditionally Protestant city had little noteworthy history of carnivalesque parading, which local culture experts told me was "really more of an American thing."[30] The EuroPride format, however, was based on an annual New York City parade commemorating the Stonewall riots solidifying the queer liberation movement in the United States.[31] To accommodate the parade format in Amsterdam, organizers revived the long-defunct tradition of staging public events on water. Amsterdam was a city of narrow and crooked streets with few squares or boulevards, and the broad canals were the only places spectators would be able see the whole show. Floats on boats turned streets and bridges into viewing platforms. They transformed sunken waterways with their long, curving footprints into highly visible stages displaying sexual emancipation.

Water as a stage with streets and bridges used as viewing platforms during Amsterdam Gay Pride, 2011. ©iStock.com/Nisangha.

This heightened visibility in space paralleled calls for "greater visibility for gay life," measured in part by the right to be visibly different in public year round.[32]

Water's capacity to visibly accommodate a parade's physical circulation through the central city also cultivated an air of social inclusivity that would have been difficult to achieve on land. According to a 2009 interview with parade organizers, moving the parade through the city—instead of demonstrating in a single cramped square—created "a sense of connectivity with the whole city."[33] The parade's circulation through many urban spaces and past several prominent landmarks gave participants "the feeling that the minority is the majority,"[34] or that queer and queer-tolerant people were the norm, at least for the day. This type of visible circulation, which was physically impossible in Amsterdam's tight streets and self-contained plazas, proved highly effective on the central city canals where the parade's extended spatial reach symbolically affirmed sensibilities of social integration and widespread tolerance.

Alongside these practices of mobilizing visibility, the novelty of floating also quickly became an important attribute of the performance. Initially, this novelty received little attention. Press announcements in 1994 and 1996 barely mentioned the events' waterborne character. By contrast, since 1997, promoters have consistently advertised floating as a salient feature distinguishing the Amsterdam parade from similar Gay Pride events in other countries. This timing suggests that the novelty of floating was an accidental discovery rather than a premeditated expectation that water ought to be culturally significant. By the event's third year, however, the novelty of water was well established. Organizers in 1997 emphasized that "above all, the fact that the parade goes through the water makes it exceptional. Other cities can't touch that. This is the proof that Amsterdam is the queer capital of Europe."[35] A 2009 parade official reiterated that message, saying, "this is the only floating parade in the world," and attributing the international cable channel MTV's interest in the event to its waterborne character.[36]

Along with these elements of visibility and novelty, water helped to depoliticize the depiction of inclusivity that the parade engendered. Political activists often hold rallies in symbolic spaces,[37] but for organizers of queer pride, the lack of political associations with water in living memory was advantageous. Some participants performed political skits, especially in the parade's later years. However, according to 1997 organizers speaking to the press, the parade was intentionally "not a demonstration. You won't see any banners." Instead, it was "a thank you that queers and straights have lived well together for 30 years in Amsterdam."[38] Choreographed revelry in an apolitical space naturalized the event, making it appear as though queer identity was an already incontrovertible and culturally valued part of society. For these reasons, the gradual increase in explicit calls for political reforms in the 2000s upset many of the earlier participants who, in newspaper editorials, lamented that calls for political change "set the clock back 15 years," suggesting that the parade was an act of protest against ongoing discrimination rather than a celebration of an assumed inclusivity.[39]

Queer parade organizers were the first cultural group to systematically mobilize water's capacities for visibility, novelty, and depoliticization, and Queen's Day partiers and Canal Festival planners quickly followed suit. On Queen's Day, for instance, water was transformed into a highly visible public promenade. Mingling on the water became a characteristic holiday pastime in the mid-1990s. In a typical explanation, college-age revelers speaking to newspaper reporters in 1995 commented, "the best thing about Queen's Day is meeting other student boats on the Amsterdam canals."[40] The canals, which at the time figured as an underused transportation space with houseboats along the edges, provided a place to see and be seen without requiring advanced planning or special permits. As another reveler explained, "look, if we went with a hundred people to a café, you'd have a problem," but, on the canals, no reservations or applications were required.[41]

Queen's Day partiers likewise embraced water for its novelty value and, in particular, the element of surprise stemming from the potential for playful misadventure. As a water historian with the Amsterdam Free University explained to me shortly before the 2009 holiday: "Dutch culture is mostly serious and boring, with endless meetings about nothing. And then suddenly we start to play."[42] Queen's Day was a day of letting go and letting loose. Partying on the water—outside of the Physical Planning Department's public space ordinances about noise, drunkenness, and decorum—created heightened opportunities for absurdity. According to one reporter covering the celebrations in the early years, groups of dozens or hundreds of partiers would rent boats, load them up with thousands of bottles of beer and a disk jockey, and then "do" the canals, throwing trash overboard, peeing over the edge, and dancing until the wee hours of the morning.[43] Water made these practices possible because, on the canals, "it's not forbidden, right? We are part of the spectacle on Queen's Day."[44] Moreover, when joyriding, people could fall in, get wet, and laugh. The water historian commented, through these activities people connected water and rituals because being joyfully ridiculous on the water "added fun. People come to see that."[45]

This capacity for heightened absurdity on water helped depoliticize the nationalistic overtones associated with Queen's Day holiday displays. Boats sported Dutch flags, boaters wore orange (the color of the Dutch royal family), and boating figured as a national hobby. However, when afloat, these expressions of nationalism and collective identity appeared playful and satirical, rather than solemn. To be sure, intentionally or otherwise, the growing significance of canal pleasure boating on such a prominent national holiday reinforced symbolic connections between canals and nationhood. However, in contrast with formal displays of national fervor, which was culturally discouraged in the Netherlands between the 1950s and the mid-2000s,[46] the spontaneous and visually chaotic displays of royal emblems on the canals helped make those performances socially palatable.

In contrast to the improvisational Queen's Day mobilizations, Canal Festival organizers made more systematic and scripted use of water's visual, novel, and depoliticizing characteristics. The tourism promoters subsidizing the Canal Festival (Amsterdam Toerisme Congres Bureau and Vereniging voor Vreemdelingenverkeer) used classical music concerts staged on water to portray Amsterdam as a hub of refined cultural taste. Water was a central feature in these performances. Promotional materials, for instance, stressed that "the water, and especially the canals, makes Amsterdam an exceptional city. This combination of bridges, trees, houses, and canals doesn't exist anywhere else in the world."[47] Festival organizers underscored this point by staging events on water and broadcasting those images internationally. For instance, when CNN first televised the Canal Festival's main concert in 1997, the architectural detailing of the waterway's visual edge was as important to the performance as the music. In the words of event promoters, for television viewers from Japan to Spain and from America to Sweden, "viewers saw a canal. [. . .] Better yet, they saw boats, flat boats, fishing boats, and punts. [. . .] What a merry anarchy, there on the water! [. . .] What a friendly people, all sitting so still. What picturesque little houses, and there's the glittering music besides. Look, that's what a Dutch Village looks like."[48] These images reinforced the symbolic associations connecting water, culture, and identity in Amsterdam. The open-air nature of the floating performances, as opposed to images of elites in stuffy concert halls, naturalized the scene as supposedly emblematic of Amsterdam street life. Using this seemingly quotidian and authentic landscape, concert planners and promoters used the media-circulated images to affirm sensibilities of their city's cultural prestige anchored in its central city canals.

These mobilizations of water's capacity to render activities visible, convey a sense of novelty, and exert depoliticizing effects helped queer partiers, holiday revelers, and concert promoters shape public life in Amsterdam. These three capacities for action, while unique to water, were not inherent to water and instead stemmed from the jurisdictional associations and customary uses connected with Amsterdam's internal canals in the postindustrial era. Moreover, these floating activities transformed collective ideas about the nature and functionality of water, recasting the shipping and squatting landscape as a de facto public open space.

Tentative Steps to Regulate Water-Top Revelry

The transformation of water into a de facto public gathering space was a dynamic process involving provisional experimentation that then engendered selective resistance and remobilizations. These activities fueled public discussions over water's acceptable uses and functional roles at the turn of the twenty-first century. By the late 2000s, those debates were prompting municipal officials to reregulate the canals to more closely align with public open space practices on land. This regulatory push followed on the heels of emerging houseboat regulations that ostensibly moved water in the opposite direction by formalizing private housing along the canal edges. These two diverging regulatory impulses nonetheless shared the common thrust of pushing water in the general direction of marketization and urban boosterism. In this instance, this change occurred both through new spatial ordinances and through the co-optation of the events themselves.

Since Gay Pride participants pioneered the festive use of the waterways, and since their parade had an organized structure, their event also became an important object for regulatory experimentation. The canals as a nautical landscape had preexisting rules that coordinated shipping and transportation. For instance, commercial skippers needed driver's licenses, large boats and risky cargo were prohibited in certain areas, and commercial traffic had the right-of-way over other vessels. However, these rules said nothing about whether boaters could travel in caravans, how loud skippers could sing, what types of clothing passengers had to wear, how much alcohol passengers could carry on board, or whether beverages had to be held in glass containers or plastic ones. These issues of noise, dress, and decorum became the fodder of several regulatory experiments from the late 1990s and continuing through 2010, focusing initially on the Gay Pride Parade.

At the time, city planners did not yet see water as a de facto public space, and so municipal efforts to control water-top events, like the Gay Pride Parade, initially focused on the participants rather than the space. In the mid-1990s, municipal officials asked Pride Parade participants to voluntarily sign "chastity declarations" promising not to expose their genitals, have sex, or masturbate during the parade.[49] In the late 1990s, the officials refined the contract language to specify that exposed "breasts and buns are fine, but not genitals. And the nakedness must be functional."[50] The coalition of queer cultural organizations and businesses organizing the parade initially enforced the rules by reprimanding and disqualifying passengers who were "too flamboyant" in their dress and decorum.[51] In exchange for compliance, participants received financial backing for their floats, formal inclusion in the parade lineup, minimal assurance that police would not intervene, and some public relations protection from potential critics.

This person-by-person strategy was generally accepted when the event was small and nuisance was the primary issue of concern. However, individual contracts soon became impracticable. Growing popular support for Gay Pride gave participants added cover to reject what some saw as repressive, heteronormative standards of costume and comportment.[52] Participant contracts also left the regulation of spectators unaddressed. Moreover, as the general public came to see water as a routine place for events and parties, the burden of writing individual contracts proved unwieldy.

City officials responded with a scalar shift, replacing individual contracts with event-permitting procedures. Although the Pride Parade motored through the waterways, onlookers viewed the procession from streets and attended after-parties in plazas. Municipal officials used these land-based activities to justify requiring permits for floating events. Media-publicized disputes between 2000 and 2007 revealed the range of issues these permits addressed. Event organizers and city council members negotiated over the volume of music played on floats, the hours that the parade ran, the number and timing of after-parties in plazas, and the exclusion of potentially dangerous glass bottles from concession stands.[53] The police department supplemented these permits with extra officers patrolling on foot and in boats to ensure compliance, direct traffic, and log complaints.[54]

The event-specific nature of these permit strategies left city council members open to allegations of discrimination. Parade organizers virulently accused the city council of homophobic "event-pestering."[55] The government-sanctioned dress code came under fire in 2002 and 2003. As one spectator noted, there was more nudity in the Rotterdam Summer Festival, but no one minded because "it's Caribbean. And straight."[56] A city council member likewise received harsh criticism for refusing to grant permits for two street parties in 2005 with the stated goal of breaking the parade's weekend "monopoly" on Amsterdam's public spaces.[57] Permit complaints spiked again in 2007 when the central city government denied permission for all Pride-related street parties because police officers said they lacked the manpower to patrol both the parade and a soccer event scheduled for the same afternoon. Denying allegations of discrimination, municipal spokespeople said they denied the permits to "protect" queers from "having to go fist to fist with a group of drunk homophobic soccer fans."[58] In this instance and most others, the requested permits were eventually granted. Nevertheless, the need for repeated requests and public confrontations left many participants feeling that city officials consistently privileged "hooligans over queers."[59]

Co-opting Floating Events and Public Gathering Spaces

As event organizers and the general public came to see water as a legitimate—if not officially designated—public open space, their expectations about its legitimate use shifted, as did the municipality's approach toward regulatory control. Queer pride participants and spectators expected to have the freedom to use their bodies, dress, and decorum to publicly display their visions of social acceptability. Additionally, residents expected that queers and soccer fans alike should have equal claim to the relevant spaces and services associated with public revelry. Moreover, with general pleasure boating and water festivals on the rise, officials began envisioning more systematic regulatory policies attached to water as a space rather than to individuals or events.

To build public support for regulatory reform, municipal officials dramatized descriptions of water as an administrative wilderness. In a series of reports, officials asserted, "there is a dangerous chaos developing on the inner city waterways" that made it "nearly impossible for skippers to navigate without incident."[60] On Queen's Day or during Gay Pride, officials said, complaints tripled, and the canals became "deathly busy."[61] These accounts depicted the Queen's Day surge in water activity as especially worrisome. "One million people celebrate Queen's Day in Amsterdam annually. That's a party, but also a sizable logistical operation."[62]

Several commentators circulated written editorials challenging these characterizations of water as a space of unregulated anarchy. Editorialists wrote that former industrial traffic was all but absent, and the canals were quieter than they had been for centuries. Critics noted that boating accidents were extremely rare. Moreover, they attributed the rise in complaints not to a spike in event-related nuisance but rather to a new and widely publicized municipal hotline established in 2006 that streamlined complaint processes and made it easier for disgruntled residents to vent their passing frustration.[63]

Despite these counternarratives, the municipality's assessments prevailed, generating popular support for a new spatial code of conduct that could be enforced full-time irrespective of the individual or event in question. In the weeks leading up to Queen's Day 2009, Amsterdam's mayor, with cooperation from several municipal offices, unrolled the first of potentially many new spatial regulations for the canals. Boats longer than ten meters were prohibited on the busiest canals. One-way traffic rules were instigated in designated portions of the city. Music played on boats could not be audible more than ten meters away, and no music was permitted after 9 p.m. Only one drink per passenger was allowed on board, and drivers could not be inebriated. These rules targeted space, applying equally to everyone occupying water within the central city. This new, comprehensive approach to the so-called canal chaos was only enacted for a few days, but if it was successful as a pilot project on that holiday weekend, regulators proposed making the rules permanent.[64]

These changes reflected the emerging expectation among municipal officials and the general public that the canals were, functionally, part of Amsterdam's public open space. The new rules echoed public space ordinances already in effect on land.[65] Moreover, by testing the rules on Queen's Day instead of Gay Pride, officials carefully sidestepped potential criticisms of homophobic intolerance.

Alongside this fledgling emergence of new spatial ordinances, business and tourism interests began co-opting the three annual floating events and turning them to city marketing ends. Once again, the Pride Parade emerged as an early and especially illustrative example of these dynamics. In something of a hostile takeover in 2006, a self-imposed external advisory group of local business leaders and politicians transferred permission to organize the Gay Pride event from the coalition of queer associations and businesses that had been managing the event since 1996 to another upstart queer organization whose members were reputed to be more sympathetic to mayoral and city council interests. This external group, which actively helped plan and fund the parade, also officially renamed the event Gay Pride Amsterdam for city boosterism purposes. Around the same time, multinational corporations began sponsoring floats displaying company trademarks, color schemes, and logos. Representatives from every major political party also felt media pressure to join the procession or risk being stigmatized as intolerant.[66]

This growing co-optation of the queer parade occurred alongside a more general push to elevate the role of water and canals in urban boosterism campaigns. For instance, some city council members began lobbying to build short-term mooring risers and other infrastructure connections that could increase the physical integration between the sunken water surfaces and the elevated commercial streets, especially in established entertainment and restaurant districts.[67] Official tourism promoters also began publicizing tourism "theme years," including the design of a full season of water-oriented attractions recurring every five years. The goal, as promoters explained to me, was to use water as the principal lure attracting as many visitors as possible to Amsterdam.[68]

The growth of floating parades, parties, and performances provided invaluable fodder for these marketing campaigns.

These functional reappropriations of water-top festivals, combined with the growing regulatory push to package them for tourism interests, transformed the once improvisational events celebrating tolerance, frivolity, and music into officially regulated activities for the sake of business. While these goals were not necessarily incompatible, this shift left many former participants feeling sidelined. Queers initially hosted a parade to celebrate tolerance and inclusivity. Holiday pleasure boaters sought spontaneous, collective revelry. Concert attendees wanted cultural edification. Business interests were important, especially for organizers pitching their events to potential sponsors, but the events were far from mercenary. Instead, they reflected a wide range of interest group objectives. However, with the growing expectation that canals were a de facto public space for the entire city, the special interests behind these events lost ground. Tolerance and pleasure on the water, once seen as ends in themselves, instead became the means to boost general economic development in Amsterdam.

The Crystallization of Public-like Water

These transitions raised important questions about the nature of public space. Although streets and plazas played an important role in industrial-era political activism, in more recent years cafés, pubs, and other nominally private but widely accessible venues have emerged as primary meeting locations involved in the diffuse cultivation of public life.[69] The sanitization and marketization of streets and plazas, by contrast, have incorporated those spaces into business-oriented city marketing campaigns.[70] Queers and partiers initially benefited from staging their events on water rather than on land, but emerging regulatory reforms have since reframed the content of those performances as well as their methods of display. These processes rescripted water as a public space for the city as an imagined whole, rather than as a space that cultural groups could use to advance individual agendas.

In just over a decade, newly invented traditions of queer parading, holiday pleasure boating, and floating artistic performances emerged as among the largest public events recurring annually in Amsterdam. These events were concentrated on central city canals, which were not officially designated as public open spaces. The festivals gained traction in part because experimenters in the early years found ways to use water's jurisdictional and material properties to escape the physical limitations, social conventions, and political associations connected with Amsterdam's streets, plazas, and parks. Water events promised unique types of visibility, surprise, and neutrality, and their success introduced new social norms for congregating and celebrating on water. These mobilizations, when repeated in subsequent years, cultivated new group identities and social visions.

The growing popularity of water-top festivals, combined with rising frustrations over their informal and potentially disruptive attributes, sparked attempts to regulate the canals by transferring land-based codes of conduct to the water surface. The partial and growing success of these measures narrowed the range of acceptable behavior on water, while simultaneously rerouting the identity performances of queers, partiers, and entertainers to more explicitly profitable ends. This regulatory push to make water function more like officially designated public open spaces reinforced efforts to make urban economic competitiveness—rather than tolerance, frivolity, or musical edification—the central objective of water-based events. Even so, this transition remained incomplete, leaving ample room for improvisational acts of self-expression, at least for the time being.

Importantly, the proposed regulatory changes stopped short of rezoning waterways as official public space. This naming issue was not purely semantic. Coding water as "public" would transfer established sets of rules governing use and access in effect on land onto preexisting spaces operating according to different standards on water. For instance, since living in designated public space was illegal, reclassifying canals as public would either put houseboats in jeopardy or would require setting the controversial precedent that people could be permitted to sleep in some types of public spaces. Some residents in canal houses also opposed official rezoning, fearing the potential nuisance that might result if transportation spaces became formally sanctioned public fairgrounds. As such, many people with entrenched interests in the extant jurisdictional system opposed an official reclassification.

Throughout this history, water was transformed from a transportation space with residential edges into a collective gathering space. Given the growing nationalistic overtones of pleasure boating and tourism advertisements, spectacle water-top events functioned as critical moments turning marginalized waterscapes into performance spaces associated with symbols of national identity and Dutch heritage. In these processes, water was not reduced to a singular nationalistic entity. Although imbued with heritage symbolism, water as a provisional stage enabled other performances as well. These events, and the conversion of water into a near-public space, then encouraged residents and city builders to rethink the practical uses and symbolic meanings of water citywide.

CHAPTER THREE

Heritage Buffs on Canals

By the late 1990s, the changing role of water in urban life was undeniable, yet its future trajectory remained unclear. Amsterdam's canals were no longer dismissed as unused, postindustrial landscapes. Houseboaters had been living on water for several decades, and their floating homes were commanding rising sales prices. Major festivals were recurring annually on water, and tourism interest in those events was growing. These activities demonstrated the cultural and economic potential of water as a meaningful and profitable element in the postindustrial city. However, these activities also generated significant ambiguity about the role that water might play in Amsterdam's future. Houseboats, festivals, regulatory reforms, and advertising campaigns pulled water in different directions. Tensions abounded among visions of water as a romanticized space and a profitable one, a counterculture space and nationalistic one, and a domestic space and a public one. These possibilities remained unresolved and widely discussed as the twentieth century drew to a close.

During this period of proliferating interpretations, a group of heritage advocates made a sustained push to transform the image of water by endorsing regulatory reforms and promoting canal reconstruction in the central city. This consortium included local history enthusiasts, preservationists, city planners, and city council representatives. They contended that water infrastructure was an integral component of Amsterdam's urban identity. The best way to appreciate the city's water heritage, they said, was to pattern the streetscape to enhance the visual interplay between water surfaces and the surrounding canal houses and bridges. In other words, instead of actively occupying water with barges, houseboats, or pleasure craft, heritage advocates favored a clear water surface that would reflect the image of the restored canal houses along its edges.

This heritage movement fit well with the ongoing structural pressure to keep property values rising even after several decades of gentrification had already renovated or replaced most of the once-devalued industrial-era buildings in the central city. The elite status of waterside living was growing internationally. In

Amsterdam, from an economic perspective, removing houseboats, regulating pleasure boats, and restoring lost canals promised both to reduce nuisance and to increase the visual and physical connection between water and real estate. The momentum of romanticized cultural activities associated with the canals, however, undercut support for market-based calls to redesign the aesthetics of the water surface to benefit elite property owners at the expense of houseboat hippies and pleasure boaters. The heritage framework, however, created a politically plausible mechanism that could link water and real estate using the rhetoric of public good.

Heritage preservationists pursued their cause through many channels. They lobbied for stronger architectural preservation laws; they refurbished old buildings and constructed new ones in historical styles; and they sought international recognition for the imagined distinctiveness of Amsterdam's cityscape, especially from the UNESCO World Heritage Centre. These long-standing initiatives reached an especially important junction between 1999 and 2005 when heritage groups launched three interrelated initiatives to reconstruct lost canals in the central city. To justify this reconstruction, advocates compiled extensive academic documentation chronicling the history of canal construction and preservation activity in the central city and especially in the medieval core and canal belt neighborhoods.[1] All three of the canal reconstruction initiatives failed from a bricks and mortar perspective since the envisioned waterways were never physically built. Nevertheless, the well-documented, widely publicized, and heavily selective heritage narrative emerging through this process fundamentally transformed public perceptions of water's symbolic legacy.

In contrast to the initially informal and subsequently co-opted houseboats and floating festivals, cultural heritage advocates have explicitly partnered with market practitioners at least since the 1950s. Heritage enthusiasts in the era of urban renewal opposed neighborhood demolition and the planned construction of office buildings that, aesthetically, could have been built anywhere. Instead, they valued historic preservation and locally derived designs that, they felt, made the cityscape pleasant, distinctive, and meaningful. By mobilizing economic logics to support preservation, advocates hoped to exert cultural influence over the market-based city development processes underway. City builders and heritage groups agreed that rent gaps existed, but rather than leaving reinvestment up to market processes, heritage groups challenged municipal planners to abandon urban renewal schemes and, instead, to close the rent gap through historical restoration, including the reimaging of urban water and the reconstruction of lost canals.

This direct engagement with market logic, which advocates vehemently underscored during the three canal reconstruction campaigns of the late 1990s and early 2000s, reinforced the growing sensibility that water and real estate were inescapably fused. The growing international interest in urban shorelines created a generalizing market logic that was difficult to escape. It seemed inevitable that restoring and rebuilding canal edges would lead to higher property values and, by extension, gentrification and social polarization. No matter the social construction of this market value, it was an international phenomenon, and Amsterdam could not simply decide to do water differently. However, instead of yielding to this seemingly inherent political impulse, residents opposing heritage preservation used the coupling of water and value to challenge the desirability of historic designations, regulatory reforms, and canal reconstruction. This process ultimately defeated the implementation of the three canal reconstruction initiatives even as the heritage interpretation of water continued to gain popular support.

During this period, the Amsterdam canals emerged as a near-hegemonic cultural landscape, albeit one that remained inconclusive. Along with the rising market interest in houseboats and the increasingly nationalistic overtones associated with water-top festivals, heritage enthusiasts added a deeply historicized narrative of water as a rich symbolic icon. If this hegemonic framework were physically measurable across space, it would be thickest in the central city canal belt where all three trends converged. The salience of this landscape cannot be overstated. Amsterdam's central city canals had long been held in high regard, and these contemporary trends reinvigorated and enriched their symbolic power. Nevertheless, despite this celebration of culture, wealth, and water in this one small subset of Amsterdam, alternative uses and interpretations of water abounded citywide, with houseboaters and partiers among others continuing to push water in more populist and colloquial directions. The salience of the canal belt did not trump the other political tensions surrounding water's present and future import, and the role of water in urban life remained decidedly unresolved.

To explore these tensions, this chapter chronicles the recent history of the heritage preservation movement in the central city, paying special attention to the cluster of three canal reconstruction initiatives launched in the late 1990s and early 2000s. These initiatives included a proposal to reconstruct a segment of the Rokin Canal, which was dismissed in 1999, a campaign to reconstruct the Palm Canal, which followed the Rokin's dismissal, and a plan to reconstruct either the Elands Canal or the Anjeliers Canal in the central city Jordaan neighborhood, which emerged in 2002. Among these initiatives, I pay special attention to the third proposal in Jordaan. That initiative progressed the farthest, and it generated both the most consolidated set of supporting documentation and the most politically charged opposition. This cluster of canal reconstruction initiatives was part of a larger heritage preservation movement, and it embodied a particularly crucial moment when narratives surrounding water as a salient heritage site crystallized.

The story of the heritage preservation movement and the canal reconstruction initiatives was preserved in several archival documents written to support, evaluate, or oppose the merits of historic preservation. One important source included the archives and self-publications of the self-declared heritage watchdog organization the United Friends of the Amsterdam Inner City (De Vereniging Vrienden van de Amsterdamse Binnenstad). This group actively supported all three of the canal reconstruction proposals, and its chairman, whom I interviewed in 2008, collaborated with academics and government personnel to advance canal-related central city heritage issues on many fronts. These archives also included academic publications that historians and city planners, with encouragement from preservation groups, generated on the water heritage question. A second archival source included public letters, reports, and other memoranda from political party officials, hired experts, and the Amsterdam City Council evaluating various preservation-related proposals. Third, newspaper coverage and editorials preserved the oppositional voice to reconstruction, which was more politically and temporally fragmented.[2]

The heritage movement, in creating this rich set of well-publicized interpretive documents, advanced an explicitly historicized vision of the canals. Moreover, the historic vision that emerged reinforced water's nascent public and nationalistic overtones at the expense of low-cost houseboats and unrestrained festivities. In response, houseboaters and partiers found new ways to justify their continued presence on the water using heritage-related terminology. Moreover, although the goal of reconstructing lost canals never materialized, the mode of seeing that this research and lobbying stimulated gained legitimacy in its own right and went on to influence water-related city building enterprises elsewhere in Amsterdam.

The Growth of the Heritage Preservation Movement

Academics and practitioners have created a wealth of secondary source documentation chronicling the rise and accomplishments of the heritage preservation movement in central Amsterdam preceding the push to reconstruct lost canals at the beginning of the twenty-first century. These accounts describe activists protesting the industrial-era elimination of picturesque canals and resisting the post–World War II urban renewal plans to demolish canal structures and fill in waterways. These groups used many strategies to advance the preservationist agenda, and they paid special attention to the medieval historic core and the seventeenth-century canal belt. Preservation advocates made slow headway for most of the twentieth century, especially in protecting water infrastructure. Then, in the late 1990s, political support for heritage preservation consolidated, which created greater opportunities to pursue canal-related projects alongside the renovation and reconstruction of buildings, plazas, and monuments.

According to secondary sources, between 1828 and 1970, the Amsterdam City Council partially or fully filled seventy-eight canals citywide as part of the municipality's industrial-era modernization impulse.[3] These canals were often filled at the request of wealthy residents living nearby who complained that water was smelly, industrial, quaint, and insalubrious.[4] Filling canals also created opportunities to widen roadways to accommodate larger-scale industry. By the beginning of the twentieth century, a small group of citizens were organizing to preserve some canals with especially picturesque arches and bridges. An especially famous example included an artist and a winemaker who collaborated in 1901 to protest the municipality's decision to replace the Reguliers Canal with a tramline. These activists saw themselves as engaged in the noble endeavor of resisting the transformation of the human city into a warehouse of slavery.[5] In this endeavor, water functioned as a symbol of the heart and soul of Amsterdam. The activists stated: "Who feels for Amsterdam feels for his canals. Amsterdam is the city of canals, and without canals there is no Amsterdam."[6] After six years of protest, a nearly unanimous city council vote abandoned the project and saved the Reguliers Canal from infill.[7]

History enthusiasts in the early 2000s often cited this victory as a direct precursor to the heritage preservation movement that coalesced after World War II. Participants in this later movement used several approaches to advance their cause, including buying historic structures, lobbying for legal reforms, and soliciting international recognition of their city's historical merits.

A private preservation group named Stadsherstel ("City Restoration") was especially proactive in developing direct market strategies. This organization formed in opposition to the municipality's urban renewal plans and, from the 1950s onward, began buying and renovating structures—especially canal-fronting buildings—that the city had earmarked for demolition. The group initially focused on individual houses fronting the most culturally prominent canals and the Amstel River. Along those waterways, they bought dilapidated buildings that they felt no one else wanted, renovated them, and rented them as apartments, offices, and shops. The group also constructed new buildings with historicized massing and facade details to replace structures that had already been demolished or that did not conform to their narrow aesthetic vision.

Although the group engaged in other restoration activities as well, canal house restorations were the group's greatest focus until the 1990s. By the mid-2000s, Stadsherstel had restored or constructed an estimated five hundred structures citywide.[8]

A second strand of the heritage preservation movement focused on strengthening legal protections of historic buildings and landscapes. This multipronged, law-based strategy advanced slowly and made the greatest headway on land. The first significant victory included the implementation of the national Historic Buildings and Monuments Act. Its adoption in 1961 granted special protections to around seven thousand buildings in central Amsterdam, or about one-third of the total buildings in the city center.[9] Preservationists urged municipal officials to designate the three major canal belt waterways as historic monuments as well, but officials worried that such a measure would prompt unpopular rent hikes at a time when the economy was slowing and the social housing movement was booming.[10] Preservationists made more progress with Amsterdam's Protected Cityscape legislation, enacted in 1999. This legislation, adopted after a decade of debate, established rules about material and facade treatments that applied to every structure in the central city regardless of its age, so that, for instance, if the city issued a demolition permit, contractors were required to replicate the facade gables and original materials of the old structure in the new building that followed.[11]

A third strand of activism focused on soliciting international recognition for the historic merit of Amsterdam's central city landscape, especially by championing an application to list the city center as an official UNESCO World Heritage Site. Preservationists began discussing the possibility of nominating a section of Amsterdam in the late 1980s, but since official recognition would have given landowners the legal right to raise their rents, the proposal remained stalled for over a decade. Between 1995 and 2006, UNESCO recognized six other heritage sites in the Netherlands, all but one of which were connected with water. When a group of academics and practitioners eventually submitted an application for the medieval city center in the early 2000s, UNESCO personnel sent the application back, saying they already had better medieval European city centers on the roster. Instead of refusing the application, however, they urged the petitioners to reframe the application to focus specifically on the seventeenth-century canal belt waterways exclusive of the rest of the central city. Following this advice, the amended application was approved in 2010.[12]

In this history, the late 1990s marked a turning point when the preservationist agenda gained tremendous political support. As the director of the Stadsherstel preservation group phrased it when speaking publicly in 2005, "historic building is again popular, complete with the rebuilding of disappeared historic buildings."[13] By that time, investors had renovated or replaced most of the central city structures that had lost value during the industrial or postindustrial era. City officials expanded preservation laws that previously protected individual buildings and monuments to also protect the spatial interrelationships among those structures and the cityscape they constituted. International heritage agencies were urging a greater focus on waterscapes, rather than monuments and palaces, as the quintessence of Amsterdam's uniqueness. Tourism events, such as the Canal Festival discussed in the previous chapter, reinforced that interpretation. These trends created an opportunity for preservationists to expand their platform and shift their focus from land and buildings to water and canals.

Shaping an Aesthetic of Water Heritage

In the late 1990s, the self-declared heritage watchdog organization United Friends of the Amsterdam Inner City emerged as an active lobbying group protecting the historic city center against the ill-defined "degradation of the cityscape."[14] The organization had connections with the Stadsherstel preservation group, as well as with preservation-minded activists promoting restaurant and business interests in the Jordaan neighborhood in central Amsterdam. Its leaders also developed strong professional ties with academic historians, municipal planners, and city council members, and they were active in generating neighborhood history documents and lobbying for regulatory reforms that they felt were compatible with their heritage cause.

For preservationists associated with this group, water symbolized the historic identity of Amsterdam. In self-published reports, the long-standing chairman emphasized that "except for Venice, there is no single other city in the world where water is so important to city image than in Amsterdam."[15] A colleague of his on the Amsterdam City Council published similar statements in a comprehensive report written to support the canal restoration agenda, saying, "the historic inner city of Amsterdam [. . .] is a water city: a city built on and in the water. From the water, Amsterdam derives its essence and its identity."[16] These statements, written for public consumption and persuasion, reinforced a perceived unity of spatial form and urban identity embodied in a rich canal landscape. "Amsterdam and water belong together."[17]

Despite these identity claims, preservationists felt that existing historic preservation laws overlooked the symbolic importance of canal aesthetics. Statues and palaces were the usual stuff of historic designation. The passage of Amsterdam's Protected Cityscape legislation created an opportunity for the United Friends to challenge this trend. This legislation, which emphasized the importance of a visual field surpassing the value of any particular monument, created a legal framework to emphasize water as an underlying spatial framework defining this holistic spatial vision. Water as a salient identity feature emerged as a principal element in the city's historic structure, if not a feature directly tied to any singular building site.[18]

Using this emphasis on the visuality of water as a heritage symbol, the United Friends advocated for a specific canal aesthetic they felt would heighten the optical potency of this terrain. For instance, spokespeople advocated for a clean and clear water surface that could mirror the image of the patrician houses that the Stadsherstel restoration group so painstakingly restored in the water surface. The group reinforced written descriptions of water's reflective capabilities with photos showing gabled facades reflected in still water canals, paired with similarly framed photos where houseboats blocked the reflection and replaced it with their own supposedly inauthentic and unattractive visage.[19] Similarly, the United Friends advocated for a highbrow interpretation of the canals as a public space, especially by criticizing officials for managing water as a nautical fairway where boaters could do as they pleased. Instead, in the organization's self-published journal, spokespeople pressured the municipality to accept water as the quintessential public space of the city, realize that the urban look of water was important, and promote a water aesthetic that was clean, spacious, beautiful, and coherent.[20]

This aesthetic vision put the United Friends and their preservation-minded allies in direct conflict with many of the houseboaters and pleasure boaters making provisional use of the central city waterways. The organization's houseboat criticisms were especially contentious. In a frankly worded political campaign, the United Friends voiced opposition to the extension of long-term mooring rights. The group also explicitly advocated to eliminate, thin out, and relocate "crap boats" lacking historic or aesthetic merit, which, by their count, included 79 percent of the total boats moored in the central city in 2000.[21] The United Friends had a more favorable view of pleasure boaters, and they actively supported the growing Canal Festival with its classical music concerts and historic walking tours. However, they pushed officials to develop more robust regulations to curtail potential nuisance.[22] The United Friends' lobbying efforts on these fronts met resistance from houseboaters and pleasure boaters, who pointed to historical precursors that gave their activities a heritage gloss, as well as from people who said their present-day water-top activities should not be subservient to the aesthetic vision of an artificial and elitist heritage theme park.[23] These arguments appear to have left heritage advocates unphased.

With this aesthetic vision as a guide, between 1999 and 2005 the United

Friends played a leading role in efforts to reconstruct lost canals in the central city. A newly reconstructed canal with no preexisting houseboating or pleasure boating associations promised to function as an important demonstration project for the organization. By using narrow widths and shallow depths, the group could design a canal that traced the path of a lost waterway but that physically precluded unwanted boating activities without requiring displacement measures or special laws. Instead, the visual effect of the reflective water surface would take priority, which proponents felt would improve the quality of the streetscape for people living, walking, and shopping nearby. Investing in canal reconstruction could also demonstrate the city's commitment to its heritage landscape, a move that reconstruction advocates felt would strengthen their ongoing UNESCO World Heritage application.

The idea to rebuild canals had been around at least since the 1930s, although proponents made no material progress on reconstruction for several decades.[24] By the late 1990s, however, urban water restoration projects were in advanced planning stages or under construction in at least nine other Dutch cities and towns. Reconstruction advocates publicized these activities in Amsterdam, paying special attention to a canal excavation project then underway in the nearby city of Utrecht. Local government officials in Utrecht had announced their intention to restore a one-and-a-half-kilometer stretch of the Singel Canal encircling Utrecht's medieval city center in 1999. Excavation advocates in Amsterdam heralded the "re-digging" plans to excavate the "vanished" canal as "the most important example of canal excavation in the Netherlands" and a role model for what they hoped to accomplish in the capital city of Amsterdam.[25] By 2006, with a third of the Utrecht project complete, supporters were already celebrating the positive visual contribution that canal restoration made to the livability of the surrounding neighborhood.[26]

For advocates of canal reconstruction in Amsterdam, their city's absence from the list of Dutch cities engaged in such practices was conspicuous. Amsterdam was the national capital, but it was not a seat of government or a global economic center. Instead, Amsterdam's status rested on its cultural cache.[27] Reporters favoring canal reconstruction proposals wrote that "in the Netherlands, Amsterdam is lagging behind in restoring ancient water structures."[28] The director of the United Friends agreed, stating publicly that "in other cities in the Netherlands, people are much farther along in bringing back historic water. [. . .] Amsterdam is trailing behind this nationwide trend."[29] Reconstructing a lost canal in Amsterdam promised to restore the city's status as the nation's leading canal city. The question that remained was how to get the local public on board with the proposal.

Justifying Intervention with a Credible Historic Narrative

Reconstructing a canal along the route where one once stood proved politically fraught. This sort of infrastructural project was costly, and advocates hoped to use public tax revenue to cover the expense. The project would also inevitably disrupt and perhaps even displace residents, businesses, and traffic patterns along the construction route. To advance their reconstruction cause, as well as to promote the UNESCO application, heritage proponents and their academic and professional colleagues generated and circulated extensive documentation that publicized the history of canal construction in Amsterdam and reinforced the cultural symbolism of water. In particular, their account framed the seventeenth-century canal belt as an especially significant cultural achievement; it blamed supposedly unsympathetic foreign invaders and misguided car-centered development models for the loss of historic waterways; and it characterized canal reconstruction as an opportunity to restore denigrated urban spaces to an imagined former glory.

These publications and public speeches painted an almost mystical picture of the construction of Amsterdam's canal belt at the imagined apex of the Dutch golden age. The story began in 1613 as Amsterdam stood on the brink of imperial ascent. Although the city was already over three hundred years old, it was said that on the land around the medieval embankment, nothing existed but a vision. A quick sentence or two later, the narrative reaches 1670. Trenches carved through the ground, water flowed through them, and an unseen hand inserted the final brick into a magnificent new landscape. At this legendary moment, the "world famous crescent canals" were born.[30] The Prince's Canal, the Emperor's Canal, and the Gentlemen's Canal formed a concentric, half-moon shape encompassing the medieval core. At this fleeting yet frozen moment, Amsterdam figured as the "navel of the cosmos"—or the administrative seat of a global empire.[31] The waterways were seen as "the jewels of the city," crystallizing Amsterdam's urban form and global prowess in one bold stroke.[32]

Construction on land ensued. City officials allocated plots for development in accordance with some basic design guidelines and taxation laws. The lots sold incrementally. Several decades passed before the grand patrician houses lining the waterways materialized, and many were refurbished or replaced over the following centuries.[33] An Amsterdam City Council report from 2004 underscored the importance of water in this development process, saying, "the buildings along the sides come from many historic periods, but the water structure forms such an important under-mat that the protection of the canals is essential" to preserving the historic fabric of the city.[34] While the architecture on land may have shifted with the sands of time, the waterways were thought to have remained constant as the heir of the Dutch golden age.

Having established this origin story connecting water, grandeur, and Amsterdam, the second phase of the historical narrative skipped ahead two hundred years to an account of a protracted, misguided assault on water. These "damaging" attempts to "make a land city out of the water city" allegedly began by French decree after Napoleon Bonaparte conquered Amsterdam in 1795.[35] His brother, appointed as acting monarch, purportedly demanded that a stinky canal behind the palace be filled and transformed into a respectable Parisian boulevard.[36] Although the Dutch golden age had been over for nearly a century already, and although Napoleon's brother reigned for less than a decade, this moment of unsympathetic foreign conquest supposedly constituted both the end of Amsterdam's global influence and the cultural abandonment of its watery heritage.

Several decades later, the canals came under renewed attack, first from industrialization peaking between 1870 and 1930, and again during the 1950s period of urban renewal. During both periods, city builders worked at a rapid pace to eliminate canals and replace them with roads and rail lines. As heritage-minded historians analyzing the changes occurring during that period explained, "the whole of Amsterdam transformed from a seventeenth and eighteenth century city with its corners and canals and small streets for handicrafts into a city with warehouses and big trade and factories."[37] The canals, as a common waste and sewage disposal location, became an infamous source of typhoid and cholera.[38] Canal reconstruction advocates generally blamed the situation on infill projects that disrupted a natural flow that once supposedly made the canals self-flushing.[39] Regardless, for the sake of modernization, the canals had to go. The grand crescent canals survived the onslaught, but nearly eighty of their watery comrades disappeared beneath piles of sand.[40]

Having established canal infill as inauthentic and harmful, these historical narratives generally ended by framing the canal reconstruction initiatives emerging in the late 1990s and early 2000s as an opportunity to repair the damage and restore Amsterdam to its former cultural glory. If canal infill erased an authentic Amsterdam, a deterministic logic suggested that reconstructing lost canals would bring the past back to life. The United Friends, for example, described rebuilding canals as "a battle to bring the inner city into a new phase, restoring as much of the old splendor of the architectural structure as possible."[41] These types of characterizations portrayed water projects as the imagined means to "bring back history," reclaiming, to paraphrase one excavation advocate, a cultural respect thought to have been lost to imperial conquest and dirty industry by re-creating the heart and veins of the waterscape forged at the city's imagined peak.[42]

These accounts framed potential canal expansion projects at the turn of the twenty-first century as excavations and restorations, not as new construction. To reinforce this cognitive frame, the two terms coined to describe building a canal where one once stood were *hergraven*, meaning "to redig," and *ontdempen*, meaning "to un-stop-up," both of which emphasized the importance of a material precursor. Similarly, the United Friends and their partners described canal restoration as a simple matter of unburying canal walls that supposedly still existed preserved underneath mounds of dirt.[43] To rally public support for canal reconstruction, United Friends leaders and their city council allies posed for photos lifting spades of soil out of the ground in the staged act of uncovering the city of the past.[44]

These heritage attributes were thought to come with economic opportunities and improvements in quality of life. For instance, heritage advocates, who knew from past experience that city council members might hesitate to financially support heritage restoration for its own sake, emphasized that rebuilding historic waterways would boost tourism, consumerism, and real estate activity. As one historian phrased it in 2005, "in Amsterdam, the number of people who put a high value on cultural heritage has increased spectacularly since the 1980s."[45] Heritage landscapes had become a source of economic and social innovation. Central city canals, as water laden with history and identity, were especially lucrative. These arguments cast canal reconstruction as "preservation through development," or the historic reconstruction of the central city via profitable investment with immediate benefits to property owners and business investors.[46]

Along with these economic benefits, heritage advocates emphasized that canal reconstruction would improve neighborhood livability. The United Friends heritage group, for instance, circulated a strongly worded editorial emphasizing that excavation was not an act of nostalgia. Instead, they said, it transformed housing on parking lots into homes on canals; it made for attractive shopping streets; and it improved the urban ecology of the cityscape. These livability improvements stemmed from the presumed human scale of urban architecture in the preindustrial era. Reclaiming the street from car-centered designs by rebuilding historical waterscapes would, by this logic, bring picturesque beauty back to Amsterdam.[47] In contrast to high modern city planning, "now, excavation is the way to expand livability. [. . .] From a historical perspective, we've come full circle."[48]

This version of history—with its linguistic, economic, and aesthetic cues—has since become a common trope in public discourse connecting water, identity, and a selective interpretation of local history. Canal reconstruction advocates recounted this narrative in public speeches and promotional literature. It appeared time and again in newspaper reports and quasi-academic publications. It was repeated nearly verbatim in government documents and municipal websites. This narrative of the past helped justify arguments for city building projects in the present. From this perspective, canal restoration was not reducible to a special interest group's aesthetic taste. Instead, restoring water figured as a means of reinforcing sensibilities of a shared cultural heritage and a unique golden age ur-identity.

Three Proposals to Rebuild Lost Canals

Heritage enthusiasts used this historical narrative to build public support for several canal improvement and preservation measures, including a cluster of initiatives to rebuild lost canals in the central city in the late 1990s and early 2000s. These initiatives both contributed to the production of this history trope and created political opportunities to publicly circulate that discourse. Although none of the proposed reconstructions were built, the heritage narrative these initiatives helped consolidate gained traction, becoming an accepted truth of the city.

The first initiative to rebuild a lost waterway proposed excavating a few hundred meters of the Rokin Canal. The Rokin, one of Amsterdam's oldest canals, once ran through the heart of its medieval center. In 1934, despite twenty-two years of civic activism to save the canal, the municipality filled the Rokin and constructed a large boulevard in its place.[49] The heritage advocates of the day continued their struggle, calling immediately for the canal's reconstruction, but those calls had extremely limited public support.

In the 1990s, when the municipality was making plans to construct a new subway system in Amsterdam, the proposal to rebuild the Rokin gained political traction. Advocates suggested removing the linear parking strip running through the center of the boulevard, building the subway line underneath, and installing a shallow canal overtop. Most of the heritage preservation community supported "letting water back into the Rokin up to the Dam so that the city's namesake, the dam in the Amstel River, would be visible from the city square."[50] Moreover, by constructing a shallow canal, preservationists could rest assured that no new houseboaters and pleasure boaters would be able to obstruct the water's reflective surface.[51] Some people, however, felt the proposed redesign was too feeble. These critics were sympathetic to the canal reconstruction cause, and they agreed that the filling of the canal had "mutilated the city's face." However, they felt the proposed design for a canal that was only thirty centimeters

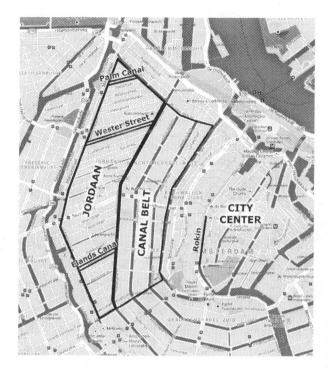

Map showing the proposed canal reconstruction sites in central Amsterdam.

deep amounted to "absolutely nothing," a "paddling pool" rather than a full canal, which was not worth its financial or political cost.[52]

The Rokin discussion ended in 1999 when the Amsterdam City Council voted against reconstruction. They cited the technical complications of turning such a major traffic artery into a waterway. The subway line took another route, and the city built a subterranean parking structure where the Rokin once flowed and installed a vegetated public plaza on its roof. Heritage enthusiasts took the defeat in stride, saying excavation was a new idea whose time had not yet come and whose implementation kinks still had to be finessed.[53] Full of optimism, they sought to apply the lessons learned in this first campaign to two subsequent urban water restoration initiatives.

The second attempt to open a filled canal in Amsterdam's city center began in 2000 with a call to excavate the block-long Palm Canal (Palmgracht) in the northwestern corner of the central city. This canal was filled in 1895, and preservationists chose it as a potential reconstruction site because one of the leading reconstruction advocates with the United Friends heritage group had lived on the block for over thirty years. With help from this organization and its city council connections, this resident organized a petition drive requesting that the city rebuild the canal. He collected ninety-three signatures from his neighbors, representing roughly half of the residents living in the immediate work area. The United Friends also used the opportunity to publicize canal restoration projects already underway elsewhere in the Netherlands, especially in the nearby cities of Utrecht and Breda. Their publicity painted Amsterdam planners as brooding endlessly over a relatively small, community-supported undertaking while leaders in other cities moved boldly forward.[54] Despite these efforts, the City Council Executive Board in 2001 decided not to rebuild the canal, citing the project's cost and traffic disruptions, as well as neighborhood concerns about the displacement of a local playground.

Despite this second setback, heritage preservation groups with help from members of two prominent political parties—the right liberal VVD and the pro-labor PvdA—continued lobbying for canal reconstruction. In response to this growing public pressure, in 2002 Amsterdam's Central Borough government agreed to formally incorporate the objective to rebuild at least one filled canal into its 2002–2006 District Plan.[55] Heritage groups quickly identified the Jordaan neighborhood as a prime location for such a project. Jordaan, which ran along the western edge of the canal belt, was a predominantly working-class neighborhood until the 1980s, when it began to rapidly gentrify.[56] Six of the neighborhood's original eleven canals were filled during the nineteenth and twentieth centuries. In 2002, only one of those filled canals was a major transportation artery.[57]

The United Friends and their allies immediately began organizing rallies, photo ops, and information sessions in the neighborhood, calling on the municipal government to open either the Elands Canal (Elandsgracht), filled in 1891, or the Anjeliers Canal (Anjeliersgracht, subsequently renamed Westerstraat), filled in 1860.[58] Central city government officials responded by commissioning a feasibility study in 2003 that returned a favorable assessment of both potential sites the following year. The report outlined the steps necessary to build a deeply sunken underground parking garage with a narrow but moderately deep canal running overtop in either of the two locations.[59] The canal would be large enough to accommodate small, slow-moving pleasure boats, but it was strategically designed to be too small to accommodate houseboats and large tour boats. A municipal survey polling residents in 2004 showed that three-quarters of citywide residents supported the plan, as did nine out of ten residents living along the proposed Elands Canal route and seven out of ten residents living along the Anjeliers Canal path.[60] Design, budgeting, scheduling, and public support appeared to fall into place. All that remained, it seemed, was to choose which of the two vetted sites would be best.

The tide turned, however, during a contentious community meeting in September 2004. Meeting organizers expected the event would be a formality,

Proposed streetscape design for the Elands Canal, including a shallow canal overtop of a subterranean parking garage, 2004. Image by City of Amsterdam, courtesy of Walter Schoonenburg, De Vereniging Vrienden van de Amsterdamse Binnenstad.

informing the public of their findings and confirming that the Elands Canal site would be best. Looking back, the city council member running the meeting described it as "a mess."[61] He tried valiantly to convey his vision of a "picturesque glittering piece of recovered city beauty" to a large and increasingly irritable crowd.[62] According to newspaper reporters covering the meeting, "advocates for the new canal spoke elegantly about 'a tourist product' and 'a unique selling point' and politely called out 'bravo' for the glory of the new canals." However, for opponents, the proposal was "reprehensible" and an "idiot plan."[63] Residents and business owners said they "dreaded living for years next to a construction site."[64] Shopkeepers were concerned that construction would prevent customers from accessing their stores.[65] Other attendees voiced skepticism that the project would finish on time and on budget: "Construction always takes longer than 'they' say."[66] Critics worried that excavation would destabilize building foundations and that the canal would interfere with established street life.[67]

The uncharacteristic rancor of the meeting caught heritage enthusiasts by surprise. No canal reconstruction project had yet succeeded in Amsterdam. However, proponents imagined the failing emerged from technical difficulties surrounding implementation, rather than from an emotionally charged public opposition to rebuilding lost waterways. With a broad base of support for reconstruction citywide, and with the international urban water craze well underway, the fierce opposition to reconstruction in the Jordaan neighborhood bucked these trends.

The Counternarrative to Amsterdam's Water Heritage

For critics of the proposal to rebuild a canal in Jordaan, the public discussions surrounding the initiative provided an opportunity to criticize broad social changes underway in the Netherlands. Residents speaking against the project challenged the historic integrity both of the heritage narrative and of the proposed design for the rebuilt waterway. These history disputes doubled as social critiques against the increasing elitism of Amsterdam's city center and public spaces. Ultimately, anxieties about gentrification in the context of a weakening social welfare state prevented reconstruction from proceeding even as heritage tropes gained widespread public acceptance.

Heritage enthusiasts who used public renditions of Amsterdam's water history trope to justify canal reconstruction necessarily presented a filtered read of the past. Residents opposing canal reconstruction eagerly challenged that reading as unfounded and selective.[68] Most significantly, critics emphasized that the canal infill era between the 1820s and the 1970s also included what they termed Amsterdam's second golden age. This era of industrial development brought significant advances in liberal government, social housing, general education, and public health. During this period, filling the premodern, antiquated, disease-ridden canals symbolized the city's progress and the country's entrance into European politics as a modern nation-state.[69] In the traditionally working-class neighborhood of Jordaan, remembering and celebrating the physical modernization of the city and the social modernization of government institutions went hand in hand.

Similarly, critics easily identified historic inaccuracies in the proposed canal reconstruction designs. Heritage enthusiasts wanted to create the visual aesthetic of a reflective water surface uncluttered by contemporary houseboats and pleasure boats. New canals designed to be half the width and a tenth the depth of their original precursors, although proportionally inaccurate, meant the most important feature from the heritage perspective—that of retracing the route of a lost canal with a clear and clean reflective water channel—would remained uncompromised by later users. For critics, however, the proportions mattered. A narrow or shallow waterway that could not accommodate boating was "a ditch, not a canal."[70] The usability of the water surface, for many residents, gave water its purpose. Without that nautical utility, water just took up space in an already crowded city. These types of projects, critics said, turned the city into a historical amusement park. "A reconstructed tower, an excavated canal, [. . .] it has no authenticity."[71]

A related point of contention was that many residents and business owners feared that reconstructing an aesthetic image of the past would disrupt local needs in the present. For residents, gentrification was the primary concern. Real estate reports from the early 2000s demonstrated that water frontage in the Netherlands added an average 28 percent premium to a property's real estate value. For a privately owned plot in the center of the capital city, the premiums would likely be even higher.[72] Transforming a dry street into a canal street would likely significantly increase the property values on either side. With the municipal government reducing its commitment to rent controls and social housing development, this level of property appreciation concerned tenants who feared displacement and who saw few attractive relocation options.[73]

Even if residents could remain in their housing, many critics felt the project put local businesses in jeopardy. Small entrepreneurs were especially concerned that storefronts barricaded behind a multiyear construction site would lose business and that their customers would forget to return once the construction was over.[74] Moreover, the expected increase in property value would likely encourage higher-end, tourism-oriented retail at the expense of resident-focused grocers and Laundromats. The incoming wealthy residents and patrons, critics said, would have "no concern whatsoever" for the local people whose labor made luxurious living possible.[75] Historical water might come back, but if it did, "the original residents [would] disappear, taking their local economy with them."[76] Similarly, while "yuppies" may like a canal in front of their door, many residents felt that other land uses—such as street parking, children's playgrounds, flea markets, and memorial squares—were better suited to the daily needs of "ordinary" people.[77]

Opposition to canal reconstruction became a means to denounce the elite-oriented future that heritage restoration enabled, as well as the general erosion of social welfare protections at the turn of the twenty-first century. To deflect sensibilities of vulnerability in the wake of welfare cutbacks and global economic restructuring, many local merchants and residents denounced canal reconstruction. Anxiety that water would undermine the interests of ordinary people who were already feeling the crunch of economic and government restructuring effectively derailed the Jordaan excavation proposal's chances of success.

The intensity of animosity during the 2004 public meeting undercut the initiative's political support. City council officials concluded after the meeting that the proposal was too controversial and needed further discussion before proceeding. According to the municipal official hosting the meeting, one by one, local political parties withdrew their support.[78] The chairman of the United Friends heritage group emphasized his sense of injustice about the meeting when I interviewed him four years later. "The city council shuffled the project away. Most people are in favor of the project, in general and in this specific form. But the silent majority was trumped by the shouting minority."[79] Although the group tried to rally support by mounting a citywide referendum in 2005, in the context of ongoing local contestation, central city officials dismissed the referendum and declared their unwillingness to consider further canal reconstruction projects in the immediate future.[80] Heritage groups and municipal officials still said they hoped to revisit the topic someday, if the political mood changed, but for the time being, discussion on the issue had closed.[81]

The Heritage Valence of Water

For preservationists, the historic canal landscape embodied the rich national heritage of an all-too-fleeting moment when Amsterdam was the world's leading imperial city. From this perspective, making water flow again through a street where a canal once stood would reproduce a lost piece of the city's golden age. Leaders of the loosely organized canal excavation movement believed that such a project would beautify the streetscape, stimulate economic development, increase the memorability of the neighborhood, and, most importantly, reaffirm their vision of a cultural heritage that made Amsterdam unique.

The economic implications of canal reconstruction proved a double-edged sword that ultimately undermined—rather than aided—the heritage cause. Deep fears about changing government priorities and market forces lay below the surface. For local businesses and working-class residents feeling the pinch, water history tropes threatened to provide an entry point for gentrification, privatization, and other exclusionary trends. Excavation opponents were not antihistory, antiwater, or anti-Amsterdam. Their criticisms merely invoked a different heritage and a different landscape that better reflected their own priorities in a context of perceived risk. In their eyes, working-class people, not water, were under siege. Therefore, at the height of the international urban water craze, residents in one of the wettest cityscapes in the North Atlantic bucked the trend and refused to rebuild a lost canal.

Despite this setback, the multipronged heritage preservation movement continued to grow and pursued other initiatives. Their opposition to supposedly inauthentic houseboats in the context of the Protected Cityscape legislation encouraged municipal officials to hold houseboaters accountable to the same design and construction standards governing housing on land. Heritage preservationists also routinely collaborated with the organizers of the annual Canal Festival, especially by arranging walking tours of the canal belt neighborhoods. Additionally, in 2010, after a ten-year campaign, the seventeenth-century canal belt and its three crescent canals were officially added to the UNESCO list of World Heritage Sites.

Most importantly, although none of the canal reconstruction projects materialized, the public discussions surrounding these initiatives solidified and popularized a standard heritage trope connecting water, identity, and history in Amsterdam. These discussions added a heritage-based interpretive lens to water's already kaleidoscopic essence. By the mid-2000s, water was a former industrial landscape still deeply embedded in jurisdictional divisions of labor from past decades. It was a domestic space with countercultural roots that was slowly being pulled into the formal real estate market. Water was a de facto public open space used for collective gathering and identity performances that were increasingly nationalistic in tone. To this mix, heritage enthusiasts added a history framework that presented water, and especially the seventeenth-century canal belt, as a culturally unique and internationally valued historic landmark.

This vision of water as a heritage landscape privileged the image of canals with open surfaces reflecting patrician houses for passive visual consumption. This narrative, although unable to galvanize support for canal reconstruction, nevertheless became a highly symbolic icon used to define and interpret city building initiatives unfolding elsewhere in Amsterdam.

CHAPTER FOUR

Planners on Harbors

By the late 1990s, the various social movements mobilizing Amsterdam's waterscapes had imbued water with new meanings. Water was associated with romantic hippy lifestyles, highbrow cultural refinement, and national heritage identities. The cultural actors involved favored central city locations, which meant that the emerging water associations were most thickly anchored in the figural forms of the central city canals. These waterscapes, rooted in Renaissance-era architectural styles, were aesthetically distinct from the industrial-era harbors, and it remained unclear how the shifting read of the canal landscape would influence public perceptions of water along the industrial wharves.

The Amsterdam City Council's decision to redevelop underused industrial shorelines beginning in the 1990s created opportunities for a heightened political discourse that mobilized, modified, and further pluralized the identity of Amsterdam water. The redevelopment areas included many discontinuous strips of waterfronts along the IJ waterway.[1] Those shorelines and harbors contained extensive, disused port infrastructure, transshipment equipment, and storage sheds. The municipal Physical Planning Department overseeing redevelopment envisioned that waterfront as a tabula rasa location. These officials had little interest in the waterfront's past life, and their redevelopment plans initially paid no attention to the water offshore. This turn away from water and its industrial past stemmed in part from the department's long-standing policy of providing affordable housing, which, prior to market liberalization measures passed during the 1990s, inadvertently discouraged water-oriented real estate investment. For several years after these reforms, planners still preferred to focus on green spaces, bicycle facilities, and other functional amenities, rather than investing in water-oriented architecture, which increased housing costs without, in their eyes, creating useful amenities.

During the course of redevelopment, however, water emerged as a significant symbolic element and financial consideration fueling an increasingly water-oriented urban growth paradigm. Squatters resisting displacement from industrial buildings used historic preservation laws to slow redevelopment and force a public recognition of the value of nineteenth- and twentieth-century nautical monuments. Architects hired from outside the municipal planning department following the shift from state-controlled development to public-private partnerships introduced new ideas about water-oriented architecture. Reporters and tourists visiting construction sites made their own connections between the brownfield shorelines, their nautical history, and the proliferating water associations emerging in the central city. Policy shifts encouraging high-end housing for elite and often foreign buyers likewise expanded the legal and economic opportunities to incorporate luxury water forms into redeveloped urban spaces.

These trends transformed the character of waterfront development in Amsterdam. Water—laden with romantic, cultural, and heritage associations from central city social movements—emerged as a useful tool helping city planners attract creative knowledge workers in business, finance, culture, and leisure industries for the postindustrial economy. The new symbolic associations connected to the canals inflected design decisions and spatial interpretations on the

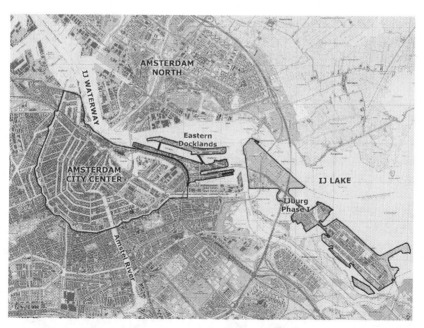

Map showing the large-scale development sites along the
IJ waterway during the 1990s and 2000s.

former industrial wharves, transforming the harbor's gritty past into the more marketable, sanitized aesthetic of the seventeenth-century Dutch golden age.

The Eastern Docklands (Oostelijk Havengebied) redevelopment project was one of many large shoreline investment initiatives that have emerged along the IJ waterway since the early 1990s. This project functioned as an especially important formative moment in the transition from urban design frameworks that ignored history and water to strategies that privileged nautical references and water aesthetics. Other noteworthy investments occurred along the Southern Bank (Zuidelijke IJoever, including Oostelijke Handelskade and Piet Heinkade), in Amsterdam North (Amsterdam Noord, including NDSM Werf and Overhoeks), and on IJburg, which is the subject of the following chapter. These projects emerged in the aftermath of sweeping policy changes that reversed past commitments to affordable housing and that established new priorities emphasizing luxury, owner-occupied development to expand Amsterdam's middle- and upper-income residential base. The Eastern Docklands, as one of the first major residential projects built after these policy changes, gave legal changes on paper a material reality on the ground. Moreover, as a successful early project, the Eastern Docklands functioned as an experimental prototype for the many waterfront projects that have followed.

From a political economy perspective, market calculations heavily influenced the timing, scale, and programmatic aspects of the waterfront transformation. Nevertheless, squatter activism, architectural whimsy, and media fantasies emerging during the implementation process encouraged market-conscious planners to change tactics in midstream. Planners knew water-oriented investment could increase real estate value, but they doubted that local buyers could sustain those premiums. Cultural groups' insistence that the redevelopment celebrate water and nautical heritage, however, generated an emphatic market response. These trends demonstrated that a larger rent gap existed on the waterfront than planners initially expected, and realtors mobilized the cultural iconography of water anchored in the central city canalscape to attract buyers willing to pay the added costs.

In these developments, the role of water varied spatially and temporally. In the Eastern Docklands and other early shoreline redevelopment projects undertaken during the 1990s and early 2000s, nautical heritage frameworks proved especially significant. Water's influence in these initial projects was often indirect, filtered through dock-related infrastructure and central city canal aesthetics. In later projects, such as in IJburg, as discussed in the following chapter, water's immediate physical properties gained greater salience. Initially, however, cultural actors and the planners co-opting their ideas mobilized water primarily through vistas, symbols, and infrastructural traces, rather than through direct engagement and occupancy.

The romantic, cultural, and heritage overtones associated with the central city canals helped nautical history frameworks take root, although invoking these water associations in the context of harbors and bays further pluralized those meanings of Amsterdam water. Vast waterscapes, seafaring narratives, and modern architecture decentered the previous focus on narrow canals, local artisans, and preserved buildings. These reinterpretations simultaneously reclaimed industrial-scale shorelines from disrepute and cloaked their imagined rust and grit in the aura of a seventeenth-century heritage.

The political debates, design shifts, and market strategies associated with these waterfront transformations were preserved in many textual sources written during the Eastern Docklands' twenty-two-year construction period. Systematic searches of newspaper archives uncovered blow-by-blow accounts of construction progress, development challenges, and market assessments. Municipal, provincial, and national government offices also generated written reports, newsletters, and promotional brochures that articulated the evolving connections between water-oriented housing and general economic growth strategies. Studies from policy advisers with the Amsterdam Federation of Housing Associations (Amsterdamse federatie van woningcorporaties) underscored the importance of the policy shifts that made water-oriented and market-led real estate development legally and financially possible during this period. These various archival sources recorded the rise of nautical heritage discourses, their grudging incorporation into municipal planning frameworks, and the emergence of a water-oriented investment paradigm in Amsterdam.

Market Liberalizations and the Shifting Value of Locational Amenities

Prior to 1989, municipal policy frameworks gave government planning institutions and social housing associations near total control over new home construction and prevented locational amenities, like waterfronts, from influencing housing prices. Water heavily influenced the price of privately owned housing in historic sections of Amsterdam, but legally it had virtually no financial impact on the majority of housing units citywide. Since 1989, however, following several market liberalization reforms, market influence over the housing sector has expanded considerably, creating the possibility for locational factors, like water, to emerge as a salient financial consideration in new home construction.[2]

Amsterdam's unique land ownership laws established at the end of the nineteenth century gave the municipality considerable influence over real estate investment and housing construction. Unlike most of the Netherlands, in 1896 the Amsterdam City Council established a land-lease system (Erfpacht) where the municipality legally owned all land developed from that point onward. Some areas, such as the seventeenth-century canal belt, predated this land-lease system, and so those areas were exempt from this law. However, geographically, most of Amsterdam's current footprint includes land incorporated into the city during twentieth-century urban expansion, which means that most residential land is publicly owned. The city sells that land to private purchasers on a term-limited basis, usually for fifty or seventy-five years, after which ownership reverts back to the municipality for potential resale.[3]

These ownership laws gave the city council considerable control over twentieth-century urban development, especially when combined with the 1901 Housing Law (Woningwet) that created a mechanism to funnel government money to social housing authorities building centrally managed, affordable housing. Social housing constituted 18 percent of Amsterdam's total housing stock by 1950. Housing authorities reached a near monopoly on new home construction in the mid-1980s when 95 percent of new housing starts citywide were destined for the social housing market and, by 1995, social housing units composed 58 percent of the housing market.[4]

In the early 1990s, just before the Eastern Docklands and other IJ waterway redevelopment projects entered construction, alongside social housing units, one-third of Amsterdam housing operated as private rentals that again were subject to strict city council controls. A senior policy adviser with the Amsterdam Federation of Housing Associations explained how this process worked during an extended interview in 2009. Under the city's Residential Assessment System (Woningwaarderingsstelsel), all rental properties in Amsterdam—both social and private rentals—received a numerical rating based on their size, condition, location, and unit amenities. The government, not the market, set the maximum rental prices for all properties receiving a rating of fewer than 142 points, which in 1995 constituted about 89 percent of all housing units in Amsterdam.[5]

Importantly, the locational component of the valuation was extremely limited, and it explicitly excluded the possibility of increasing housing prices based on "nonfunctional" environmental amenities, such as water frontage. The total number of points awarded for location could not exceed 25 points or 18 percent of the total rating, which significantly reduced housing costs in desirable neighborhoods. Moreover, only functional locational factors, such as proximity to a public transit stop, counted. Other characteristics, like average household incomes, ethnic composition, and proximity to social-cultural spaces like canals, were excluded.[6] As a result of these policies, for 89 percent of housing units in Amsterdam in the mid-1990s, water was not legally permitted to influence housing prices. By contrast, location was the most important determinant of property values and sales prices for owner-occupied housing. However, since only 11 percent of housing units were owner occupied at that time, the importance of water in real estate in one of the wettest cityscapes in the world remained significantly circumscribed.[7]

A series of market liberalizations implemented since 1989 changed both the process and the end goals of new home construction, creating greater opportunities for water to influence housing markets. One set of reforms reduced the monopoly of the municipality and housing authorities on new home construction by shifting from state-led development models to public-private partnership approaches. This shift took policy-based decision making away from the city council and let market considerations play a larger role. A second set of reforms changed the proportion of new housing units destined for the social housing market. Instead of 95 percent of new housing starts earmarked as social rentals, as was the case in the mid-1980s, from the 1990s onward only 30 percent of units were required to go into that sector, and the rest could be sold through the land-lease system to private buyers. As a result, the owner-occupancy rate in Amsterdam increased dramatically from 11 percent in 1995 to 20 percent in 2002 and then to 31.5 percent in 2009.[8]

Concurrent with these policy changes, a growing subset of Amsterdam residents experienced an increase in their household income and disposable wealth. By 2006, 90 percent of Amsterdam's workforce was employed in the service industry, and over half of those residents worked in lucrative knowledge and creative professions.[9] Their rising incomes brought new urban investment opportunities. In the municipal planning department's self-published magazine *PlanAmsterdam*, planners proclaimed, "You are rich!"[10] As they explained, after fifty years of economic underperformance, "Amsterdam has now entered calmer waters and is now prosperous enough [. . .] to invest substantial resources" in luxury infrastructure and cultural amenities.[11] Although other analysts have emphasized the simultaneously declining incomes for a growing subset of households working in low-wage service jobs, for the residents on the upper-income end of the spectrum, higher incomes propelled a shift in housing demand.[12] As the Eastern Docklands master planner phrased it, "people have had more than enough of the painful mediocre houses that past decades of state repression have built."[13] Affordable housing, which was crucial to postwar urban development paradigms, seemed out-of-step with twenty-first-century creative class expectations. Instead, high-quality, privately owned housing became de rigueur.[14]

These shifts in policy frames and income levels created the possibility for water as a locational factor to exert greater influence on real estate markets. By 2009, the growing, seven-year waiting list for a social housing unit in Amsterdam, combined with the expanding supply of new owner-occupancy units along the IJ waterway, had decidedly changed the city's housing culture. Young people and newcomers with limited resources often "got stuck with less desired housing on the periphery in poor condition," if they could get anything at all.[15] By contrast, creditworthy residents who could assemble financial resources for a down payment—that is, Europeans with promising jobs and rising incomes in the information economy—could jump the housing queue by buying a home on the burgeoning private market.[16] For those homes, locational amenities, including water, heavily influenced the value of real estate.

Building Amsterdam's Industrial Waterfront

The IJ waterway was once a bay on Amsterdam's northern shore.[17] For sixteenth-century sailors, passage through the bay signaled the beginning and end of long voyages to Asia and the Americas. The majestic vista of Amsterdam's urban waterfront welcomed and intimidated foreign diplomats, monarchs, and warlords arriving by sea. This grand arrival reinforced Amsterdam's symbolic status as a globally powerful, imperial city.[18]

The industrialization of the IJ changed the spatial relationship between the city and this shoreline. By the mid-1800s, remittances from colonial operations in the Dutch East Indies constituted one-third of the Netherlands' annual federal revenue.[19] These resources helped fund the construction of new harbor facilities and coastal rail lines in Amsterdam. This infrastructure, which soon monopolized the waterfront, introduced new physical barriers dividing the growing city from the industrializing wharves.[20]

The history of the Eastern Docklands exemplified these processes. The Docklands included two artificial islands, Java and KNSM, and two man-made peninsulas, Borneo and Sporenburg. The municipality built these landmasses at the beginning of the twentieth century as Amsterdam's industrial and colonial activity reached its peak. This harbor infrastructure expanded the city's network of transshipment loading docks and storage hangers. The Royal Dutch Steamship Company (Koninklijke Nederlandsche Stoomboot Maatschappij, or KNSM) maintained its headquarters in the Eastern Docklands for over eight decades.[21]

The Docklands were, by design, disconnected from the central city. Java Island, which is a special focus of this chapter, was built to be 1,300 meters long and only 130 meters wide, giving it the shape of a long parking medium surrounded by water on all sides. Around 1910, as the Docklands were nearing completion, 1,600 ships from the Dutch East Indies and the Americas anchored there annually.[22] Since bridges interfered with nautical traffic, and since Java Island and the other Docklands landmasses had a double-stacked corridor design that allowed ships to anchor on both sides, no roads or bridges connected these islands to the rest of the city. Many dockworkers lived in Amsterdam North, on the opposite side of the IJ waterway, and commuted by boat to the harbor for work. From the city center and suburbs to the south, the rail lines along the southern bank effectively screened the harbor from view. This physical isolation meant that few residents beyond harbor employees had much familiarity with this newly built landscape, and few residents living in growing suburban areas to the south had much interaction with the working-class residents living in the north.[23]

In the 1970s, transoceanic shipping companies shifted from break-bulk cargo to containerization carried in ever-growing vessels. During this transition, the businesses operating along the IJ waterway either closed or relocated to the wider, deeper harbors to the west in the present-day Port of Amsterdam or to the extensively modernized and significantly larger Port of Rotterdam. The collapse of the local shipping industry and the end of commuting patterns to the noncontiguous islands augmented their isolation from the rest of the city.[24]

Planners observing the decline in the 1970s advocated razing the harbor and expanding the land area to build a large New Manhattan business district for 350,000 residents, or five times the number of people then living in Amsterdam's city center. Development of this magnitude proved untenable for financial and ecological reasons, but a scaled-back version of this city on the waterway began moving forward in the 1990s, beginning with the Eastern Docklands.[25] Initially, other than characterizing the harbor as blighted brownfield, the municipal planners proposing redevelopment made almost no reference to the harbor's past life. Instead, redevelopment was simply characterized as a way to build new housing on existing, underutilized land near the city center. City planners and newspaper reporters described the Docklands of the 1980s as physically inaccessible and socially marginalized. These accounts painted the waterfront as "an industrial wasteland" of "coal piles, ship yards, strange buildings, drug trade, and cops."[26] These strategic characterizations symbolically emptied the wharves of meaningful infrastructure and occupants, discursively wiping the landscape clean for future redevelopment.

The onset of market liberalization policies, which allowed locational factors to influence housing prices for a growing segment of the market, coincided with the beginning of the municipality's sustained push to redevelop the former industrial wharves. Hippy houseboats, floating parades, and canal heritage had already elevated interest in shoreline living, recreation, and aesthetics in the central city. Those practices shaped the meaning of water in important ways, but those meanings were geographically clustered and aesthetically rooted in the central city canalscape. Legal reforms and rising consumer incomes created opportunities to expand these water resonances, reinterpreting them through the lens of redeveloped industrial shorelines outside of the city center.

From the 1990s onward, the Eastern Docklands became one among many sites of large-scale housing development along the IJ shoreline. For two decades, the Docklands constituted the largest single construction site in the city. Enthusiastic reviewers glowingly described the redevelopment as an entire city springing forth—seemingly autonomously and overnight—complete with 8,300 housing units, 20,000 residents, and fully formed community organizations.[27] Each new block opened to tremendous public acclaim. On Java Island, five- and eight-story apartment buildings soon lined the waterfront, encircling large internal courtyards filled with grassy knolls and jungle gyms. Cyclists whizzed along the wharves and across newly constructed bridges that carried them into the city center in ten minutes or less. These changes gave the Docklands a new economic life and, for the first time, physically integrated the islands into the surrounding cityscape.

Emerging Nautical History Development Narratives

During the redevelopment process, rhetoric of a "harbor conversion" coalesced slowly after the plans were drawn and construction was underway, and over the Physical Planning Department's strong objections. The process involved several small shifts in design and implementation that planners had not anticipated. By the 1990s, squatters displaced from central city neighborhoods lived in the harbor buildings, and they used heritage preservation laws to slow demolition. Concurrently, private sector architects, who gained greater autonomy with the rise of public-private partnership models, incorporated water into their designs in unexpected ways. Similarly, media reporters and tourists observing these trends made their own discursive connections between the former harbor, its nautical history, and the canal heritage of central Amsterdam. As construction progressed, celebrations of water through these history frameworks became key in overcoming squatter opposition and enhancing public enthusiasm for the redevelopment agenda.

Three brief examples from Java Island and other Eastern Docklands locations illustrate the types of dynamics at work in the early years. The first example demonstrated the unintended making of relics. For efficiency's sake, municipal planners preparing the Docklands for redevelopment preferred to bulldoze the warehouses, cranes, and administrative buildings to create as much of a tabula rasa design slate as possible. This strategy reduced health and safety liabilities. It also provided a technical justification to evict the squatter communities of self-proclaimed artists, counterculturalists, travelers, and struggling families who moved into the Docklands between the time the harbor closed in the late 1970s and the time that the redevelopment project entered construction in the early 1990s.[28]

Some of those squatters occupying a few dozen warehouse-style buildings organized themselves into a collective called the Industrial Buildings Guild (Gilde van Werkgebouwen). This group lobbied the national Ministry of Education and Culture to list their structures as official National Monuments, which stripped the municipality of their authority to evict squatters for demolition purposes and delayed displacement. In some instances, such as the former cafeteria building named The End of the World (Einde van de Wereld), planners justified demolition anyway, citing soil contamination underneath the foundations that could not be remediated without structurally damaging the building. In other instances, such as the Grain Silo (Graansilo), development remained stalled until private investors secured permission and funding to restore the monuments, usually by converting them to luxury apartments targeting wealthy foreigners willing to pay premiums to live in a registered historic monument on the waterfront.[29] Despite this eventual, profitable co-optation, heritage preservation began as a defensive strategy that squatters used to slow development and resist displacement.

A second example of unplanned heritage activity involved the mobilization of canal aesthetics generally associated with Amsterdam's seventeenth-century golden age. Java Island's master planner, Sjoerd Soeters, was a private architect hired to design the island's layout and to coordinate the work of other private architects commissioned to design and construct the island's individual blocks. Soeters was an avid proponent of pedestrian-scale urban development, which he publicly described to the media as the antithesis to Amsterdam's "painfully average" and "socially indiscriminant" postwar social housing blocks.[30] While designing Java Island, he read a book on Japanese hillside villages, and he had the idea that the arched bridges and sunken waterways in Amsterdam's city center constituted a "sort of thrilling mountain walk" with each bridge functioning as a transition point between charmingly distinct, small-scale, Japanese-style communities. Soeters hoped to re-create this ambience on Java Island, "so we wanted strongly curved bridges to break up the long map of Java, and if we then also needed to dig canals, then so be it."[31]

Soeters's resulting master plan called for the construction of four new ca-

Newly built canal lined with "modern" canal houses on Java Island, 2010. Image courtesy of Zoltan Vass.

nals through Java Island. Along the canals, he commissioned individual architects to build housing that explicitly mimicked the rhythm and massing of the seventeenth-century canal belt, albeit using modern building materials and finishes.[32] The municipal planning department purportedly responded angrily to the proposal, which added ƒ10 million (€4.54 million) to the construction cost. Similarly, contractors initially refused to build the canals and homes, fearing that Amsterdam residents would be unwilling to pay the ƒ2,000 (€910) rental price needed to offset construction expenses. Despite these reservations, residents jumped at the opportunity of living in a canal house like those inaccessible to them in the high-priced and closely guarded central city markets, so construction proceeded.[33] When complete, some critics hailed the new canals as an urban design innovation while others decried it as nostalgic namby-pamby kitsch.[34] These aesthetic judgments aside, critics on both sides described Soeters's waterways as the first canals built in Amsterdam in four hundred years. Also, instead of seeing the bridges as inspired by Japanese hillside settlements, commentators focused on the water and publicized it as "an ode to the old Canal Belt of Amsterdam," transposing the symbolism of the seventeenth-century golden age onto the postindustrial shores.[35]

Media reporters and visiting tourists underscored the cultural significance of water in the redevelopment process as well. The enormous scale of the

Docklands project combined with the utopian allure of an incipient city-in-the-making attracted scores of visitors, tourists, and home buyers even before the old structures were cleared or the new foundations poured. To manage this widespread interest, the Amsterdam Physical Planning Department published field guides and organized walking tours of the construction site. Marina de Vries, an architecture and art critic chronicling the Docklands redevelopment for several newspapers, reviewed one such guide in the late 1990s. In her description, the journey began spectacularly with a short boat ride from Amsterdam's Central Railway Station to the Docklands' Java Island. From there, the guide led sightseers through the spectral city of a "future marina," past the "still invisible bridges," to the island's "fallow head, reserved for one or another foggy cultural purpose."[36] These characterizations emphasized the romance of the water-based experience of arriving at the redevelopment site and navigating around its noteworthy features.

Among people following these guides or visiting the construction site independently, foreign tourists were especially insistent on perceiving redevelopment not as a housing project but rather as a harbor restoration. Many Dutch residents touring the Docklands expressed bewilderment at the aquatic abundance. As one resident asked a reporter, "why wasn't [the water] filled in? You could have built more."[37] Similarly, many locals wanted green spaces instead of blue ones. "Water is nice, but you can't play soccer on it."[38] The international response, by contrast, embraced water as a quintessential icon of the harbor's past life and global connectivity. For foreigners, the mystique of the Netherlands as a seafaring nation was an important hallmark of Dutch folklore. Municipal planners organizing tours of the Docklands in the early 2000s told reporters that foreign visitors of all nationalities spoke at length about the water, describing it as pretty, Arcadian, and novel. Foreign buyers were also willing to pay high prices for a place in a seemingly authentic—that is, aquatic and nautical—Dutch environment.[39]

These examples illustrated some of the many ways that diffuse, haphazard mobilizations of waterscapes generated new ways of reading the municipality's housing development agenda. Media coverage of the squatters' defensive deployment of preservation laws forced planners to grapple with the potential cultural value of a landscape they had previously dismissed as a desolate terrain of rusting rails and neglected shipyards forsaken by God and city.[40] The architects' desires to incorporate water structures and canal symbolism into the housing landscape introduced new water identity markers into the emerging neighborhood. Reporters, visitors, and tour guides further publicized the nautical heritage tropes, propelling waterscapes to the forefront of the Eastern Docklands' public image.

Co-opting Waterscape and Nautical Heritage Frameworks

After initially opposing historic preservation and water-oriented development, municipal planners eventually shifted tactics and embraced the financial and symbolic opportunities arising from mining the harbor's nautical past. By the 2000s, the planning office was heavily invested in publicizing the traces and vistas of the Docklands' seafaring history. Their emphatic—if not always tangible—aesthetics and narratives sutured memories of a global heritage with visions of Amsterdam's imagined international future. These history frameworks also provided an entry point for contemporary global real estate trends that placed economic premiums on water-oriented housing.

Instead of reversing their opposition toward building preservation in the Eastern Docklands, the municipal planning department launched a public relations campaign to instruct people to see historical fodder in traces and specters, rather than in preserved structures. For instance, in the late 1990s, planning officials commissioned or self-published several field guides, architectural books, and walking tours of the Eastern Docklands touting the area's early twentieth-century relics. The book *Discover the Eastern Docklands*, published in 2009, was among the most popular of these field guides to hit the shelves.[41] Like the pamphlets and tours that preceded it, this guide described the Docklands as a public demonstration site of nautical inheritance. The walking tours gave lavish attention to the few original harbor buildings that remained—such as the Loods 6 transshipment and customs shed and the KNSM Administration building, both turned artist workspaces. Another celebrated landmark was the Figee Hoisting Crane, the only crane not demolished during redevelopment, which stood like a sculpture on the shore. The emphasis placed on these relics implied that preservation was the rule, rather than the exception. None of these relics stood on Java Island, but where actual preservation was scarce, new artwork and staged sculptures filled the gaps. For example, the "Heavenly Jewel" gateway and the "Transit" plaque, both completed in the late 1990s, paid homage to the long, uncertain farewells and surprising intellectual exchanges associated with oceanic sojourns of centuries past.

In contrast to this emphatic preservation narrative, the names used in the redeveloped harbor created a nearly unpublicized yet highly effective reference system turning street signs into heritage plaques of global connectivity. The islands' names—Java, Borneo, and KNSM (the acronym for the Royal Netherlands Steamship Company)—reflected the tempo of a seafaring nation.[42] Java Island's four new canals were named after prominent Indonesian rivers and cities, and its block-scale garden courtyards took their names from Indonesian hamlets, palaces, and royal graveyards. This strategy permeated the Eastern Docklands. A short twenty-minute bicycle ride, like the ones outlined in municipal field guides, brought cyclists to Java Wharf, Sumatra Wharf, Levant Square, Piraeus Square, Surinam Wharf, Barcelona Square, Panama Square, Shipwright's Street, Helmsman Wharf, Signal Watcher Street, and Oar Wharf. It was not uncommon elsewhere in Amsterdam to see an occasional street or plaza named after former colonial strongholds and nautical heroes. In the Docklands, however, the practice occurred in an especially intense form with one exotic destination following another in rapid succession to create an entire tapestry of seventeenth-century exploration in miniature. These names applied narrative content to the landscape, creating a living public memorial of a globally connected city.

Press releases and project descriptions also used colonial nomenclature to describe the contemporary Docklands residents. During the construction phase, planners characterized the pre-redeveloped harbor as a no-man's-land and as the refuge of "nomads" and "hut builders," suggesting that squatters were a modern variant of an imagined tribal Other living outside government oversight and conventional social norms.[43] Visitors touring the construction site were cautioned, somewhat tongue-in-cheek, to be on the lookout for animal-like roving cranes and cement trucks, to pack provisions for their journey through a precapitalist landscape devoid of ATMs and restaurants, and to be cautious of pirate-like pickpockets exploiting the wilds of the unfinished landscape.[44] Similarly, neighborhood boosters characterized new businesses and home buyers as waterfront "pioneers" who were "discovering" the exotic islands of Java and Borneo on their "ventures beyond more settled territory."[45] These colorful tales of huts, danger, and East Indies exploration—all located a convenient seven-minute tram ride from Amsterdam's city center—cast waterfront redevelopment as a modern-day expedition civilizing an untamed wilderness within the national heartland.

By the late 2000s, as construction ended, these guidebooks, names, and colonial references had created a spectral air surrounding the way people saw and spoke about the Eastern Docklands. In the words of the architectural critic Marina de Vries, "the ships to England and Java, to Africa and America, have disappeared, it is true. But the memory of their activity on the landscape of yore remains."[46] These ghosts lurked in aged photographs depicting rows of ships anchored along the shores. It existed in "the sturdy bricks on the sidewalk and streets, and in the open wharves, and the clear view of the water."[47] It existed in statues and street signs, in acts of urban recolonization, and in the occasional preserved building and staged monument.

As a finishing touch, the construction of new bridges to Java and KNSM Islands provided opportunities to celebrate water directly without requiring a historicized, nautical intermediary. The planning office commissioned twelve new bridges in total, all decidedly modern and impressionistic in form. An especially prominent bridge connecting Java Island with central Amsterdam was designed to look like a lizard complete with a head, tail, and feet creeping over the water.[48] Similarly, on Java Island, the small bridges crossing the newly built canals used abstract metal ribbons inspired by the letters of the alphabet to turn the act of crossing the narrow channels into celebrated moments of whimsy and caprice.[49] These bridges quickly emerged as new, water-oriented icons defining Amsterdam's evolving shoreline.

Within these harbor waterscapes, houseboats and party boats were notably absent. In the written record of government documents and newspaper accounts, the term *houseboat* is nearly invisible. In addition to this discursive silence, the newly constructed canals built on Java Island were too narrow and shallow to accommodate houseboats. Large tour boats and fast-moving pleasure boats were likewise excluded. Smaller boats could physically enter the canals, and for the first few years, some residents and visitors moored boats along the canal edges. However, in 2009, the district government proposed closing the canals to boat traffic entirely, citing noise-related nuisances and maintenance expenses.[50]

Instead of being a site to occupy, water in the Eastern Docklands was mobilized to offer respite and clarity. Architectural critics emphasized the immense feeling of freedom summoned by the water. The new internal canals mimicked the ambiance of central city canals, but the surrounding IJ waterway acted as a buffer between central city "chaos" and domestic tranquility. In the words of one resident, "nothing is more lovely, for instance, than to leave the madhouse of the inner city behind you and to realize that a peace will wash over you only two streets and a bridge away. Water offers this pleasant protection when the exuberant city life becomes too much."[51] This critical distance also afforded picturesque vistas of the historic city. As one city planner explained publicly, "from the head of Java," at arms-length from the city center, "you find the finest overlook for Amsterdam."[52] From that location, residents saw the city from the perspective of sixteenth-century sailors and dignitaries arriving by sea, complete with the imagined lingering aroma of "tar and port."[53]

The various celebrations of water and nautical history in the Eastern Docklands emerged haphazardly from planners' perspectives. Squatter resistance forced building preservation. Architectural whimsy gave rise to a canal aesthetic. Architectural tourism prompted planners to organize tours and brochures, creating written guides to heritage destinations. These unplanned dynamics then became opportunities to reimagine housing development as a harbor metamorphosis.

Since the rhetoric emerged during, rather than before, the Eastern Docklands' redevelopment process, nautical references on that site assumed primarily spectral forms rooted in a handful of small relics and new monuments rather than in an extensively preserved harbor infrastructure. In this figural revalorization, seventeenth-century seafaring emerged as an important narrative, albeit an anachronistic one since the Eastern Harbor was not built until the end of the nineteenth century. Planners consolidated these specters and narratives after the fact into water- and history-focused neighborhood referents. These frameworks connected real estate development with water, nautical heritage, and an imagined legacy of global cosmopolitanism that helped guide and sell subsequent property investments along the IJ shorelines.

Water-Oriented Real Estate Development in the IJ

By the late 2000s, municipal planners were celebrating what officials called the "return" of Amsterdam to its "natural" orientation facing the IJ.[54] According to planners, the IJ shores were "back on the map. [. . .] Amsterdam has been oriented toward the IJ waterway from time immemorial," and, thanks to large-scale real estate investment during the 1990s and 2000s, the waterfront was "gradually being brought back under development, thus 'giving back' the IJ to the city."[55] This rhetoric of a return featured prominently in planning documents, newspaper reports, and local government newsletters. These heritage-oriented narratives cast postindustrial reinvestment as an opportunity to correct supposedly shortsighted industrial-era decision making and to reclaim water as a wellspring of Amsterdam heritage. "Where train sheds and railways once lay, a real 'island city' is now springing up. [. . .] So grows Amsterdam again back to its roots: the IJ."[56]

This imagined process of a return to the waterfront involved significant social and spatial transformations along the banks, and the Eastern Docklands project was only the beginning. During a 2008 interview, a director with the International Institute for Social History headquartered in the recently completed Eastern Docklands explained, "there is a new prestige to having an office on the waterfront and an apartment on the IJ, which was non-existent before the 1990s."[57] An elderly resident who had lived in Amsterdam for over eighty years expressed similar statements when touring the Docklands with her granddaughter and a reporter, asking, "Are you certain we're still in Amsterdam, child?"[58] From the central city canals, it looked as though nothing had changed, but on the open water, nothing seemed the same.

As construction on Java Island and the Eastern Docklands neared completion in the mid-2000s, architectural critics, real estate agents, and market analysts called the project Amsterdam's preeminent "success story."[59] As one of the first large-scale housing projects constructed in the wake of market liberalizations, the Docklands presented an opportunity to test new development models. Unlike past projects where municipal planners and social housing corporations had near total control, the Docklands began the process of gradually transitioning to public-private development models, a trend that deepened with each subsequent redevelopment occurring along the IJ banks.[60] Similarly, in sharp contrast to the nearly exclusive focus on social housing in previous decades, 70 percent of the Docklands' housing units were intended for private sale, a condition that allowed locational factors, such as water amenities, to exert a significantly larger influence on consumer prices.

These private properties—with their canal, harbor, wharf, and island inflections—functioned as an experimental market for water-oriented investment. Valuing water in real estate had precedent outside of Amsterdam where private homeownership had a stronger presence. A study from the Alterra Department of Landscape and Spatial Planning published in 2000 found that, nationwide, housing with views of water, proximity near water, or green spaces that fronted water sold for an average 28 percent premium over equivalent privately owned homes without those amenities.[61] Other government sources concurred, putting the benefit between 15 percent and 40 percent.[62] By comparison, the sales premium for other environmental features, such as proximity to open parks and green spaces, was negligible. These numbers suggested that homebuyers saw water as culturally unique and not interchangeable with other nature-like amenities.

Moreover, government analysts recognized that water might be especially salient among creative knowledge economy workers. According to a 2006 municipal survey, 95 percent of Amsterdam's "creative economy" employees were "of the opinion that the canals, the Amstel [River], and the IJ [waterway] make Amsterdam exceptional."[63] The study also noted that many knowledge workers expressed "a notable preference for 'more modern' water," which created opportunities for real estate developers to capitalize on water-oriented investment opportunities beyond the historic central city, since, for this group of people, modern "water-rich environments, such as the Eastern Docklands, do just as well."[64] These trends justified preserving and celebrating water features that had no technical value for drainage and flood control but that functioned as important economic catalysts in real estate and knowledge economy development.

Through these processes, the Eastern Docklands emerged as an important local experiment testing the willingness of upper-income buyers to pay luxury prices for water-oriented housing in Amsterdam. Municipal officials and contractors initially balked at the suggestion that they build new canals through the former harbor, but those new canals became "an excellent place to erect expensive housing," adding "just the right sex appeal" for high-end buyers.[65] The long-distance water vistas likewise generated a strong market response.[66] Although the elevated costs of water-oriented real estate exceeded the spending capacity of many Amsterdam residents, the homes most closely associated with water sold most rapidly and at the highest prices.[67] Many of those properties also nearly doubled in value within their first few years on the market, suggesting that consumer willingness to pay increased even after the initial novelty of the neighborhood wore off.[68] By the late 2000s, real estate along the IJ waterway was valued at €6,000 per square meter, or a 33 percent increase over the €4,500 citywide average. This price equated to approximately €1.2 million to buy an apartment on Java Island or between €1,100 and €1,600 in monthly rental fees, an exorbitant sum at the time by Amsterdam standards.[69] Similarly, one of the Eastern Docklands' first established social organizations was an antifoliage association founded to prevent planners from planting trees along the open wharves that could obstruct residents' views of the IJ.[70]

These economic dynamics transformed the Docklands into an investment prototype for the many shoreline redevelopment projects that quickly followed, influencing the municipality's decision to continue treating the IJ shorelines as a major city building opportunity. During the 2000s, housing units, cultural institutions, and office buildings emerged in a flurry of construction along the waterfront. On the Southern Bank, for instance, investors constructed the largest science center in the Netherlands, a lavish concert hall billed as the most important stage for contemporary music nationwide, and one of the largest public libraries in Europe.[71] In Amsterdam North, city planners celebrated the establishment of artist workspaces and demonstration halls in former industrial warehouses while, farther up shore, a public-private consortium erected sumptuous residential towers that promised to provide "the most expensive housing in the city."[72] In sum, since the 1990s, investment along the IJ has transformed the postindustrial shorelines into a major center of new residential neighborhoods, cultural centers, and retail spaces.

In these sections of Amsterdam, the importance of water, which emerged in a haphazard and stilted manner in the Eastern Docklands, subsequently became a taken-for-granted cornerstone of redevelopment. For instance, in Amsterdam North, in an effort to accelerate the pace of revitalization, architectural boosters in the early 2000s began aggressively promoting a "hands-on-the-water" approach where, instead of filling internal water structures as was previously discussed, architects advocated widening the canals to make them more visually dramatic. Stated one advocate, "We have to protect the water structures. Not only because we would drown otherwise, but especially because it's the most important quality of the district."[73] The specter of seafaring ships likewise became a metaphor for urban development. Rhetoric of a "home harbor" and a "city as hull" design concept transformed visions of rootlessness and incompleteness into comforting notions of flexible domesticity.[74] These concepts melded seamlessly with images of a post-Fordist global economy where corporations and elite residents were expected to be transient.

Through these processes, high-end housing construction with literal, symbolic, and metaphorical water inflections emerged as the centerpiece of the municipality's urban growth agenda. Water propelled these processes by increasing the market value of newly built housing and by functioning as a quality-of-life amenity marketed especially to knowledge economy workers. From these modernized shorelines, commentators said, "the city looks more worldly and wiser than ever seemed possible on the small canals."[75] It scarcely seemed to matter that many locals could not afford these waterfront homes. High-end housing with a decidedly water flavor emerged as a major symbol of the imagined future of an internationally competitive and livable capital city.

The Economic Utility of Urban Waterscapes

By the mid-2000s, real estate development had emerged as a key urban economic growth strategy in Amsterdam. Newly constructed residential neighborhoods with high-end housing and quality-of-life benefits sold at high prices. Even more importantly, the urban boosters promoting these neighborhoods advertised them to potential knowledge economy entrepreneurs who might be interested in relocating to Amsterdam. These neighborhoods became opportunities to expand the city's human capital, which officials saw as an important growth strategy in the postindustrial era of international urban competition.[76]

Water initially had no place in these real estate growth strategies as they emerged in the early 1990s. Planners described the postindustrial shorelines as a "hidden reserve,"[77] or as rent-gap space where city builders could erect new cultural, housing, and office structures. In these characterizations, the cultural symbolism of water and shorelines was absent. Moreover, historically water played a legally constrained economic role in the housing market.

By the mid-2000s, however, water had become a central element and organizing feature in large-scale municipal development projects. The rise of this water consciousness emerged from several sources. The houseboat hippies, floating parades, and canal excavation efforts discussed in previous chapters expanded the cultural valence of water in the central city. Then, on the industrial shores, squatters resisting eviction publicized the cultural value of harbor relics, private architects replicated canal aesthetics in modern forms, and tourists and architectural critics interpreted housing construction through these nautical history lenses.

Alongside these cultural dynamics, municipal policy shifts created new opportunities for water and real estate to intertwine. Market liberalizations that expanded home ownership gave social landscape amenities greater influence over housing prices. The rising incomes of knowledge economy workers—especially among foreigners for whom the cultural value of water was especially pronounced—increased prices further and consolidated a market of buyers willing to pay high premiums for water-related neighborhood aesthetics.

These diffuse reinterpretations of the former harbors, combined with new financial mechanisms of valuing locational factors in real estate, elevated the significance of water in redevelopment processes. Stories and traces of the nineteenth-century industrial past were mixed with narratives of a seventeenth-century global heritage and an imagined twenty-first-century urban future. Small-scale canals and vast open waterways connected seafaring legacies with the newly developed neighborhoods and increased their marketability.

Although the significance of water in shoreline redevelopment appeared coherent—and perhaps inevitable—by the late 2000s, from the perspective of municipal planners in the 1990s, this water-oriented framework emerged largely by accident. No comprehensive government program or developer agenda stipulated the incorporation of water or nautical history into these emerging neighborhoods. On the contrary, this water nomenclature emerged despite planners' efforts to resist water- and heritage-oriented investments, which added cost to development processes and home prices without, in their eyes, adding utility for residents.

Nevertheless, an array of cultural and legal influences created a situation where water-oriented symbols and narratives gained market traction. Residents, architects, commentators, visitors, and real estate agents forced the issue of water's importance, and physical planners who previously ignored water or advocated for its elimination instead began embracing water as a key driver of urban economic growth. By the mid-2000s, the literal and figurative harbor structure, with its quality-of-life aesthetics and sensibilities of global connectedness, figured as a new point of departure not to distant lands but to an imagined future prosperity for the water city of Amsterdam.

CHAPTER FIVE

Ecologists on Islands

During the 2000s, water occupied a privileged position in Amsterdam. Cultural movements and market interests had resuscitated the canals and the harbors from the bins of tourism kitsch and industrial obsolescence. Instead, water had become the focus of comprehensive real estate investments, heritage interests, and public events.

The historical rescripting of water that occurred between the 1960s and the 2000s followed a distinctive geographic pattern. Early cultural groups and small-scale mobilizations of water initially focused on the inland waterways and central city canals. Concurrently, real estate development in these areas proceeded through in situ infrastructural upgrades across several separately managed properties. In the 1990s and 2000s, however, city builders shifted their attention to "big water," or the industrial-scale waterways and their extensive brownfield shorelines, which could accommodate expansive, centralized, total neighborhood redevelopment.[1] On those postindustrial waterfronts, alongside newly emerging modes of property tenure and real estate valuation, the cultural and financial resonance of water continued to evolve.

With the real estate market growing, these big-water shorelines absorbed enormous amounts of capital investment. However, as extensive as these shorelines were, the push to extend the urban footprint beyond the brownfields and into the water was mounting. Previous generations of city builders in Amsterdam had filled central city canals to enable economic growth.[2] By the 2000s, this approach was politically implausible given the centrality of water for houseboat romance, public festivals, pleasure boating, aesthetic ambience, identity symbolism, and real estate value. Moreover, the inland waterways were too small and too entangled in preexisting uses to constitute a financially attractive redevelopment site. By contrast, big water lay outside the city's existing footprint, and as a vast open space, big water was not so heavily laden with the cultural and symbolic weight associated with the sculpted historic canals. From

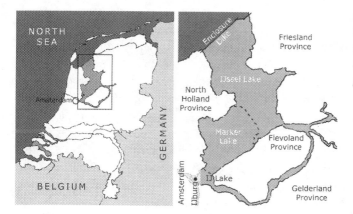

Map showing the IJssel Lake District and its component parts.

municipal planners' perspectives, big water figured as a potential space for future urban expansion.

The IJburg development project in IJ Lake off Amsterdam's northeastern shore was the first big-water urban land reclamation project in the region in several decades.[3] Its implementation generated extensive political controversy that centered on concerns about the negative environmental consequences of the city's expanding footprint. IJ Lake was part of an internationally celebrated bird sanctuary anchored in the IJssel Lake District (IJsselmeer), the largest fresh water body in Western Europe. The controversy, and the negotiations, concessions, and synergies that emerged, significantly modified the shape of IJburg infrastructure and the conception of urban water, giving both an ecological valence that they had not previously held.

This greening of water was one in a series of shifts redefining the character of urban water between 1960 and 2010. Squatting skippers domesticated water, and heritage enthusiasts historicized it. Floating revelers transformed water into a public space, and lawmakers and city planners working in tension with cultural groups incorporated water into real estate markets. To this shifting web of identities, nature preservation groups and urban ecologists "environmental-ized" water, reworking the ideological and structural relationships among water, nature, and real estate. Until this point, the public image of nature was green and rural, not blue and urban. Amsterdam's geographic expansion into IJ Lake, a space widely recognized as a protected ecological site, forced city builders to grapple with the environmental functionality of water. The resulting reconceptualization of the water-nature-city nexus influenced the process of urban expansion. Equally important, it created opportunities to reevaluate existing inland waterways, bringing a more pronounced green point of view to the central city canals.

From a political economy perspective, the disputes, concessions, and experiments surrounding the IJburg urban expansion project demonstrated both the capacity for cultural groups to push market investors in new directions and the potential profitability that can emerge from accommodating, rather than denying, cultural concerns. Environmental opposition to the project was insufficient to prevent market-based real estate decision makers from moving forward with their expansion plans. However, given the public relations concerns and legal challenges that environmental groups posed, municipal officials felt it was tactically and financially prudent to broker an agreement with the advocacy groups, partly by funding supplemental environmental mitigation initiatives to offset expected damage, and partly by modifying their infrastructure designs to create ecologically vibrant spaces within the newly built neighborhood. Accommodating these concerns came with financial costs, but those investments reduced barriers to long-term urban expansion in IJ Lake, and they led to unanticipated design innovations that increased the development's overall marketability.

The resulting urban form of Amsterdam's IJburg neighborhood brought the assemblage of water, infrastructure, and nature into a reworked and explicitly self-conscious articulation. At a basic level, the greening of water elevated the public recognition of water's ecological attributes alongside its role as a memory trace, reflective surface, public space, and market asset. Even more importantly, this greening process cast water as an active element within a web of people, birds, fish, plants, waves, sediment, technology, and money. This reconceptualization transformed shorelines from static dividing lines containing inert water into a generative interface producing environmental qualities, political possibilities, and market opportunities. Water and shorelines emerged as recognized active elements in development processes, rather than overlooked boundary lines marking the limits of capital.

This ideological shift away from water as a flat, reflective surface to conceptions of water as an enlivened, thick substance cast waterscapes in a new light. While many cultural and market practices over the preceding decades had emphasized the visual attributes of the inland canals, the experience of water emerging through IJburg involved the scent of water in the air, the feel of water on the skin, the sound of water in the ears, the calm of water in the mind, and the thrill of water for the heart. Water no longer appeared confined to canals, ditches, and lakes. Instead, it seemed connected with birds flying through the air, mist carried in the breeze, and fish served on dinner tables. Water traveled through these embodiments, creating new political valences and sensory perceptions of urban water citywide.

This chapter explores this greening of urban water and the implications for city building as they emerged through the first phase of the IJburg development project, which was built in the IJssel Lake District between 1997 and 2009. The findings are based on an extensive review of written environmental, governmental, and media sources generated during IJburg's planning and construction process. Environmental documents included public speeches, press releases, advocacy brochures, and editorials written during this period, especially from two key organizations: Nature Monuments (NatuurMonumenten) and the Friends of the Earth Netherlands (Milieudefense). Governmental sources included brochures, reports, maps, and directives generated primarily, but not exclusively, from the municipality's Physical Planning Department and its IJburg Project Bureau (Projectbureau IJburg), which was established to oversee and manage the IJburg urban expansion. Given the project's large scale and the intensity of environmental opposition, archived newspaper reports and radio broadcasts also provided invaluable insight into the shifts, uncertainties, and negotiations as they emerged and evolved during the development process. Along with these archival sources, in 2010 I interviewed two spokespeople with Nature Monuments, two project managers with the IJburg Project Bureau, and the head city ecologist in the Physical Planning Department.

These sources vividly chronicle the greening of water and its figurative emergence as an ecological agent within an assemblage of law, property, capital, nature, sensuality, and symbolism. After losing the political campaign to prevent urban expansion, some environmental advocates shifted tactics and pushed planners to use new island construction to finance habitat restoration, stimulate ecological resiliency, and use nature-like landscape aesthetics to promote an ecological consciousness among Amsterdam residents. IJburg emerged as an experimental garden, a place where city builders developed new technological skills and conceptual frameworks that brought water to life in unanticipated ways. This crystallization of the ecological dimensions of waterside living galvanized public support for urban expansion when combined with habitat restoration in big-water contexts.

This conceptual retooling of water built selectively on past cultural and financial mobilizations of water, and it created opportunities to reread the central city waterways through an environmental lens. Given the growing market interest in houseboats, canal houses, and home harbors, planners used small sub-neighborhoods in IJburg to test the market potential of these and other forms of shoreline living in official, regulated, and commodified forms. Designers also explicitly integrated public space amenities into waterways and bulkheads even as they steered those spaces toward low-intensity leisure activities rather than crowded festivals. Similarly, from narratives of Amsterdam's water heritage and nautical past, planners framed IJburg as an opportunity to envision the future environmental evolution of the water city. Moreover, instead of constraining shoreline symbolism to traces, specters, and vistas, water in IJburg emerged as a multisensory entity actively produced through urban investment. These processes, with their attention to formal, market-mediated, and leisure-oriented practices, narrowed public conceptions of shoreline living associated with the central city canals while simultaneously expanding the political valence of wet urban spaces to include nature, sensuality, and agency.

Ideas of Nature and Environment in Amsterdam

The concept of nature in the Netherlands shifted during the second half of the twentieth century, beginning with the emergence of a strong environmental movement advocating for green space protections in the 1970s and 1980s. Unlike in the United States, Dutch environmental thought has long recognized the historical interconnection between nature and culture. Even so, Dutch environmental groups favored pastoral visions of nature as meadows and forests outside urban centers. This perspective shifted in the 2000s with the rise of green-blue environmental thinking that expanded this image of nature to include water. Moreover, as the IJburg project in Amsterdam demonstrated, by the late 2000s environmentalists, government leaders, and urban practitioners began fundamentally reevaluating the imagined antithesis between nature and cities, in part by envisioning water as a new intermediary connecting these conceptually polarized spheres.[4]

Environmental thought in the Netherlands has long emphasized the active role of human activity in shaping the natural world. As the chairman of the Amsterdam chapter of Nature Monuments explained to me in 2010, unlike the United States, which he characterized as "a young country," the Netherlands "is an old country. Nature and culture are interwoven here. They cannot separate."[5] Secondary source environmental studies, as well as a gray literature on nature tourism promotion, affirmed this sentiment. The popular—albeit misleading—image of so-called pure nature in the United States, imagined as a place standing apart from people and society, never held such ideological sway in the Netherlands, where the landscape has instead been understood as deeply malleable. In the words of a historical geographer reflecting publicly on this malleability, "Nothing in the Dutch landscape is super human. [. . .] If we want to change the landscape, we turn a button, and the landscape adjusts itself."[6] Other historians and city planners have echoed these sentiments. In the Netherlands, where one-third of the nation's footprint includes artificially reclaimed land masses, "you see almost nothing natural, almost everything is made by the hands of men."[7]

This image of malleability has infused the Dutch concept of nature with expectations that nature has a history of production, making it an inherently cultural entity. Marketing brochures encouraging nature tourism in the Netherlands in the 1990s through the early 2000s, for instance, described protected nature zones as World Heritage Sites that visualized past human interventions in ur-Holland landscapes. These places included artificial drainage systems, pastures, and farmhouses that were as central to the nature experience as the wind, puddles, meadows, and clouds.[8] Nature preserves often existed in areas where industry used to be or where attempts to reclaim land from the sea had failed. The obsolescence of direct human intervention created opportunities for nature to reemerge as the dominant landscape element, but where traces of human activity remained visible.[9]

These characterizations, while allowing natural and cultural categories to intertwine, nonetheless placed nature squarely beyond the purview of more intensively humanized landscapes, like cities. Nature was something urban residents experienced on camping trips and hiking expeditions. Cities, by contrast, were thought to be too humanized to count as wild.

Similarly, these nature imaginings emphasized green spaces rather than blue ones. According to secondary studies, in the early 2000s, nature areas constituted 14 percent (or 483,000 acres) of the Netherlands' total landmass, which equaled the acreage devoted to industrial, residential, and commercial uses combined. Among all land use designations, only agriculture exceeded nature in size.[10] These officially counted nature areas included "dry natural areas," such as forests, heaths, dunes, and beaches. They also included the dry portions of "wet natural areas," such as swamps, marshlands, mudflats, and meadows. However, in legal terms, water itself did not count as nature. "As the CBS (Central Bureau for Statistics) data on nature explicitly refer to *land* use, open water is not included."[11] Moreover, even if lakes and rivers were reimagined as potential nature zones, popular conceptions of nature emphasized that water had to include reeds, birds, and fish—as well as people engaged in leisure and recreation—before it constituted a meaningful natural element.

Municipal planners in Amsterdam, who used these cultural and legal interpretations of nature as a guide in city building processes during the mid-twentieth century, understandably focused their attention on parks, plants, and other types of green infrastructure. Prior to World War II, planners encouraged the construction and preservation of separate nature zones outside the city limits. These nature preserves included green parklands and grazing pastures where residents from Amsterdam and other nearby towns could seek refuge from city life. From the 1950s onward, the municipal planning department adapted this vision, retaining the notion of discrete green parklands but incorporating those spaces as "green lobes" penetrating into urban neighborhoods from the larger outlying preserve.[12] In these contexts, urban water figured as a sanitation concern, flood issue, and industrial space, but not as a nature zone.

In the 1990s, this vision of nature as a green, bounded space separate from the city began to change, not only by allowing for a finer-grained interweaving of natural and urban spaces but also by tentatively rereading canals and waterways through an explicitly environmental lens. In smaller cities around Amsterdam and in less densely utilized outlying residential areas, environmental advocates pushed officials to soften canal edges by replacing vertical concrete and brick walls with vegetated slopes more hospitable to frogs and rabbits.[13] In dense areas like Amsterdam's city center, where soft edges were deemed impractical, municipal officials built experimental "floating marshes" that tested the potential to use floating gardens to mitigate pollution and expand habitat. The dangling roots of willows, reeds, bulrush, and buttercups arranged on open-bottomed rafts absorbed waterborne pollutants and oxygenated the water, which benefited fish populations. The rafts also created safe nesting sites for birds. Similarly, three-corner mussels, which could each filter several liters of water a day, lived on the raft frame.[14]

Despite some measurable success, the rising competition for space among houseboaters and pleasure boaters, as well as the heritage preservation interest in keeping the water surfaces clear, meant that floating marshes did not gain a strong presence in Amsterdam. Instead, a pronounced green read of urban water only gained traction in the 2000s when municipal officials began expanding the city's footprint into the adjacent IJ Lake.

The IJssel Lake District

The collaboration of city planners and nature preservation groups on a large urban expansion project in the IJssel Lake District in the 2000s generated a robust environmental framework that crystallized the capacity to view urban water through the lens of nature. As with houseboats, pleasure boats, heritage preservation, and harbor enthusiasm, this environmental lens initially emerged in tension with city planning objectives and then gradually became integrated into core understandings of urban water identity. City planners at the time were acutely concerned with environmental issues, as evident by the municipality's overt commitment to reducing its environmental and carbon footprint by building compact neighborhoods, promoting alternative transportation, and pursuing energy-neutral housing options.[15] However, sustainability rhetoric was virtually silent on the topic of wet urban nature. The political negotiations over IJburg dramatically changed this mentality, bringing nature and cities into explicit articulation.

The history of the IJssel Lake District functioned as a prime example of the *longue duree* interconnection between environmental and human processes in the Netherlands. According to secondary environmental histories, in the early Middle Ages bogs, moors, and fens covered the land where the IJssel Lake District would eventually stand. Farmers built drainage ditches and a few small freshwater lakes across the region over a six-hundred-year period. By the twelfth century, most of the land was under cultivation.

Then, "the tragedies" began. Drainage caused the ground to subside while warming climates caused sea levels to rise. A series of strong storm surges between the thirteenth and fifteenth centuries broke through dikes and flooded the region on several occasions. Pop-culture references to these events in the 2000s said these inundations covered up to seventy towns at a time and swept as many as a hundred thousand people and the land underneath them out to sea. Academic scholarship has shown that these legends exaggerated casualty tolls by a factor of ten or more. Geographically, however, the myths were instructive. By the fifteenth century, storm surges had transformed the medieval agrarian landscape into an inland saltwater bay, the Zuider Zee (South Sea), the same bay that Amsterdam's nautical seafarers would later traverse en route to the East Indies and the Americas.[16]

This oceanic landscape, the Zuider Zee, remained in place until the early twentieth century when the region was geographically transformed yet again. After a 1916 storm surge crushed dozens of local dams, claiming lives and damaging property, national government officials oversaw the construction of the Enclosure Dike (Afsluitdijk), a sea wall that divided the inland saltwater bay from the outlying Atlantic Ocean. The national government and its engineering team initially planned to gradually reclaim the entire bay to make developable land. By the 1970s, four large reclamation areas had been completed, but further infill efforts floundered in the wake of fiscal shortfalls stemming from deindustrialization, as well as from antidevelopment pressure stemming from the burgeoning environmental movement.[17]

By the late twentieth century, rivers and rainfall had flushed the salt out of the remaining 1,800 square kilometers of open water, and the IJssel Lake District had become the largest freshwater body in Western Europe. The IJssel Lake District included three jurisdictionally distinct but physically contiguous lakes: IJ Lake, Marker Lake, and IJssel Lake. The lakes were one of the few areas in the temperate European climate zone that rarely froze in the winter. Over several decades, freshwater fish colonized the lakes. Hundreds of thousands of northern birds began breeding there in the cold winter months or stopped to feed on mussels and fish on their migratory journey to Africa.[18]

In its freshwater form, the IJssel Lake District became a prominent and protected European nature district celebrated internationally as an avian rookery.[19] Several loosely coordinated national and international laws protected these birds and their aquatic habitat. The portion of IJ Lake near Amsterdam, where municipal planners hoped to expand the city's footprint, lay within the National Ecological Network (Ecologische Hoofdstructuur) and adjacent to a Natura-2000 European Union nature and biodiversity area. That area was also subject to the 1971 Ramsar Convention on Wetlands of International Importance and the 1992 European Bird Directive.[20] Additionally, the Dutch government had enforced a no-intervention policy in the area since the 1970s, a policy based on the expectation that human intervention into natural habitats was inherently destructive and that the environment would thrive best when left alone.[21]

Despite these legal protections and non-intervention approaches, throughout the 1990s and 2000s environmentalists repeatedly voiced concerns that the ecological quality of the IJssel Lake District was declining. Concerned advocates wrote that a deathly calm was slowly spreading across the water. Environmentalists had long been aware that twentieth-century urbanization along the shorelines had hardened the boundary between water and land, eliminating marshes and reducing ecological diversity. The Wetlands in IJssel Lake Foundation, which was formed to investigate the situation, uncovered several additional factors exacerbating ecological vulnerability as well. One issue was that the strong tidal currents that once flowed inland from the Atlantic Ocean scouring grooves in the underwater bedrock no longer penetrated beyond the Enclosure Dike sea wall. Instead, sediment buildup was turning the lake floor into a smooth, shallow, frying pan–like surface. The loss of grooves meant the loss of habitat for mussels. A second problem was that warmer water temperatures on the sheltered side of the sea wall were negatively affecting fish populations. Since mussels and fish were the birds' primary food source, the avian population was falling in turn. Third, in the absence of strong ocean currents, the lake experienced a constant, low-grade turbulence that left the water cloudy, making it difficult for birds to see their prey. Given these dynamics, environmental scientists warned that the lakes were "silting up into lifeless water."[22] They cautioned that if nothing were done to stop the decay, the shorelines and skies would become "sterile."[23]

Planning for the IJburg Urban Expansion Project

In Amsterdam, the municipality's decision to expand the city's footprint by building new islands for housing, office, and retail in the 1990s brought municipal planners into direct conflict with prominent environmental groups working to preserve and restore the IJssel Lake District. The public controversy surrounding the proposal emerged as a generative moment of negotiation and innovation. These discussions challenged city planners to modify their treatment of water and to bring nature, water, and real estate together in new ways.

Ideas for urban expansion into the Lake District were not new. Planners in the 1970s envisioned filling IJ Lake and building a massive, Manhattan-style business center overtop. Fiscal shortfalls and environmental legislation confined this idea to the drawing board for several decades. It was only in the 1990s that the municipality could afford to build a smaller-scale version of this island city. The IJburg Project Bureau, which oversaw the project, included employees from the municipal Physical Planning Department, as well as engineers, accountants, and advertisers from other municipal offices citywide. This municipal team was tasked with building an artificial island and establishing the programmatic requirements that private contractors would follow when building housing and retail amenities on top. Although the IJburg neighborhood was more modest in scale than the 1970s New Manhattan vision, it was nevertheless a significant undertaking. The 1990s design called for eighteen thousand housing units for forty-five thousand people, which would create a brand-new neighborhood that was over half the size of Amsterdam's existing city center.[24] As with the Eastern Docklands project discussed in the previous chapter, 70 percent of the housing units were destined for private market buyers. The goal at the time was to maximize housing construction, and the plan did not include a nature restoration component.

Environmental opposition to urban expansion peaked in 1997 just as the planning office was about to begin island construction. Two national environmental groups, the Nature Monuments environmental society and the Friends of the Earth Netherlands, were especially proactive in organizing public opposition against the project. The group mounted a rigorous public awareness campaign that highlighted the potential negative ramifications on the Lake District's ecological health. Campaign materials asserted that such a large urban extension into the already vulnerable Lake District would do irreparable ecological damage. Pro-development spokespeople countered the argument, in part by invoking references to a local heritage of building housing in wet landscapes since Amsterdam's golden age.[25] The controversy led to a citywide referendum requesting a permanent ban on IJburg construction. A quarter million people cast their votes, and nearly 60 percent of the ballots cast opposed the project. However, voter turnout was a few thousand votes shy of the threshold needed to make the election legally binding, so the project moved forward.

The IJburg Project Bureau recognized that their victory was somewhat hollow. Legal authority was on their side, but public perception was working against them. Officials worried that environmental groups would take their case to international courts, which could lead to costly time delays. Many planners were also genuinely sympathetic to the ecological concerns, especially given the planning department's general interest in sustainable development, which had become de rigueur during this period.

Given these concerns, the IJburg planning team offered to make a deal with the environmental groups, proposing to incorporate nature restoration into their housing project in exchange for the environmentalists' political and financial support. This offer divided the two environmental organizations that until that point had been united in their opposition to urban expansion. The Friends of the Earth Netherlands retained its staunch antidevelopment position. Over the following decade, the group continued to distribute leaflets, publish editorials, and host public events protesting urban expansion in the IJssel Lake District.[26] The Nature Monuments society, by contrast, accepted the municipality's partnership offer. Despite lingering reservations, Nature Monuments decision makers felt that inaction would only lead to further environmental degradation.[27] Ultimately, three organizations—the Amsterdam Physical Planning Department, Nature Monuments, and the North Holland Province—signed an agreement to establish the IJ Lake Nature Development Fund (through the ROM-IJmeer covenant) with each organization committing a third of the total €15 million budget to "compensate nature" for the negative side-effects of IJburg construction.[28] Still, as city planners explained, one vexing question remained: "Compensate water, how do you do that?"[29]

Mobilizing Water in IJburg

Around the time that the Physical Planning Department made promises to compensate nature and water for urban expansion, the department also began hiring urban ecologists as full-time staff members. Starting with a single ecologist and gradually expanding to a team of eight, these new municipal employees were asked to advise on several development projects citywide. Their primary goal, according to the first ecologist hired, whom I interviewed in 2010, was to help the planning department incorporate genuine, innovative, and profitable nature-creation undertakings into building plans already in motion. Ecologists could improve project designs, but ecological goals did not dictate which projects would or would not be pursued. For IJburg, these ecologists, along with other governmental and environmental partners, designed a series of landscape interventions and planning strategies that fundamentally transformed the design of water and shorelines in that district.

The Hoeckelings Dam was one of the first environmental improvement measures that the IJburg planning team implemented. This 1.6-kilometer, freestanding, sandbar-like dam was built off IJ Lake's northern shore a few kilometers north of the primary IJburg construction site. Municipal planners explained the rationale behind the dam's design in an undated promotional booklet published in the mid-2000s. In that document, project managers described the dam as an attempt to create "space for spontaneous nature development. [. . .] Yeah, it looks a bit like you are playing god. But nature is dynamic. [. . .] We only created the conditions for new nature, and these were surprisingly well picked up by nature itself."[30] The dam's above-water land area was envisioned as an avian rookery. Its underwater footprint running parallel to the coast would shelter water near the existing shoreline from the lake's constant turbulence. This underwater wall created a small habitat zone in the sheltered water between the existing shoreline and the Hoeckelings Dam. With cleaner water, new plants, and more fish, birds building nests on the dam would have an easier time finding food.[31]

After construction was complete, the municipality conducted an environmental survey of Hoeckelings Dam and publicized its successes. The sheltered waterway and island rookery, which cost €10.5 million over four years to build, stimulated bird breeding activities. As public relations material explained, "already in the first year that the dam stood above water, Common Terns settled there in a large breeding colony." Black-Headed Gulls, Mediterranean Gulls, three types of Plovers, several Avocets, and the first pair of Little Terns known to nest in Amsterdam built nests alongside an estimated eight hundred Common Tern breeding pairs. Urban ecologists celebrated the dam as "a real bird paradise" in line with the European Union's legal vision of the lakes as an internationally valued avian rookery. The dam was a boon to birdwatchers as well, since some of these breeding pairs were rare in the Amsterdam region. Birdwatchers have shown their support for Hoeckelings Dam by joining the citizen volunteer group that maintains the dam by annually hand-clearing young saplings from its surface, an activity that illustrates the ongoing role of human hands in stimulating nature development.[32]

Following this initial environmental success, the IJburg development team attempted to replicate it on a larger scale in IJburg proper. City ecologist Remco Daalder explained their strategy to me in 2010. The first step, he said, was to decide what kind of nature to make. The answer for the municipal planning office was, unquestionably, to make "nature that sells," which in their eyes meant nature that looked wild and unkempt. Well-manicured urban parks, while nice, were considered passé from a market perspective and bland from an ecological viewpoint. Instead, they hoped to create a self-regenerating landscape that made people think, "Wow, this is real!"[33] This picture of nature, the planning office believed, would boost sales and galvanize public support for urban expansion among environmentally conscious residents.

Once planners settled on this landscape vision, ecologists developed the design modifications and construction strategies that would bring this seemingly wild nature into being. They decided to start with water. The charge to design water in the late 1990s was a significant undertaking. Dutch engineers were used to working in a wet environment, but standard professional approaches made land the object of focus and designed water-management devices—such as canals, pumps, and dikes—so that the land object remained dry.[34] By contrast, the IJburg project team shifted focus from managing water in a terrestrial setting to designing water as the primary object. With a strong aquatic ecosystem as a starting point, ecologists hoped to initiate a chain of biophysical events that would help the nature born in the lake to climb onto the ground and fly into the air.

A project leader with the IJburg Project Bureau publicly explained some of his team's water design innovations in a 1997 newspaper interview on the cusp of the citywide referendum that nearly curtailed the project's construction. Instead of building one large island, as was originally planned, they broke the development into an archipelago-like constellation of seven smaller islands. This change maximized the length of shoreline, which was the most ecologically diverse part of the island. Then, by placing these islands close together, the narrow channels between the shores would accelerate currents between the banks. This quickened movement would prevent algae growth and create small grooves in the lakebed that mussels could grip. Similarly, using strategies tested at Hoeckelings Dam, the planning team introduced several internal marshy waterways traversing each of the islands to fragment their landmass even further. Artificial reed beds planted along these shores would create sheltered environments where wild water plants could take root. These wild plants would provide habitat for fish. They would also calm turbulence and filter sediment, making the water clean and helping birds see underwater prey.[35]

The interconnectedness of these incremental steps was an important feature in the overall design. IJburg planners did not want to create a fully completed landscape in one fell swoop. They did not want to physically insert each plant into the ground, dump fishery-raised fish into the lake, or import bird breeding pairs from other places, which were common strategies used when designing urban parks and completing environmental restorations elsewhere. Instead, they wanted to activate biophysical processes associated with water and shorelines so that the shape of IJburg's underwater infrastructure would spontaneously create a self-produced—and self-reproducing—vibrant ecology in the future.[36]

Once construction was complete, IJburg planners created several interpretive devices to heighten the visibility of the emerging underwater ecosystem to people on land. Municipal ecologists were acutely aware that the greatest ecological creation in the world might do little to advance an environmental agenda if no one ever saw it or appreciated its value.[37] Lakebed grooves, mussels, and fish had unquestioned ecological significance, but as ecologist Remco Daalder explained to me, "you can't see it. [. . .] It is very important to have things people can see. Things people can enjoy. And then they love nature. Otherwise, they won't love it."[38] In IJburg, ecologists strove to make underwater nature visible and pleasurable to people on land by cleaning the water and boosting fish counts near the city instead of only in distant locations, like Hoeckelings Dam. This local focus meant that people sitting at their breakfast tables could watch cormorants swooping through the sky searching for food. Residents could also fish for themselves from the walkways alongside their five-story apartment buildings. Similarly, planners designed the islands' shorelines to accommodate everyday leisure activities. For instance, although the interior waterways were too shallow for large public events, the water was deep enough that kids could swim and sail small boats, and the bridges were high enough for people to ice skate.[39] According to Daalder, "you don't have that in the city. That's why people live here."[40]

Helping vegetation climb banks and encouraging birds to swoop past kitchen windows was only one part of the challenge of making nature visible. The second step was to get people to cognitively process these things as nature. Municipal press releases and public relations materials played an important role in this endeavor. Municipal field guides, such as the popular *50X Outside!* neighborhood brochure, mapped several water-rich locations on IJburg that were described as "perfect [locations] for a mid-day sail, lounge, stroll, or cycle."[41] The brochure drolly described birds that, like humans, had trouble finding homes in Amsterdam and so squatted in whatever attic spaces they could find. It talked about sea creatures sunning themselves on rocks near IJburg's beaches where people were doing the same thing. These upbeat stories used humor and short jaunts from front doors—instead of science and extended hikes from remote trailheads—to encourage people to physically engage with IJburg's environmental amenities and to interpret those amenities as genuinely natural. All the better, Daalder said, if those stories led to "a nice little article in a local magazine or a TV spot" that got "people talking," building momentum for further nature restoration elsewhere in Amsterdam.[42]

Evaluating IJburg's Environmental Successes

In 2009, twelve years after municipal contractors began building the IJburg islands, the construction process reached its midpoint. Three newly built islands of dredged sand were complete, as were the high-density row houses, apartment buildings, retail structures, and office buildings overtop. Construction on phase two, including four additional islands, was scheduled to begin in 2013 pending the successful outcome of a European Union court case reviewing the project's ecological performance to date. Planning officials and media outlets took the opportunity to reflect on the neighborhood's economic and ecological performance and to publicize success stories among potential future homebuyers.

From a market perspective, IJburg was very successful. This project, billed as "one of the most ambitious urban projects to appear in the Netherlands in a generation," quickly emerged as "one of Amsterdam's most popular quarters," winning urban design awards and fetching stable sales prices at a time when the general housing market was entering a recession.[43] The neighborhood also offered distinctly new types of shoreline housing. Although no houseboats were permitted in IJburg, the neighborhood included a small marina exclusively devoted to high-end, custom-designed floating homes. Private buyers had purchased 73 of the 110 available water lots by 2007, paying €135,000 for the lot and between €200,000 and €300,000 for the floating homes.[44] Other luxury units had direct private access to the marshy inland waterways where owners could anchor boats near their back doors.[45] Similarly, investors experimented with expensive villas on beaches, a novel architectural form in Amsterdam.[46]

From an ecological perspective, in the late 2000s the Amsterdam Physical Planning Department directed its in-house city ecologists to quantitatively assess whether the design adaptations implemented in IJburg's phase one had successfully offset the negative environmental consequences associated with urban expansion. Municipal employees spent several months collecting water samples and other data sources and then published their findings in an assessment report entitled "IJburg: A Guest in Nature."[47] Their overarching conclusion was that large-scale housing development in the cherished and fragile Lake District had improved the lake's environmental health.[48] The environmental benefits listed in the report were long and varied. Lake ecology had purportedly recovered in full from construction-related disruptions. More plants and animals lived in the area in 2009 than was the case in 1997 before construction began. Fish diversity had expanded. The number of grass snakes had increased. Water quality had improved. Perhaps most importantly, the number of conventional and exotic birds breeding in the lake area had grown substantially.

Based on these findings, the report asserted that nature was "makeable."

Nature-friendly shorelines lined with high-density urban development in IJburg, ca. 2009. Image courtesy of Remco Daalder, Dienst Ruimtelijke Ordening.

In other words, beyond simple landscaping and habitat zoning, the authors argued that city planners could shape edge conditions and biome patterns so that some types of fish, birds, or mollusks would flourish while unwanted pests would flounder.[49] This framework shifted attention away from a discussion of habitat loss and refocused attention on a discussion of which types of plants and animals planners should invite into the expanding urban infrastructure. From this point forward, the IJburg neighborhood, which only months before was still troubled with negative press from antidevelopment critics, became a celebrated aquatic nature-making prototype that municipal ecologists hoped to replicate elsewhere.[50]

Their notable successes aside, city ecologists stated in interviews that their most prized accomplishment had less to do with the raw numbers of snakes and birds. Instead, they prided themselves on changing public expectations about the extent to which city builders could and should engineer ecosystems. The Lake District's millennial history showed that people could make freshwater lakes and bird breeding grounds by accident. By 2010, IJburg planners felt they had demonstrated that experts could make spaces for spontaneous nature development both on purpose and through urban expansion as well. In addition to IJburg being a nature restoration undertaking, planners soon began discussing it as an "experimental garden" and "a big nature development laboratory" where practitioners pursuing other development projects could test ideas about how to incorporate water and nature into urban spaces.[51]

For residents, water also gradually emerged as an important neighborhood amenity. In a 2010 interview, IJburg project managers emphasized that renters and buyers who moved to the area often initially had little interest in the neighborhood's watery characteristics. In a crowded and expensive city, residents had few choices about where to live. They moved to IJburg because its newly built units were available while the rest of the city was full. "But, once there, in satisfaction surveys, people want to live there, because it is close to the city, but also, to enjoy nature and water."[52] Residents enthusiastically described water as a defining characteristic of the place, saying that the scent of water in the wind and the sound of water sloshing around the island made people feel as though they were out at sea. Moreover, they described their new homes' closeness to the soft water edges as fundamentally distinct from their interactions with the hard, narrow canals permeating the rest of Amsterdam. If central city water was historic, IJburg water was seen as natural, dynamic, and wild, a nice contrast to the carefully manicured and blatantly artificial canalscapes elsewhere in the city.[53]

Despite these successes, the notion that city building and habitat preservation could operate on equal footing—let alone with environmental considerations taking priority—remained deeply uncertain, especially in light of unresolved ecological concerns connected with IJburg's development. One issue involved the question of scale. IJburg was the largest urban expansion project underway in the Netherlands, but the enormous Lake District still dwarfed it in size. IJburg's phase one footprint of two hundred hectares comprised less than one half of one percent of the entire freshwater Lake District.[54] Additionally, the most significant ecological gains in terms of water quality and wildlife diversity occurred immediately adjacent to the newly created shorelines. Even if new home construction could generate localized environmental benefits, experts were uncertain whether those gains would have a measurable impact on lake functioning as a whole.

A second concern was that the proliferation of some fish and bird species did not mean that every species had thrived. This issue became especially pressing with the adoption of more stringent European Union environmental standards in 2005 that affected urban expansion into IJ Lake. Under the new requirements, before receiving construction permits, planners had to demonstrate that the population count of every creature already living in the vicinity of the work area would not be negatively affected by the proposed construction. According to interviews with IJburg Project Bureau officials, by 2010 the planning team felt they had remediation strategies in place to protect or replace all plants, fish, and mussels in the phase two construction area. They were also confident that all but three bird species would remain unaffected. However, with mitigation plans to protect the last three bird species difficult to envision, European Courts had delayed their construction permits several times pending further study.

A related concern was that housing construction had many environmental consequences beyond immediate habitat loss and reductions in species diversity. Spokespeople with the Friends of the Earth Netherlands noted that urban expansion increased vehicular traffic and impervious surfaces, which increased nonpoint source pollution, storm water runoff, and climate change.[55] Critics were also concerned that the emphasis on species population counts overshadowed the Lake District's equally important unique environmental aesthetic. "IJ Lake is an open, spacious area in the middle of the North Wing, the northern section of the Urban Ring. It is the place right by Amsterdam where you can still see the horizon and still feel the wind."[56] This aesthetic interest in preserving a wide, open waterscape formed the backbone of the Friends of the Earth Netherlands's 2008 and 2009 public campaigns to keep IJ Lake visually open and recreationally accessible. "IJ Lake is no large 'white' area that has to be filled in with new development. It is a valuable 'blue' area. [. . .] Keep IJ Lake open!"[57]

Another unresolved tension stemmed from concerns that so-called copycat projects might be less genuinely sensitive to environmental considerations and less rigorously scrutinized by permit-granting agencies than the initial IJburg trailblazer. Even in IJburg's phase two, the ecological measures of success had shifted. With costly delays and public perception problems draining the city's shaky financial resources in the context of an international economic recession, the IJburg Project Bureau hired the internationally renowned green building consultant William McDonough to review their schematics. Based on his feedback, the revised environmental priorities for phase two emphasized the use of recycled building materials, carbon-neutral architecture, and mixed-use zoning, alongside nature creation, to make the development sustainable.[58] These aspirations, while commendable, were also potentially problematic. Habitat preservation, which was so crucial to environmental groups, was recast as one among many potential green attributes to consider. This shift sparked concerns that future urban expansion projects might cherry-pick carbon neutrality or mixed-use zoning as their preferred environmental focus, leaving the immediate relationship with lake ecology unaddressed.

These trends left the Netherlands' leading environmental groups acutely concerned. The most agitated opponents, including spokespeople with the Friends of the Earth Netherlands, emphasized that IJburg had set a disturbing precedent by allowing urban expansion to proceed.[59] Even among sympathetic groups, such as the Nature Monuments society whose members collaborated with city planners on IJburg's design, spokespeople worried that their support for IJburg might be misinterpreted. During a 2010 interview, for instance, an organization representative emphasized that unlike the city ecologists on staff with the Physical Planning Department, they viewed IJburg as a site-specific solution that should not be exported to other places. After the 1997 referendum opposing development failed, phase one of construction was going to proceed no matter what environmental groups thought. Moreover, restoring the vast and decaying Lake District was bound to be pricy. The severity of the situation motivated Nature Monuments to compromise, but the organization still preferred to restrain urban growth in most other contexts.[60] Even though IJburg generated disagreement within the environmental community on some fronts, both advocacy groups remained opposed, in principle, to the preservation-through-development ideology that the city planning office had come to embrace.

Nature Restoration through Urban Development

Despite ongoing concerns, by 2010 the general public appeared to support the municipality's assertion that water-oriented urban development was ecologically legitimate. The IJburg project provided opportunities for a public debate over the relationship between water, nature, and housing. These discussions led to immediate changes in the physical form of urban expansion, as well as to a growing environmental consciousness surrounding water in cities. These developments created opportunities to consider further human intervention in the IJssel Lake District, and they created new cognitive schemas that cast existing urban shorelines in a new light.

Despite some continuing disagreement, by the late 2000s planners, environmentalists, and politicians of many stripes agreed on two points: the ecological quality of the IJssel Lake District remained perilous, and society could take steps to improve it. Newspaper reporters described the rise of unprecedented interest in the region's ecological vitality.[61] Some environmental groups advocated for a "robust, spectacular, new nature" zone to be constructed northeast of Amsterdam along the Lake District's eastern shore.[62] Others pressured government officials at the provincial and national levels to invest in a "massive ecological boost" commensurate with the lakes' exceptional scale, value, and vulnerability.[63] The State Secretary of the Ministry of Transport, Public Works, and Water Management lent national credence to these endeavors in 2009 by publicly voicing enthusiastic support for plans to improve the lakes' ecological health.[64] With silt deposits accumulating, and with no end to the decay in sight, even the most ardent hands-off conservationists felt that continuing the 1970s no-intervention policy would only exacerbate the problems.[65]

Many possible solutions were considered. Some people proposed physically partitioning the Lake District into two large zones, with the northern half partially tied back into tidal ocean systems and seasonal storm cycles while the inland areas closer to Amsterdam would remain heavily regulated for flood control purposes.[66] Other people suggested using eco-friendly techno-science to convert the aging Enclosure Dike sea wall into a vegetated terrain surrounded by floating homes and attractive minilakes.[67] By 2009, the idea gaining the most traction envisioned transforming a portion of the Lake District into a national water park surrounding a man-made, six-thousand-hectare marshy wetland and flanked by an extensive series of coastal reed beds similar to IJburg's Hoeckelings Dam. By recontouring the lake floor, creating vegetated dunes, and sheltering shoreline bulkheads, wetland designers proposed using IJburg-style construction to stimulate self-perpetuating current flows and habitat zones. Advocates hoped the resulting wetland would then function as an ecological "beating heart" for the region, nation, and continent.[68]

Financing the wetland would require political collaboration. Ecologists estimated that a wetland system substantial enough to restore ecological health to the entire Lake District would cost €800 million. According to Amsterdam's head municipal ecologist, "no government will give so much money to make nature."[69] Nature Monuments spokespeople agreed, saying, "if there is no building, the government will never spend that much for nature."[70] As they explained, however, new home construction could generate the revenue streams needed to amass the requisite capital. The IJburg experience demonstrated that €800 million for nature restoration seemed expensive when considered in isolation, but the expense "is peanuts" when compared to the cost of a new bridge, tunnel, or island associated with urban expansion.[71] When incorporating wetland restoration as a subcomponent of urbanization, "officials say, sure, throw it in."[72]

The exact form that preservation-through-development should take, however, remained undecided. Some developers hoped to connect the envisioned wetland with a tourism center of casinos, hotels, and adventure outriggers built on a series of themed vacation islands.[73] Many rural residents living near undeveloped sections of the waterfront criticized that vision and instead advocated for small-scale marinas and recreational fishing amenities catering to existing local residents. Some people envisioned building a large reservoir that could provide a secure source of fresh drinking water in the context of projected climate change–related shortages.[74] However, the most promising scenario by the late 2000s was an IJburg-inspired project. City planners hoped to build new homes on strip islands interwoven with the wetland.[75] If IJburg ecologists were correct that shorelines—not land surfaces—mattered most from an environmental perspective, then it followed that "if there are houses on the islands, it doesn't matter."[76] From a financial perspective, the total projected cost of €3 billion for several thousand new hectares of housing would include a €500 million savings achieved by combining wetland reconstruction with housing development. Those savings could pay for over 60 percent of the envisioned wetlands system independent of other funding sources.[77]

In addition to shaping future growth plans, the redefinition of urban water as an environmental entity in IJburg influenced the way planners and residents interpreted other water features in Amsterdam. The Physical Planning Department's extensive public outreach campaigns built excitement around the notion of looking for nature in the city. Urban ecologists publicized that there were 10,000 species of fauna and flora, 30 types of mammals, 130 species of birds, 60 breeds of fish, and 1,5000 varieties of mushrooms in Amsterdam.[78] To enhance these counts, planners used urban park renovations as opportunities to transform existing ponds from aesthetic water follies into rich habitats for frogs, rabbits, and salamanders.[79]

This ecological lens inflected the public's perception of the central city canals as well. Media sources reflecting this change reinforced expectations that "decades ago, the canals were dead," but by the beginning of the twenty-first century, Amsterdam canals had purportedly become "an idyllic spot for plants and animals."[80] City ecologists measuring life in the canals in the late 2000s popularized notions that the central city waterways had greater biodiversity than the Netherlands' Veluwe National Forest. More crabs lived in Amsterdam than people. With antipollution measures improving water quality, formerly rare birds, such as blue herons, became increasingly common sights along the inland waterways. The municipality also proactively publicized laws written to protect this ecosystem—for instance by reminding pleasure boaters not to disturb birds nesting in the canals, a legal measure explicitly aimed at Queen's Day partiers who often uncovered their boats for the first time on that early spring holiday when nesting activity was at a peak.[81]

Around the same time, members from several liberal and green political parties created the new Natural Water (Water Natuurlijk) advocacy group to support ecology-minded candidates in Water Board elections. This consortium, which controlled about 20 percent of Water Board seats by the late 2000s, campaigned explicitly on the platform of creating nature-friendly shores in urban areas and making safer, cleaner, healthier, and lovelier waterscapes in residential neighborhoods.[82] These political shifts occurred in the wake of IJburg construction and in the context of a growing national environmental consciousness, and they created new opportunities to give nature a stronger voice in city management processes.

The Greening of Urban Water

The IJburg urban expansion project emerged as a key moment in the construction of a shifting eco-consciousness in Amsterdam. The contestation and innovation during the development process transformed city planners' vision of nature, cities, and the role of water as a connecting element stitching these spheres together. Ardent environmentalists and innovative city ecologists gave aquatic habitat a voice and presence in planning circles. They devised infrastructure construction techniques and public awareness campaigns that transformed island-based urban growth into an opportunity to restore an internationally renowned, water-based avian rookery. These efforts creatively recast birds, currents, and water plants as entities created through urban investment that could play an active physical, legal, and emotional role in future water-oriented real estate development.

The tense but generative collaboration between environmental groups and municipal officials challenged long-standing expectations in Amsterdam that nature and cities were fundamentally opposed. By the late 2000s, physical planners—long seen as enemies to the environmental health of the IJssel Lake District—assumed the role of patrons and midwives for the lakes' avian rookery and the underwater ecology necessary to sustain it. Newspaper editorialists, provincial officials, sports fishermen, and many but not all environmental advocacy groups began to consider preservation-through-development as a potentially genuine solution to ecological decay. Building large-scale housing projects over portions of the lake began, tentatively, to read as a cost-effective, ecologically sound strategy to finance environmental restoration across the entire Lake District.

This potential hinged on fundamental shifts in the imagined functionality and identity of urban water. Nature discourses, once confined to the aesthetics of rural green spaces, embraced notions of water and cities as potentially nature-rich and nature-generative sites. This reframing of water prompted further reassessments of water's ecological capacities in already existing wet urban spaces. Crabs in canals, frogs in ponds, and birds on boats became evidence of a latent ecological potentiality that green and liberal residents, planners, and politicians hoped to nurture citywide.

The vision of urban water as an ecological entity complicated other cultural associations connecting water with housing practices, public space, and heritage identities. For homes floating on water or built on reclaimed land, the environmental lens elevated the importance of the edge interface between housing and water as zones of potential biofiltration and biodiversity. Similarly, instead of seeing the city center as a convenient and historically charged site for public festivals on the water that could also occur elsewhere, the historic city reemerged as a bounded entity where large-scale events were reasonable in contrast to newly built areas where smaller-scale leisure activity was seen as a more appropriate use of the environmentally rich waterscapes. Moreover, the identity symbolism of water expanded beyond visions of hard-edged canals and restored harbors to include marshy channels, aquatic scents, and urban beaches, which reinforced the theme of a water-based Amsterdam identity while expanding it beyond the iconography of its seventeenth- and nineteenth-century physical forms.

To this mix, the greening of water transformed waterscapes into a connecting tissue weaving nature and cities together.[83] Investing in nature through water-oriented infrastructure created the necessary legal preconditions for Amsterdam's continued expansion. Urbanization became an environmental laboratory, and the proliferation of so-called wild nature spaces increased the market attractiveness of newly built neighborhoods. Water, as a combined cultural landscape and ecological medium, became an important focal point where new rationales for shoreline living emerged.

CHAPTER SIX

Investors on Floodplains

Reflecting the escalating scale of shoreline urban redevelopment in the Netherlands, this chapter shifts focus as well, moving the discussion away from Amsterdam to consider a new water-oriented development paradigm at work on a national scale. By the early twenty-first century, water was central to the urban growth strategies of many Dutch cities. In Amsterdam, this centrality emerged gradually, entangled with the cultural logics of squatting skippers, floating partiers, and heritage enthusiasts. It grew through regulatory reforms that redefined the character of water as a living space, public space, and locational amenity. It involved large-scale construction projects on deindustrialized shorelines and in ecological lake districts. These trends prompted diffuse, ongoing public discussions about the nature of water and its desirable urban form. By the 2000s, water-oriented real estate development in Amsterdam, combined with similar trends following their own trajectories in other nearby cities, had become a nationally recognized driver of economic development.

Also in the 2000s, technological advances in floating architecture were enabling new possibilities to mobilize water as the foundation for growth. These technologies brought the logic of living afloat full-circle, supplanting the image of squatting skippers in rickety houseboats with the image of high-tech, speculative, luxury neighborhoods built entirely afloat, complete with apartment buildings, offices, roads, parks, and beaches bobbing on water surfaces. As technologies advanced, industry experts began speaking seriously about the potential to build new floating cities in the Netherlands.

Despite growing enthusiasm, constructing sprawling, floating cities on existing big-water surfaces was politically contentious. For instance, although the IJssel Lake District could theoretically support floating architecture, international environmental regulations challenged that vision. Unlike Amsterdam's IJburg neighborhood, where architects used underwater island infrastructure to restore natural habitat functions,[1] floating architecture made no demonstrable environmental contribution, and it visually interrupted the aesthetic of a wide-open nature space. Other, smaller lakes also had preexisting environmental, economic, and symbolic associations that city builders had difficulty overcoming.

Instead, floating architecture made greater headway on greenfield sites. In the late 2000s, Dutch government officials were encouraging the transformation of green environmental areas and agricultural land into lakes and floodplains as part of an emerging national climate change adaptation plan. This rhetoric of disaster preparedness justified compulsory land sales. Then, once the land was lowered and flooded, the newly created lakes figured as blank canvases, erased of their preexisting ownership claims and environmental functionalities and awaiting a new identity. For city builders, this logic of land de-reclamation provided opportunities for urban expansion on greenfield sites that were otherwise off-limits. Conversely, for national officials with the Ministry of Transport, Public Works, and Water Management (Verkeer en Waterstaat), market-oriented redevelopment through floating architecture provided a revenue source to finance climate change response measures. Together, these mutually reinforcing discourses consolidated into a development model that would supposedly turn the largest physical threat facing Dutch cities into the most profitable urban development paradigm of the next hundred years.

From a political economy perspective, real and perceived flood risks became a political mechanism for overcoming agricultural and environmental resistance to growth. Greenfield development had a long, contested history in Amsterdam and its peer cities in the Urban Ring.[2] Although the declining profitability of many Dutch farms created greater economic incentives for redevelopment, antisprawl policy regulations shielded those areas from encroaching cities. The emerging culture of climate change responsiveness, however, loosened those protections. It created new opportunities for city builders to propose lake and wetland creation, which they financed through new housing sales on those locations.

These practices gave water new life in land management and city building processes. National climate change discourses cast water as an intermediary transforming atmospheric warming into a localized threat to lives and infrastructure. Concurrently, floating architecture inverted historic urban expansion practices, replacing water infill and land reclamation with flooding and de-reclamation. These trends literally and figuratively mobilized water to naturalize land reform and urban expansion.

Officials used the cultural history of water in places like Amsterdam to naturalize these land reforms and building practices in the face of opposition from environmental groups and agricultural landowners. The romance of living afloat, the legacies of water as a public space, and the claims of a water-based heritage identity reinforced the perceived authenticity of the newly created lakes and their water-oriented housing. Past investments in harbors had proven the market value of water in real estate, and investments in new island shorelines reinforced expectations that water connected people with nature. These narratives, which emerged incrementally in Amsterdam, were combined with similar narratives emerging through other paths and from other locations outside of Amsterdam to form a national campaign to redevelop farmland and green spaces for water storage and floating cities.

This chapter explains these processes by tracing the interconnections between the de-reclamation movement and the floating architecture movement. The term *de-reclamation* (*ontpoldering*) refers to the process of turning land into marshes, wetlands, floodplains, and lakes. Contracting the national footprint in one of Europe's most densely populated countries may sound counter-intuitive, but when combined with floating architecture, de-reclamation emerged as an important strategy that increased rather than decreased the acreage available for real estate investment. These land reforms ceded ground, but not territory, and innovative architects were eagerly preparing to turn the newly created lakes and wetlands into new, large floating cities.

The history of these two movements was preserved in written archives documenting shifts in government policy objectives and architectural building practices. Government sources included cabinet-level speeches, press releases, policy reports, and promotional videos that the Ministry of Transport, Public Works, and Water Management prepared between 2000 and 2010. Similar material from other agencies—including national entities such as the Ministry of Housing and the Living with Water Foundation, as well as local entities such as the Amsterdam Department of Inland Waterway Management and its contractor Waternet—also helped shape the de-reclamation debate. Architectural sources included documents from professional and educational institutions, such as the Royal Institute of Dutch Architects, the Rathenau Institute, and the UNESCO-IHE Institute for Water Education, as well as a growing body of gray literature developing around the concept of floating architecture. Dutch language reports and editorials in left-leaning national newspapers also gave climate-related adaptation plans and experimental design solutions extensive coverage.

These sources brought water's climatological attributes to the foreground and, simultaneously, recast water management as the technical justification for land appropriation and greenfield development. Advocates mobilized cultural legacies of shoreline living, water heritage, and floating public celebrations in places like Amsterdam to frame these changes as the simple continuation of living with water in the Netherlands.

These dynamics demonstrate that the imagined international paradigm shift from industrial to postindustrial urban water remains incomplete and open-ended. Shoreline and harbor redevelopments often look formulaic from a distance, as though developers follow the same investment recipe and create the same placeless festival markets on every postindustrial shore. Ongoing innovations in Amsterdam, however, illustrate the opportunities and competing influences that push redevelopment projects in new directions and put water to work for an ever-evolving set of political agendas.

Urban Expansion and Real Estate Investment

The market success of real estate investment in places like Amsterdam's Eastern Docklands and IJburg neighborhoods in the 2000s reinforced a national policy goal of using high-end, water-oriented, new home construction to enhance the Netherlands' international economic competitiveness. Geographically, housing development focused on the Urban Ring (Randstad), which included Amsterdam, Almere, Utrecht, Rotterdam, and The Hague. These cities formed a loose circle around a central green zone reserved for environmental tourism and low-intensity agriculture. From the 1950s through the 1990s, suburban expansion in these cities threatened to infringe on both this internal green space and rural areas outside the Urban Ring. The shift to water-oriented development in the 2000s, instead of alleviating development pressure on those green spaces, increased pressure to redevelop greenfield sites by transforming parks and pastures into urbanized lakes and floodplains.

By the mid-2000s, real estate investment had become a lynchpin in the Netherlands' national economic development agenda. The Ministry of Housing, Spatial Planning, and the Environment (Ministrie van Volkshuisvesting, Ruimtelijke Ordening en Milieubeheer), for instance, gave real estate a prized role in its thirty-year structural growth plan. In this plan, titled "Randstad 2040," officials called on city builders to construct at least five hundred thousand high-end housing units in the coming decades. To paraphrase from its report, the ministry identified cities as engines of the global economy. Since cities purportedly competed internationally for business investment and top-notch entrepreneurs, officials promoted investments in "green, attractive, and climate-resilient living environment(s)" to expand their creative- and knowledge-industry base.[3] As an example of successful development projects to emulate, ministry personnel pointed directly to Amsterdam's IJ waterway to illustrate the economic merits of high-density, mixed-use, water-oriented investment. Alongside the laudable reuse of brownfield sites, officials praised the IJ shorelines for their interweaving of nature and water amenities, which added an aesthetic of health and pleasure, and which increased property values.[4]

Calls for rapid housing construction and urban expansion were not necessarily new. Only a decade earlier in the mid-1990s, the Ministry of Housing had set the goal of constructing six hundred thousand new homes by 2015.[5] From the 1950s through the 1990s, urban expansion often included greenfield, suburban-style development. Some agricultural land was affected, but the legacy of postwar food shortages across Europe lent farmers significant support to resist urban encroachment for several decades. Green nature zones, however, remained vulnerable. By the mid-1990s, leading national newspapers frequently printed reports, editorials, and rebukes debating the merits of environmental preservation, as well as the advantages and disadvantages of allowing housing construction in large open spaces.[6] Arguments in favor of urban expansion often characterized green preservation spaces as inaccessible, polluted, or agro-industrialized, attributes that challenged the perceived merit of protecting those parklands as recreational nature zones. This logic fully acknowledged the environmental harms associated with suburban sprawl, but it challenged that the market demand for single-family homes in green rural settings would make better—or at least justifiable—use of those allegedly already degraded spaces, a stance that environmentalists vocally refuted.

By the mid-2000s, with demand for water-oriented neighborhoods rising, it seemed for a time that big-water lakes might divert development pressure away from greenfield parks and farmland. For instance, the IJburg urban expansion project in Amsterdam discussed in the previous chapter emerged as an important benchmark case illustrating the potential to build high-density, mixed-use neighborhoods in wet areas. Its eco-friendly amenities encouraged some environmental groups and city builders to consider collaborating on more joint marsh reconstruction and urban expansion projects in the future.[7] Similarly, building interests in Almere, Amsterdam's so-called smaller sister city on the opposite side of IJ Lake, advocated expanding Almere into the lake and allowing Amsterdam and Almere to grow together across the water. These campaigns advertised water as the front yard and showpiece for the city, a rhetorical turn that discursively domesticated water as an already urbanized entity and, therefore, a logical place to invest.[8]

Although urban expansion into the Lake District may proceed, that location as the site for future urban growth was suboptimal for many reasons. Financially, complying with environmental regulations that protected the lakes' ecological vitality add time and cost to urban expansion projects, and as it was an international legal issue, the Dutch government had limited ability to grant exceptions to the rules. Additionally, the Lake District lay to the north of the Netherlands' Urban Ring and far from the existing transportation, communication, and cultural infrastructure concentrated farther south. The pressure to expand urban areas onto greenfield sites has continued mounting, and the rise of floating architecture unexpectedly created a mechanism to shift development away from the lakes and refocus it back on greenfield locations.

The Rise of Floating Architecture

The aesthetic and technology of floating architecture has evolved considerably since the decades of the squatting skippers and their self-built houseboats in Amsterdam. Advances in floating platform technology and lightweight construction methods have led to a series of scalar jumps from floating villas to floating apartments, offices, beaches, parks, and roads. The capacity to build floating infrastructure, like roads, has proven especially significant in the plausibility of constructing entire cities afloat. Despite technological advances, the challenging political question of deciding where to locate these floating cities has continued to linger and, unexpectedly, has returned the question of greenfield development to the center of urban expansion debates.

Experiments with floating architecture have taken several forms. As an early example, in 2004, contractors working for the engineering company Dura Vermeer constructed forty-six homes in Maasbommel, a small riverfront town about a hundred kilometers south of Amsterdam. Although this strip of homes was a comparatively small undertaking for the company in terms of project size, it netted Dura Vermeer considerable international media attention. A string of feature stories published in the *New York Times*, the *Guardian*, and *Der Spiegel*, as well as aired in the United States on National Public Radio, followed reporters knocking on doors, talking with residents, and touring homes.[9] Reporters described the homes as well-appointed, if otherwise fairly typical, single-family houses. However, each home had a remarkable feature that was the object of curiosity. About 70 percent of the housing was "amphibious." These units were built on hollow platform foundations anchored to vertical steel posts, a mechanical arrangement that allowed the structures to rise off the ground and float on water up to five meters deep. The other 30 percent of housing units floated full-time in a sheltered recreational area in the Meuse River. According to company spokespeople, these engineering experiments with amphibious and floating architecture would keep the homes and residents safe from the river's periodic floods. More significantly, Dura Vermeer's engineers used the project to develop the technological capability to build secure, weather-resistant cities as a routine part of their business operations.

The Royal Institute of Dutch Architects (Bond van Nederlandse Architecten) became an avid promoter of floating architecture in the mid-2000s. A brief glance at the association's special website devoted to this issue, "H$_2$Olland: Architecture with Wet Feet," revealed the range of water dwellings and floating architecture typologies emerging nationwide.[10] For example, the association's project list included the "Six Water Houses" project constructed in 2001 in Amsterdam's IJburg neighborhood, which included a collection of architecturally playful housing units built on a floating Styrofoam platform wrapped in a thin shell of concrete.[11] It included the "All Hands on Deck" project constructed in Almere the same year that featured sixteen houses built on floating concrete shells on designated water plots. The houses as purchased offered a basic, minimal set of living spaces with the expectation that buyers would use do-it-yourself labor to add additional rooms and amenities of their choosing.[12] The website also featured many designs for prototype projects, such as Aqua Domus and Aqua Villa, which were floating house designs advertised as "superior to traditional Dutch houseboats in quality, durability, technical equipment, outlook, and their relation to the surrounding water."[13] Digital renderings of the housing designs depicted aesthetically modern, high-end facades, terraces, fireplaces, bridges, and walkways all built on a supposedly durable, stable, unsinkable, fireproof, and maintenance-free floating foundation.

Floating architecture existed in a tense relationship with houseboats. Unlike houseboats, floating architecture lacked an internal motor or the ability to move from place to place independently. Floating architecture also tended to be expensive and explicitly commodified. Despite these differences, architects and engineers promoting the technology frequently referenced houseboats in places like Amsterdam. On the one hand, these references naturalized and romanticized living afloat by mobilizing traditions of architectural uniqueness and cultural distinction. On the other hand, the emphasis on floating architecture's physical stability and market luxury co-opted the romance of living afloat without requiring residents to commit to small home sizes, labor-intensive maintenance processes, or the imagined nuisance of waves and tour boats.

By 2010, the market for floating homes and office spaces had expanded considerably. According to secondary sources, several companies performed technical and market tests during this period. Those experiments often occurred as subcomponents within larger, more conventional projects already underway, which meant that the amphibious and swimming communities completed by 2010 were mostly small-scale and distributed around the country. For instance, seven floating homes constructed in Leeuwarden in 2004 received international media attention as being the first official permanently inhabited floating homes in Europe, a distinction that was not quite accurate but that nonetheless illustrated both the relative novelty of the architectural form and its initially small-scale implementation. A handful of other projects followed, including, for example, 19 floating homes constructed in Almere in 2008, 14 floating homes for sale in Utrecht in 2009, and 73 floating homes sold in Amsterdam's IJburg neighborhood by 2010, plus the 46 amphibious and floating homes in Maasbommel.[14]

Although these projects were small in size, their growing technological and market successes lent credibility to the architectural concept of building entire neighborhoods afloat. The amphibious homebuilders Dura Vermeer, for example, also publicly circulated design schematics for "The Floating City" ("De Drijvende Stad"). Their sketches have undergone several iterations in the dozen or so years since company employees began considering the idea in the late 1990s. One ambitious and widely replicated computer rendering depicted a new town of twelve thousand people envisioned as a new suburb for Amsterdam built overtop of existing agricultural land located near the Schipol Amsterdam International Airport. Design images showed a radial layout with freestanding housing and greenhouses encircling a consolidated town center with schools,

Design proposal for a floating city to be built over de-reclaimed agricultural land outside of Amsterdam. Image courtesy of Dura Vermeer, 2001.

shops, and transportation hubs. The entire imagined city bobbed serenely on buoyant platforms in a sparkling sea of blue. Advocates asserted that this urban planning vision embodied the "Water Landscape of the Future."[15]

Although city-scale plans of this magnitude remained unrealized in the mid-2000s, the pressure to expand construction and build full-fledged floating cities was mounting. In 2007, in a cross between a serious development proposal and a sales gimmick, the company Dutch Docklands proposed constructing a floating city for sixty thousand people on the edge of Amsterdam within ten years.[16] In 2008, the architectural firm Waterstudio launched their more serious "New Water" project (Het Nieuwe Water) with the announcement that they would submerge twenty-three hectares of marshland outside The Hague in 2010 to create a large water storage area, which they planned to finance by building luxury floating housing and apartment buildings on top.[17] Similarly, the engineering company DeltaSync envisioned building 1,300 floating homes and highways in Rotterdam on large blocks of polystyrene foam. They collaborated with the design firm Public Domain Architects in 2010 to build their "Floating Pavilion" project ("Drijvend Paviljoen"), a sample slice of the proposed development that they exhibited to the public in a prominent office area in Rotterdam.[18] Developers soon began speaking of these scattered projects as the tip of a growing research and development agenda preparing industry experts and the general public for a new urban planning paradigm embodied within the floating metropolis.

The goal of consolidating floating architecture from a handful of small exhibition houses into full-fledged floating cities raised the important question of where those cities should be built. Existing open water areas, such as the IJssel Lake District, were unlikely candidates. In the IJburg urban expansion project, the shorelines and underwater portions of island infrastructure were critical in improving wetland functionality and restoring ecological diversity to the area. That underwater infrastructure was pivotal in securing international legal permission to build in the protected Lake District. Floating architecture, which lacked an underwater eco-restorative infrastructure, also lacked the legal mechanism that would have made urban expansion into the lakes politically viable.

Other possible building sites included nationally protected environmental areas and sheltered river areas. Environmental law in those spaces was controlled nationally, rather than internationally, giving developers greater leeway to lobby for exemptions. In the Maasbommel project, for instance, national officials lifted antidevelopment environmental protection laws for companies willing to build climate-proof demonstration projects, such as floating and amphibious homes.[19] Although valuable test sites, those linear, isolated locations lacked the expansiveness and centrality needed to accommodate a full floating city near the Urban Ring. Quickly, city builders turned their attention away from existing water bodies and back onto pasture areas and farmlands as the most attractive potential locations to build floating cities, a logic that gained significant political traction through emerging national discourses of climate change readiness and land de-reclamation.

National Climate Change Adaptation Plans

Water management has a long history in the Netherlands, but the notion that Dutch residents live in partnership with water, rather than protect themselves from water, is a relatively new phenomenon. According to the Ministry of Transport, Public Works, and Water Management, as repeated in over one hundred public statements and press releases issued between 2000 and 2010, water management has proven critical to economic development nationwide. "Three-quarters of our land," including most of the national capital, "lies below sea level." Half of the nation's total acreage consists of land reclaimed from the sea floor, and "about 65% of the Gross National Product is earned there."[20] Several ministry state secretaries reiterated this message. "Without our dams, dikes, and dunes, two-thirds of our country would regularly lie under water."[21] The Netherlands, they said, includes an estimated one hundred thousand kilometers of coastline organized into "a fine-grained network of hundreds of different water levels" with "monitoring stations, pumps, windmills, and drains" that "precisely regulate the water level in even the smallest ditch."[22] These statistics, for ministry officials, were sources of pride.

Despite technological advances in managing water, flood risks in the 1990s and 2000s were growing. According to Crown Prince Willem-Alexander— affectionately dubbed "the Water Prince" and an internationally recognized water expert with the United Nations—"flooding is far and away the biggest risk threatening the Netherlands. It is a hundred times bigger than the chance of a terrorist attack, avian flu epidemic, tunnel failure, and all other such incidents combined."[23] Dutch folklore contains copious references to legendary inundations, including the St. Lucia's Flood of 1287, the St. Elizabeth Flood of 1421, and the All Saints' Day Flood of 1570. When speaking casually, Amsterdam residents often said these events killed more people than the plague, which, although perhaps inaccurate, underscored the profound emotional weight associated with flooding narratives in the Netherlands.

According to government sources looking back from the late 2000s, efforts to solidify the land-water divide and to triumph over flood risks once and for all were central to the Netherlands' twentieth-century water management policies. For example, the 1953 Delta Works initiative was the largest and most expensive of several large-scale engineering projects completed during that period. Dubbed a "magical concept" and a "titanic work of hydraulic engineering," the national government launched the project less than three weeks after a storm surge at high tide drove the North Sea inland, leaving 1,835 residents dead, 72,000 people homeless, and 200,000 hectares of land below water.[24] Swearing an oath of "never again," government-backed engineers designed a network of coastal dikes that eliminated 675 kilometers of an undulating, 700-kilometer coastline, closing the Netherlands' major estuaries from the sea.[25] Thirty years and €2.5 billion later, according to media sources in the United States, "the American Society of Civil Engineers counts [the Delta Works] among the Seven Wonders of the Modern World."[26] This image of industrial technology promised to eliminate flood dangers by hardening the boundary between ocean and nation and by making the barriers against water absolute. "By the end of the 1980s, the Netherlands breathed a sigh of relief. The battle against water was nearly won."[27]

These engineering initiatives, by the mid-2000s, carried a tinge of irony. According to secondary sources circulating through the popular press, the need for such dramatic defenses was self-produced. In the words of a local environmental historian, "our land hasn't always been so low; there was a time when it was higher than the sea. What's crazy is that we ourselves made it sink."[28] Geological histories showed that nearly a millennium of human activity compounded flood risks. Clearing vegetation, plowing fields, and extracting peat destabilized riverbanks and coastal dunes. Draining marshes caused soil to compact and erode. Dike construction accelerated sedimentation and caused water levels to rise. These activities perpetuated a chain of events where attempts to keep land dry increased long-term flood risks, which spurred new rounds of more extreme diking and reclamation, leading to heightened concerns about catastrophic failures and inundation. In the words of a geographer with the London School of Economics, "truly the Dutch were the engineers of their own disasters!"[29] Experts with the University of Amsterdam, University of Groningen, and the Netherlands' national government concurred, saying, "because people protected the land against water, it fell prey to water."[30]

The Delta Works project, born from the mantra of "never again," illustrated the ongoing difficulty of controlling floods despite extensive water management expertise. In the mid-1990s, only seven years after the completion of the final Delta Works dike, residential neighborhoods lay once again underwater, this time due to rainfall and snowmelt flowing through the Meuse and Rhine River valleys. These river floods shook public optimism that technological solutions would ever prevail. Government studies later revealed that 30 percent of sea dikes failed to satisfy existing safety standards and that the risk of river inundation was rising rather than falling.[31] As one prominent water management expert commented publicly in the late 2000s, Dutch residents had "the idea that the government ensures that buildings stay dry. But that is no longer the case. We no longer have water a hundred percent under control."[32]

National "Living with Water" Campaigns

As visions of total water management lost credence, government spokespeople, water engineers, and floating architecture advocates began to change the conversation surrounding water to emphasize the need to "make room for water." This emerging chorus resonated with the dozens of government and government-funded reports outlining the objectives of the soon-to-be-released 2015 National Water Plan and the efforts to prepare for the hydrological changes associated with global warming. Despite the best technology available, officials warned, "in the years to come, we will be faced with so much water that technical measures alone, such as raising dikes, will no longer be enough" to keep people safe from floods.[33] Instead of trying to keep the Netherlands dry, national agencies said, "we must give water more room" by "committing the once arduously drained lands back to the water."[34]

The Ministry of Transport, Public Works, and Water Management, one of thirteen ministries within the national government, has been spearheading campaigns to expand the country's water storage capacity since the late 1990s. This project involved extensive publicity measures intended to challenge visions of water as an enemy requiring technological domination and recasting it as a friend calmed by land-water integration. A promotional video released in 2008, for instance, depicted images of kids playing on a beach. Children scooped sand with plastic buckets to create miniature walls and drainage ditches lining the coast. The film then cut to footage of professional engineers at computer stations designing the excavator machinery, windmill arrays, and high-tech dikes that stand like sentinels along the Netherlands' shore. Within these defensive borders, the film showed images of towns, pastures, and fairways with water lapping demurely against sidewalk curbs and backyard gardens. The voiceover informed viewers that this was Holland, a land still protected by strong border defenses but soon to be made even more healthy and prosperous as calm waters, once banished, returned to rehydrate the national heartland. In case anyone doubted the importance of this task, video clips of hurricane-flooded New Orleans during 2005 were interspersed with tranquil scenes from the Netherlands.[35]

This video contributed to several "Make Room for Water" and "Living with Water" ministry initiatives implemented during the 2000s. Former state secretary Monique de Vries, for instance, launched a precursor campaign in 2000 with the allocation of ƒ2.8 billion (€1.3 billion) for the Make Room for the River project, a twenty-year initiative to conserve and expand wetland and water storage areas. This measure, which was a direct response to the river floods of the mid-1990s, advocated giving rivers "requisite space for 'controlled flooding'" to prevent uncontrollable overflows.[36] Two years later, de Vries instigated the related Netherlands Lives with Water campaign "to give water space and let it again into our daily lives."[37] The goal of this extensive public awareness campaign involving television, radio, and newspaper advertisements was to remind complacent citizens that flood dangers posed a significant threat to Dutch citizenry. Those documents also popularized expectations that accommodating floodwater, instead of eliminating it, could reduce the likelihood of all-out disaster.[38]

The ministry's next two state secretaries continued these campaigns and gave them a more explicitly climate-oriented framework. In a series of public speeches and advertisements, former state secretary Melanie Schultz van Haegen underscored the need to reconsider water management in the context of global warming. During her administration and with her ministry's support, the national cabinet established the Living with Water Foundation in 2005. This five-year, €45 million knowledge program was tasked with finding ways to integrate expanded water storage capabilities into other spatial, social, and economic development objectives.[39]

Her successor, Tineke Huizinga, turned these water and climate initiatives into a central career objective from the moment she took office in 2007. Within her first three months, Huizinga established the Netherlands Water Land program, a commission of independent experts charged with developing water management alternatives to dike construction and with raising awareness of the social importance of water in the Netherlands.[40] Huizinga encouraged developers to transform land areas into waterways, and she publicized claims that making room for water made room for employment, housing, and leisure development as well.[41] Floodwaters would come, she said, but there was no need to wait for another disaster before taking action.[42] To this end, shortly before her 2010 promotion to Minister of Housing, Spatial Planning, and the Environment, Huizinga launched yet another Living with Water campaign by directing the Water Canon program to draft legislation to turn the credo Make Room for Water into official government policy.[43]

To support these climate-related Make Room for Water aspirations, government officials provided financial, legal, and technical support for combined urbanization and de-reclamation undertakings. For instance, in 2005, the Ministry of Housing in partnership with a handful of other organizations agreed to finance 45 percent of the €1.2 million design cost for Dura Vermeer's envisioned Floating City to be built on the outskirts of Amsterdam.[44] That same year, officials with the Ministry of Transport agreed to lift development restrictions on fifteen previously protected ecological wetland areas for developers willing to build waterproof demonstration projects on the environmentally sensitive shorelines.[45] Similarly, government-funded ministry spin-offs, such as the Living with Water Foundation, provided research and development assistance to municipal planners and private investors considering de-reclamation as an urban development approach.[46] This government support helped nascent floating architecture experiments gain traction.

Water as a Mechanism for Greenfield Urban Expansion

By the late 2000s, these efforts to expand water storage sites in low-lying areas were prompting several land-use changes and demonstration projects nationwide. Three examples will illustrate the range of interventions at work. One early, government-funded project completed in 2008 emphasized the environmental and leisure potential associated with de-reclamation. That year, the so-called Water Prince, Willem-Alexander, presided over the opening of a wet nature reconstruction zone on the edge of Biesbosch National Park about an hour's drive south of Amsterdam. For this project, the national government purchased six hundred hectares of pastureland and lowered the ground level to thirty centimeters below the high-water line to create a combined nature, recreation, and fishing ground.[47]

Two other, larger, and explicitly urban projects also captured significant media attention. First, in 2005, Queen Beatrix of the Netherlands presided over a groundbreaking ceremony for the Blue City (Blauwe Stad) urban development project near Groningen. Instead of plunging a spade into the ground, the queen turned a ceremonial bathtub-style faucet that began the process of transforming eight hundred hectares of farmland into a lagoon-style lake. To finance the project, the private developer, who bought the land at market rate from sixty farmers, had already begun building 1,400 homes on seventy-five newly constructed islands within the emerging lake. Although Blue City housing was built on islands instead of afloat, the project emerged as an important market benchmark testing the profitability of speculative de-reclamation and the ability for water-oriented home sales to offset lake construction expenses.[48]

Three years later, in 2008, the architecture company Waterstudio announced the start of construction on their New Water project outside The Hague. The

New Water project was the first large-scale floating city endeavor to enter construction in the Netherlands. The project involved de-reclaiming the formerly agricultural Westland polder by lowering the soil to 1.8 meters below the water line to create a 75,000-cubic-meter water storage area. Waterstudio architects then planned to build 1,200 luxury floating homes, including a large floating apartment building, on the lake.[49]

These three demonstration projects, as exemplars of the range of projects underway, illustrated several key dynamics at work during these processes of land reform. De-reclamation during this period focused primarily on agricultural land where investors or officials purchased land from farmers through state-negotiated, compulsory sales at near-market rates. Although early demonstration projects involved a range of economic drivers and architectural models, by the late 2000s floating architecture was quickly emerging as the preferred building approach. Through these developments, water became the mechanism of transforming greenfield sites around the Netherlands' Urban Ring into newly developed spaces for water-oriented living.

The general decline of the agricultural industry over the preceding decades enabled this process. From an economic perspective, the consolidation of farming into high-density agribusinesses, combined with competition from European Union agriculture, reduced the political clout of small pasture–based farmers.[50] The rhetoric of climate change likewise undercut farmers' previous positions of privilege. For instance, the extensive pumping and drainage required to artificially lower groundwater to the optimal level for agricultural productivity increased the salinity of the water, causing environmental damage and potentially contaminating the nation's supply of fresh drinking water. With the Netherlands' environmental consciousness on the rise, these levels of contamination appeared increasingly unsustainable from a political perspective.

Emerging national climate adaptation policies similarly encouraged farmers to reevaluate their willingness to live with water in new ways. For example, in the mid-2000s, as global warming flood risks continued to rise, national officials abandoned their previous goal of eliminating flood risks for everyone and instead decided to prioritize protections for densely settled urban areas at the expense of low-occupancy rural environments. Under the new model of stratified risk, pastures would be allowed to flood once every 10 years and agricultural fields every 25 years. By contrast, low-density residential districts would only flood once every 100 years, metropolitan areas like Amsterdam's nineteenth-century neighborhoods would flood once every 1,250 years, and historic areas like Amsterdam's seventeenth-century Canal Belt would only go under once every 10,000 years.[51] These policy changes guaranteed that floodwater would eventually come to low-lying farmland in one form or another, increasing farmers' willingness to support compulsory land sales rather than live with flooding likely to recur with every ten-year storm.

Simultaneously, the de-reclamation process, as a market-mediated act of creative destruction, encouraged project instigators to reinvest in flooded land rather than to leave the water surface open and undeveloped. De-reclamation struck an emotional blow to many farmers who denounced it as decapitalization. The process, they said, destroyed the drainage, cultivation, soil, transportation, and memory infrastructure they and their ancestors had built into the landscape over several generations.[52] From another perspective, the goal of fair compensation for farmers increased de-reclamation costs, which encouraged the redevelopment of the de-reclaimed area either for leisure and tourism or for urban expansion. These emotional and financial considerations pressured proponents to find ways to frame de-reclamation as a positive investment, rather than a capital loss, in part by emphasizing the safety benefits and economic payoff of the subsequently reused, urbanized wetlands and lakes.

In these political discussions, floating architecture and climate adaptation came together to form a politically justifiable and economically profitable model for greenfield urban expansion. The language of national safety concerns, combined with the declining economic profitability of low-tech pasture farms, weakened farmers' control over land use and water management decision making. These factors created opportunities for land de-reclamation agendas to advance. Architects and city builders saw opportunities to develop their own de-reclamation projects financed through urban expansion. Politically, however, it appeared as though climate concerns, rather than city building agendas, were pushing the land transformation forward.

Naturalizing Urban Expansion through De-reclamation

The floating architecture movement had significant business potential on its own merits, and government pressure to use these technologies to "climate-proof" the Netherlands against global warming flood risks added poignancy to the discussion.[53] The perceived environmental need for variable water levels and expanded water surfaces became the mechanism to advance greenfield development despite longstanding opposition from environmental groups and agricultural landowners against anything resembling greenfield suburban sprawl.

The discursive framing of global warming as a hydrological issue was central to these urban growth processes. This framework contrasted with carbon emissions talk common in the United States and concerns about agricultural parasites and human disease in the Global South. The term *climate change* in these narratives somewhat indiscriminately referred to rising sea levels, continuing ground subsidence, and harder and more frequent rainfall. According to former state secretary Huizinga, in preparing for "the consequences of global warming that we will inevitably face, we mainly speak about water management."[54] She elaborated on the issue in several domestic and international speeches emphasizing the need to bring water management and climate agendas together. Water played a primary role in climate adaptation because, she stated, "water is the primary transmitter of climate change impacts on societies and the environment."[55] For domestic audiences, the Ministry commissioned billboard signs reading "Another Climate, Another Policy" and "Higher Temperatures, Higher Water Levels."[56] In public speeches, officials said climate change adaptation would spur innovation and creativity.[57] "Because of climate change, we have to go about water in another way: no longer fighting against water, but living with water."[58] The environment was shifting, officials remarked, and "we have to move along with the water level," at least "if we don't all want to move to Germany."[59] To underscore the urgency, public officials since 2005 have liberally salted their speeches and promotional materials with references to Hurricane Katrina and New Orleans underwater.[60]

These climate narratives used the language of cultural heritage to naturalize their envisioned response plan. For example, in 2008, ministry officials launched a renewed round of the Netherlands Lives with Water campaign. The formal announcement came during a visit to a local elementary school outside The Hague. The day began with an informal, video-recorded conversation between the state secretary and the students about the importance of water management. It ended with the kids wearing matching "Living with Water" shirts while standing on a floating foam raft cut in the shape of the Netherlands.[61] The decision to launch the program in a school underscored the connection between the past and the future. "Our water heroes and inventors of yore are icons of our past worth remembering. It is important that we pass on this consciousness to children, the future generation of water managers."[62]

In this campaign, as in the others that preceded it, tropes of history, place, and identity cast water and Dutch-ness as two sides of the same coin. The refrain "Holland-Waterland" recurred throughout many public speeches, investigatory commissions, research reports, and legislation drafts.[63] According to government spokespeople, "the Netherlands without the sea, without rivers, lakes, ponds, ditches, and canals. That is unthinkable. Water belongs to the soul of the

Netherlands and of us Dutchmen."[64] From an airplane, it was said, "you realize immediately how exceptional our country is. What water! It is everywhere."[65] In this mix, landscape and culture were equally saturated.

> Water flows through our entire history, from the first farmers who settled here in the early Middle Ages until now. [. . .] In the middle ages, our ancestors dug ditches to drain the peat so that the muddy land would be habitable and fertile. [. . .] Our ancestors built windmills, innovative wonders of their time, with which they could artificially pump wet areas dry. [. . .] They built the Amsterdam canals, which the government has recently nominated to the UNESCO heritage list. In 1932, our ancestors laid the finishing touches on the Enclosure Dike, a dike we are currently renovating into an innovative work of art. Etched in our national memory is the flood of 1953. [. . .] After this disaster we said, "Never again!" and we began construction of the Delta Works. [. . .] All these events and interventions have shaped our landscape into what it is today. [. . .] This is a history to be proud of. Few nations can boast of such a close bond with water. We know the power and beauty of water.[66]

These oft-repeated narratives—presented as so self-evident that even children knew it—celebrated a supposedly uniquely Dutch experience premised on a grand water heritage. These discourses naturalized claims of an intimate, privileged knowledge of all things aquatic. Even critics who disagreed with the premise that Dutch water history was truly unique acknowledged the pervasiveness of this commentary. "We go on as though we had heaven's patent on water."[67]

Invocations of water heritage lent credibility to assertions that physical solutions would solve the mounting flood concerns. References to living with water in bygone eras conveyed a sense of familiarity to the new and potentially frightening challenges that climate change posed. Officials said that nine million people in the Netherlands lived below sea level on land that had been low for over eight centuries.[68] Moreover, water had long been rising. "Sea levels have risen 20 centimeters in the past century, and, according to the Delta Commission, it will certainly rise another 65 centimeters and perhaps 1 meter and 20 centimeters this century."[69] This rhetoric was not intended to minimize the dangers associated with rising water levels, nor did it explicitly discount the human contribution to global warming. Even so, such statements asserted that the Netherlands was "well versed in tackling water issues," having "for centuries [. . .] successfully controlled water and adapted ourselves to its whims."[70] Problems of rising seas and imminent floods read as old hat in a place with a thousand years of experience seemingly sitting in a memory bank just waiting to save the day.

These invocations of a hydrological heritage were more than simple invocations of an identity emblem or origin story, and the strength of these narratives was not based on whether history actually happened as described. Instead, this heritage discourse justified assertions that hydrological concerns in the present should supersede other possible objectives guiding infrastructural development and gauging its success.[71] These assertions functioned as a territorial strategic essentialism.[72] Mobilizing hydrological explanations of seemingly innate risk and instinctive knowledge narrowed the debate, justifying the land reforms and development subsidies that advanced de-reclamation and floating cities.

Perpetuating the Urban Growth Paradigm

Although floating architecture demonstration projects promised a novel urban water paradigm, they left several troubling city building priorities unexamined. The emphasis on the biophysical process of flooding rather than the social production of risk naturalized some climate change response plans over others. This perspective prioritized industry innovation and land reorganization over development restrictions as the preferred risk management strategy.

While the effect of climate change on hydrological cycles was undeniable, the emphasis on biophysical imperatives diverted attention away from the social production of risk and, by extension, other potential mitigation measures. The role of human activity in global warming was only one such consideration. Urban expansion pressure after World War II pushed people deeper into low-lying areas and unstable regions. According to government spokespeople, residential and commercial building in flood-prone areas around the Urban Ring nearly tripled between 1970 and 2000. The population living below sea level had also grown sharply since the 1950s. The value of buildings and infrastructure in those areas was rising, as were people's expectations of safety. Moreover, in those areas, human-induced subsidence outpaced the rate of rising seas.[73] Officials cited these trends as reasons to revamp water management, but not as sources of risk deserving reconsideration in their own right.

The biophysical framework of risk and response strategically precluded many political questions. Casting hydrology, rather than capitalism, as the self-evident cause of growing flood dangers kept criticisms of sprawling cities off the table. Similarly, since the need for a total management overhaul appeared to emanate from unforeseen biophysical circumstances, the professional acumen of water engineers remained safely ensconced. This emphasis on the environment overshadowed questions of ideology. The Make Room for Water approach simply seemed "much more natural" than pumping and diking.[74] It was merely "a better fit" for the newly emerging reality of a warmer, wetter world.[75] Similarly, it seemed that the sooner this vision materialized, the better, because the climate was changing, the risks were mounting, and "eventually nature always wins."[76] The supposedly inevitable and overwhelming specter of climate change dangers generated political support to unlock farmland from past ownership patterns inhibiting urban expansion. These changes created new buildable areas in the region where officials were actively promoting extensive real estate investment as a national economic driver.[77]

The envisioned mix of land reorganization, de-reclamation, and floating architecture was as responsive to expected market imperatives as it was to the anticipated water challenges. For government officials, accelerating water-oriented urban development had other payoffs, as well. Developers touted shoreline living as a way to lure creative knowledge workers to the Netherlands.[78] Similarly, de-reclamation and floating architecture, combined with assertions of a Dutch water identity, helped Dutch companies gain an advantage when bidding on city building contracts in other countries. Flood-proof construction technologies were expected to be relevant across Europe, where "the greatest natural threat in the coming years will be flooding as global warming sends more water gushing through passageways bordered by densely populated areas."[79] Innovative city building approaches that expanded river catchment while creating new construction sites figured as a "splendid export product in favor of our country."[80]

These economic advantages made land reform and floating architecture financially inviting even in the absence of atmospheric concerns. Nevertheless, combining these innovations with biophysical perspectives blunted political opposition to de-reclamation and loosened government purse strings for development subsidies. Such projects, it was hoped, would demonstrate how to keep coastal cities like London and New York dry when sea levels rose. They would illustrate how to rebuild the world's cities so floods merely tickled the understories of housing serenely rising and falling with the storms and tides. The social production of risk was obscured, and alternative solutions to problems of greenhouse gas and urban sprawl were not pursued. Instead, narratives of biophysical dynamics and national heritage promised to keep people, infrastructure, and economies afloat by finding new ways to live with water.

These trends raised the question of whether de-reclamation and floating architecture constituted the "radical change" and "historic turnaround" that government officials proclaimed them to be.[81] In physical terms, there was some truth to these assertions. Homes and highways no longer needed to be tethered to terrestrial topographies. They could instead bob in variable, undulating seas of blue. Similarly, for the first time in history, developers began intentionally putting land back underwater. Floodwaters, once deemed dangerous, now read as wellsprings of tranquility and profit. These changes dramatically altered the layout of new towns and the technologies used to build them.

In social terms, however, these land reforms and architectural innovations may have been little more than business as usual. Through these discourses, water became the primary object of focus while other economic, political, and ecological considerations were sidelined. Market expansion was perhaps the strongest argument in favor of the floating city planning paradigm. Cast as biophysically inevitable irrespective of human choice, these water management visions had little to say—and none of it negative—about the continuation of sprawling, speculative, greenfield urban development.

Urban Expansion through De-reclamation

Urban water has undergone many shifts during the postindustrial era. From squatting and counterculturalism to heritage and green development, the domestication of water as a dwelling space has, in some respects, come full circle. By the late 2000s, government spokespeople were heralding de-reclamation as the Netherlands' "biggest spatial undertaking of the twenty-first century."[82] The rise of floating city demonstration projects reflected a new urban planning vision linked to national government climate change policies. The Living with Water approach, based on the premise that letting feet get wet can keep heads dry, reflected a loosening of the rules about where water was allowed to stand and how much it was permitted to fluctuate. Instead of focusing exclusively on engineering projects that locked water in place, government officials and creative architects envisioned a waterscape that varied from year to year and season to season. These emerging wetlands and lakes then became prime building spaces for urban expansion.

Pro-growth government officials combined market, heritage, and environmental logics in mutually reinforcing narratives to advance de-reclamation and urbanization. The invocation of national flood risks justified compulsory land sales from multigenerational farmers facing declining revenues from their agricultural activities. New home construction emerged as a financial logic transforming de-reclamation from the destruction of rural infrastructure into an economic investment opportunity of national importance. The rhetoric of a millennial-long history of water management expertise naturalized this development agenda as the imagined continuation of an older water-oriented heritage that surpassed the cultural romance of farmland aesthetics and emphasized water-oriented living as a nationally shared legacy. References to a history of water-oriented housing, the cultural worth of Amsterdam's canals, the expertise of the IJssel Lake District's Enclosure Dike, and other water heritage tropes added credibility and visual iconography to these heritage claims.

These narratives embraced water as a symbolic public space and heritage icon while, simultaneously, domesticating water as a tamed and inhabited terrain. Through a process of accommodation, water, once feared as a threat, was repositioned as an ally. Water became the literal foundation for floating architecture experimentation. These processes superimposed residential activities onto water surfaces while elevating the novelty, romance, and marketability associated with water-top living. Wrapped in an environmental discourse, these processes built on emerging conceptions of water as a potent intermediary weaving human experiences and biophysical processes together into a rich socio-spatial assemblage.

For would-be city builders, through these discursive and material framings, water became a mechanism for overcoming limits to growth. Climate change risks justified land appropriation that was otherwise politically fraught. Flooding that land with water created the illusion that the project was environmental, rather than economic. Moreover, the act of flooding decisively severed existing property from its previous ownership patterns and environmental functions. On these tabula rasa sites, before new ecological processes could emerge, architects, engineers, and pro-growth government officials had carte blanche permission to build floating architecture. These processes enabled otherwise politically untenable urban expansion on greenfield sites. Moreover, they created opportunities to realize visions of large-scale floating cities that were more difficult to achieve on existing open water surfaces, like the IJssel Lake District, with their preexisting environmental regulations.

These mobilizations of water in urban expansion processes connected water-oriented cultural interest in places like Amsterdam with land reforms and heritage discourses unfolding at the national level. At the same time, climate change–related de-reclamation added new symbolic import to water. Narratives of golden age canals and nineteenth-century harbors continued to carry weight. However, instead of being interpreted narrowly as lovely but antiquated waterscapes, those heritage discourses gained added value as exemplars of an ongoing, still evolving, and fully modern Dutch experience of living in water-rich environments. The emergence of floating architecture elevated, rather than displaced, public awareness of these older modes of shoreline living, even as they expanded the range of locations, styles, and costs associated with water-oriented development.

CONCLUSION

The Everyday Politics of Urban Water

The most visually dramatic moments of urban waterfront transformations are often the moments of demolition and reconstruction. For many postindustrial cities, that physical process marks an unmistakable transition away from the legacies of ports and factories, and it embodies the arrival of new leisure- and consumer-oriented modes of shoreline living. Those moments, when city builders give future waterfronts a concrete form, are also capital intensive. Infrastructure construction is a costly affair, and the importance of market calculations and profit considerations is unavoidable in that context.

The visual and financial drama surrounding those moments of large-scale infrastructure redevelopment nonetheless constitutes only a small—albeit important—flashpoint in the much longer and varied lives of cities and their shorelines. Internationally, squatters, partiers, artists, scavengers, fishermen, and children from nearby communities frequently make informal use of devalued waterfronts, and their actions influence public understandings about the nature and meaning of urban water. Similarly, civic, environmental, and regulatory groups influence the programmatic constraints and funding availability for large-scale reconstruction endeavors. Moreover, in the decades after construction, waterfront sites continue to evolve as economic trends and cultural practices redefine their market dynamics and public spaces. In sum, waterfront transformation is about much more than photogenic moments of physical reconstruction and instead involves countless small, distributed shifts in social norms, policy frames, and investment practices.

When looking at urban waterfronts through this broader lens, it becomes clear that a wide range of social processes bring city shorelines to life. Cultural mobilizations occur alongside market ones. Infrastructural projects play a role, but shoreline transformation also emerges through the reconstruction of laws, social norms, symbolism, and spatial props. These reinventions follow messy, incremental, and rhizomatic pathways, and they generate countless subtle shifts in waterscape assemblages. These assemblages diversify the stakes

Leisure, nature, and real estate coming together on an Amsterdam waterway, 2007. ©iStock.com/rglinsky.

of shoreline redevelopment. Market interests may choose to ignore the vast subsurface of nuanced, pluralized meaning that congeals in city shorelines, but bringing those latent undercurrents to the surface creates new ways of thinking about wet urban spaces. Excavations of waterscape politics, like the account of Amsterdam presented in this book, provide one route for conceptualizing the complex relationship between culture, capital, and water, as well as for developing greater opportunities for social actors to gain an expanded civic voice in the undercurrents and side channels shaping city shorelines.

In this chapter, I conclude by suggesting a few ways to foster the visibility of water as an inherently pluralized landscape assemblage that, while engulfed in hegemonic market logics at certain moments, remains productively multivalent and open-ended. Rather than proposing a new recipe for shoreline redevelopment or delineating a set of best practices that feign to collapse cultural goals with real estate interests, I focus on three attitudes that are integral in foregrounding the social practices that bring spaces to life. First, given the tendency for market logics to elide alternative social visions, there is a need to revalue the logic of everyday practices that connect water with local norms and subjective identities. Second, there is a need to reorient conventional discourses that portray water as a fully developed, self-contained entity to instead recognize that waterscapes exist as an evolving bundle of attributes, only some of which are made meaningful at specific moments. Third, there is a need to shift attention away from land-based development that treats water as a passive neighbor to instead allow for a greater recognition of the formative work that water itself is made to perform in the politics of urban life. These everyday, selective, and mobilized aspects of urban water demonstrate how people act through water for many different political purposes, as well as how those mobilizations generate unexpected economic potential and cultural meaning.

The rich history of water in postindustrial Amsterdam exemplified the innovations and opportunities that brought water to new life, adding cultural richness and economic significance to the city's pluralized waterscape. Qualitative evidence of these mobilizations beginning in the 1960s and accelerating in the 1990s and 2000s was preserved in the written records of media outlets, government offices, advocacy groups, and a wide range of experts and scholars. As industrial uses of shorelines declined, cultural actors mobilized water as an informal living space and a de facto public gathering site. Water's historical significance received new narrative frames, and its ecological functionality was brought to the fore. These mobilizations, and the political discussions they prompted, generated shifts in the legal definitions, policy frames, and technological approaches defining how people could act through water. Within this mix, megascale, market-dependent infrastructure constituted one mode of intervention alongside many others. These diffuse practices congealed over time, consolidating into a recognizable but fluid urban water milieu saturated with plural political possibilities.

This plurality of water, while especially apparent in Amsterdam, is an inherent trait that can be nurtured and leveraged to diversify shorelines in other cities. Water, like any cultural landscape, is an activated entity. It is a bundle of material, legal, economic, and symbolic attributes that people selectively and strategically bring to life. This plurality of waterscapes expands the political potentiality of water beyond techno-managerial questions of its efficient control and profitable use. Instead, cultural groups of many stripes can, and do, mobilize water to advance a wide range of social causes. These causes vary across space and time, even within the same city. In Amsterdam in the late twentieth and early twenty-first centuries, people acted through water to advance their interest in affordable housing, creative expression, identity symbolism, market development, environmental protection, and public safety. At these moments, water sometimes functioned as a direct object of intervention, and other times water served as a lateral witness naturalizing visions of place, self, and society. These practices, some large and market-centered, others small and intimately subjective, jointly influenced the evolution of urban shorelines, pluralizing water, as well as the housing, festivals, and identities associated with urban waterfront living.

Although centralized municipal planning paradigms sometimes opposed these informal and complicating impulses, the emerging dialogues, while not fully inclusive or equitable, generated richer urban spaces than planners envisioned when unchallenged, resulting in a diverse, valued, livable, and resilient cityscape.

Urban Water as an Enacted Environment

The political economy literature on land use, infrastructure, and real estate emphasizes the tendency for market-based capitalism to override and marginalize alternative modes of living, a message that the subliterature on water and shorelines reiterates as well. In this context, one of the most daunting tasks of urban reformers involves enlarging the decision-making influence of everyday politics in the economic life of cities. Moving beyond visions of domination and resistance creates greater opportunities to recognize the agonistic—or the generative, rather than exclusively adversarial—relationship between quotidian cultural practices and market-based city building. Development is a multiscalar, multimodal process that remains entangled with provisional practices, agendas, and subjectivities. Recognizing these practices as pervasive and generative, rather than frail or disruptive, creates conceptual space for practitioners to mobilize everyday politics to enhance the diversity, salience, and marketability of urban water.

The enactment of water politics in postindustrial Amsterdam involved both the consolidation of waterscapes into consumer-oriented territories of profit and a series of cultural movements that connected water, subjectivity, and everyday practices together in new ways. Reshaping shorelines, literally and symbolically, gave water new modes of life in market-dominated tourism and real estate industries, a process that contributed to the city's international competitiveness and also, unfortunately, to the increasing socioeconomic inequality among Amsterdam residents. At the same time, improvisational mobilizations of everyday waterscapes loosened water from market dictates and generated alternative uses and visions of shoreline spaces. Water as a cultural landscape evolved with self-built houseboats, improvised water-top parties, selective heritage discourses, and creative ecological reassessments of wet city spaces. In these endeavors, water was one element among many that residents and activists used to advance calls for social change, generate symbols of group identity, and expand the economic imagination guiding urban growth.

This characterization of waterscapes in Amsterdam resonates with political economy research that recognizes the significance of hydrological engineering in class- and state-based politics of control while also attending to the connection between water-mediated labor and everyday subjectivity. Water politics writ large includes government entities repatterning watersheds to fuel the growth of cities, factories, agribusiness, and trade.[1] It also includes privileged social groups that use their economic and political clout to monopolize access to potable drinking water and displace risks of thirst, disease, flooding, and fire onto other more vulnerable groups.[2] These processes demonstrate that water is a powerful political tool and that interventions in waterscapes are, necessarily, interventions into the social order.

At another level, alongside these geopolitical questions of wealth generation and humanitarian ethics, people—including groups with limited official rights or economic assets—act through water in ways that shape subjectivity, autonomy, and sensibilities of belonging. In many countries in the Global South, for instance, women use daily tasks—such as carrying household water buckets and cultivating wetland subsistence crops—to develop social capital and generate cash resources beyond the purview of the repressive male gaze. Similarly, in the United States, Native American groups use subsistence fishing to anchor cultural identity and economic independence in opposition to white capitalist domination.[3] These examples of everyday mobilizations of water-related labor illustrate the importance of mundane, culturally mediated, and process-oriented landscape practices in forming subjectivity and eluding domination.

In Amsterdam, although the extremity of risk and inequality was substantially less pronounced, countless provisional activities used water to spark public discussions about how people should live, relax, and cultivate distinction. Houseboat hippies, queer partiers, heritage enthusiasts, and environmental advocates explicitly connected water-related activities with the development of social norms, group identities, and development priorities. Their interventions reshaped understandings about the functionality and meaning of water, which pulled urban waterfronts in new directions, expanded the range of values incorporated into urban development, and pluralized the salience of water in everyday life. These processes involved conflict, and new water, new cities, and new societies emerged through those agonistic tensions. These practices were not utopian. Some groups continued to benefit at the expense of others, and market interests continued to dominate infrastructural decision making. Nevertheless, the everyday practice of water politics meaningfully advanced visions of social reform that redirected and democratized—rather than derailed—the political economic development of Amsterdam.

Selective Mobilizations of Water's Attributes

Recognizing the everyday mobilizations of urban water is an important first step toward understanding the plurality of the social mechanisms bringing water to political life. Urban water is not a pregiven entity. It exists, in Amsterdam and elsewhere, as a bundle of properties and associations. Physical spaces, policy frames, leisure habits, status symbols, folklore narratives, and ethical commitments converge from many locations, perspectives, and historical moments. Their articulations congeal into plural, frayed landscapes that, from a quotidian perspective, are rarely seen or valued for their entirety. While a full portrait of water may be interesting from an academic perspective, cultural actors and market investors mobilize only certain elements of the water assemblage at a time. This partiality is advantageous since it enhances people's ability to turn water to targeted political ends.

Written with these insights in mind, this book may not always look or feel like a book about water in Amsterdam. There are no long, preamble chapters on the local history of land reclamation, the legend of polder model consensus politics, the provision of clean drinking water, the reformulation of governing water boards, or the role of water in Dutch landscape painting.[4] Those elisions are deliberate on my part. Although those issues are important to the question of water management, those strands of water's identity did not emerge as important rallying points and mobilization mechanisms in the cultural and economic processes transforming urban waterfronts in Amsterdam between 1960 and 2010. Similarly, some pieces of water's identity emerged in unexpected sequences, with zoning considerations and heritage tropes preceding discussions of pumping and diking, which, from a techno-managerial perspective, would seem fundamental to the water question. Again, this presentation format was intentional on my part. The chapter sequence reflects the chronology of water's cultural mobilization in the present rather than the making of water management policy in the past. Any attempt to sketch a total picture of water or a singular beginning point for action that included these elements as meaningful prior to their mobilization would be deeply misguided. The story here is not about how people manage water in general but is instead about how cultural groups mobilize select aspects of water at certain moments for specific ends. Understanding the everyday politics of water involved narrating the experience of water from everyday perspectives. At any moment, only some historic legacies, material properties, governing entities, and symbolic elements figured as significant.

This framing of water politics resonates with political ecology studies that approach water as a natural-social medium through which people act, rather than a preexisting object on which people act. Although often treated scientifically and bureaucratically as discrete matter, water gets its shape and utility from a mix of biophysical properties, infrastructure technologies, political aspirations, knowledge schemas, and provisional uses. The ability to build a dam, travel through a desert, grow monsoon crops, or navigate a river depends on the cultural capacity to mobilize these milieus in a selective, targeted manner. Water is complicit in these actions, filling reservoirs, hydrating bodies, and conveying boats. However, neither water nor people act alone. Instead, processes of selective engagement bring water to social life, modify its political salience, and put water to work.[5]

The everyday politics of urban water in Amsterdam involved precisely this type of mediated action. Cultural groups domesticating water and seizing it as a public space put the jurisdictional distinction between water and land to new political uses. Heritage groups brought the history of canals and harbors to new light. Environmentalists greened water, connecting it to scientific discourses about ecology and climates. City builders, lawmakers, and urban growth boosters explored its market potential. Although policy, history, biophysicality, and markets mattered in every instance, advocates pursuing specific political agendas benefited from enacting a filtered perspective of water that overlooked the full picture of water to instead emphasize only the specific traits of interest that advanced their specific agendas.

Waterscapes, congealed in part through selective mobilizations from the past, constrained the range of actions people could pursue, but these constraints did not necessarily limit the variety of political objectives those actions could advance. For instance, water existed as a buoyant substance, but people used the act of floating to meet transportation needs, advance countercultural agendas, develop identity symbols, and appropriate agricultural land. As another example, water had a social history, but the political messages implicit in narratives of fifteenth-century floods, seventeenth-century canals, nineteenth-century miasmas, and twentieth-century sea trade were put to many—even competing—social purposes. The capacity to act through waterscapes hinged on legal understandings of public space and housing laws, historic legacies of spatial forms and jurisdictional structures, physical properties of water surfaces and environmental webs, and narrative frames of identity formation and cultural symbolism. However, it rarely hinged on all of these attributes at once, and those attributes did not predetermine any singular political end.

Social Practices Bringing Water to Life

Everyday politics and selective mobilizations of space create opportunities to bring cultural landscapes to life in new ways. Not every provisional use of water is progressive, which means that these practices require negotiation rather than carte blanche encouragement. Nevertheless, interventions that loosen space from entrenched modes of market-based management and that explicitly disrupt the status quo create the potential to rethink measures of livability, inclusivity, and equity. These actions generate small, incremental shifts in social life and urban forms, gesturing toward opportunities to do water and cities differently in the future.

The visual aesthetic and ideological import of urban waterfronts has shifted significantly during the transition from industrial to postindustrial economies. Festivals and housing replaced factories and barges as the mechanisms used to extract profit from landscapes, but shorelines remain fully enmeshed in capitalism just the same. Notions of sustainability and resiliency have replaced discourses of domination and improvement, but market objectives have remained in the driver's seat. Nevertheless, the transition from one economic paradigm to another created a substantial and prolonged period of uncertainty. That interim phase, when water was released from one capitalist paradigm and not immediately subsumed by an emerging model, was a period of rich cultural exploration giving rise to new, local, and unexpected modes of shoreline politics.

Embracing the capacity to bring water to life through provisional uses, evocative references, and improvised appropriations created opportunities to incorporate a wide range of cultural objectives and lived experiences into Amsterdam's postindustrial waterscapes. These processes indicate that the serial reproduction of market-dominated, man-proofed, seemingly placeless spectacle environments occurring in many European and North American cities need not define the future of urban water. In Amsterdam, incremental, experimental, and even seemingly disruptive practices deepened both the cultural value and the subsequent economic profitability of the shorelines. The productive negotiation of these tensions enriched market processes, deepened spatial symbolism, and pluralized the cultural import of the redeveloped spaces.

As an activated assemblage rather than a self-contained substance, many different types of actions brought water to life in Amsterdam. The chapters in this book recount acts of floating for housing affordability and social diversity. They describe the socio-spatial impacts that public space ordinances and rent control laws had on the marketability of water surfaces. They recount the narrative frameworks that imbued waterscapes with heritage sensibilities and environmental salience. These actions, when performed repeatedly with iterative differences by many social groups for various social ends, made use of water's plural political possibilities and reinforced the continued multivalency of waterscapes in that city.

Creating new forms of urban shorelines may seem like a heroic endeavor, but these stories of squatting skippers, queer partiers, heritage buffs, home builders, nature preservationists, and creative architects illustrate the humble roots and provisional influences of everyday practices on city building processes. Mobilizing water was partly about engaging with water, but, more significantly, engaging with water enabled cultural voices to be heard in new ways. Water was transformed into a stage, symbol, and mechanism enabling a wide range of political interventions in social life. These political possibilities lingered in public memory and wet urban spaces even after the instigating cultural movements were disbanded, co-opted, or displaced. These practices, emerging through the plurality of urban water, illustrate the potential for other people in other places to do space differently, mobilize water to unexpected ends, and shape new modes of shoreline living.

Notes

Introduction. The Politics of Urban Water

1. Desfor and Keil, *Nature and the City*; Dovey, *Fluid City*; Illich, *H$_2$O and the Waters of Forgetfulness*; Kaika, *City of Flows*; O'Neill, *Rivers by Design*; Schubert, "Waterfront Revitalizations."
2. Desfor et al., *Transforming Urban Waterfronts*.
3. For more on the concept of genealogies of praxis, see Foucault, *The Essential Foucault*.
4. For more on the concept of the assemblage, see Deleuze and Guattari, "Becoming-Intense."
5. Illich, *H$_2$O and the Waters of Forgetfulness*, 10.
6. See also Deverell, "Remembering a River"; Kaika, *City of Flows*; O'Neill, *Rivers by Design*; Oliver, "The Thames Embankment."
7. Illich, *H$_2$O and the Waters of Forgetfulness*, 76.
8. Desfor and Keil, *Nature and the City*. See also Heynen et al., "Introduction"; Katz, "Whose Nature, Whose Culture?"; Lave, *Fields and Streams*.
9. Baviskar, *Waterscapes*; Desfor and Keil, *Nature and the City*; Stevens, "The German 'City Beach.'"
10. Buiter, "Transforming Water Infrastructures"; Deben, Salet, and Van Thoor, "Heritage and the Future"; Kloos and De Korte, *Mooring Site Amsterdam*.
11. For more on the concept of loose space, see Franck and Stevens, *Loose Space*.
12. Desfor and Keil, *Nature and the City*; Desfor et al., *Transforming Urban Waterfronts*.
13. Smith, *The New Urban Frontier*.
14. Mele, *Selling the Lower East Side*.
15. Deverell, "Remembering a River"; Osman, *The Invention of Brownstone Brooklyn*; Shaw, "The Place of Alternative Culture"; Zukin, *Naked City*.
16. Merrifield, *Dialectical Urbanism*, 24; Hannigan, *Fantasy City*, 51; Harvey, "From Managerialism to Entrepreneurialism," 13–14. For more on the social inequity resulting from these sorts of investments, see Levine, "A Third-World City" and "Downtown Redevelopment."
17. Desfor et al., *Transforming Urban Waterfronts*.
18. Latour, *Reassembling the Social*. See also Mitchell, "Can the Mosquito Speak?"
19. Winner, *The Whale and the Reactor*.
20. Carter, "Elysiums for Gentlemen"; Raffles, *In Amazonia*; Winichakul, *Siam Mapped*.

21. Matless, *Landscape and Englishness*; Mukerji, *Territorial Ambitions*.
22. For more on shape-shifting landscapes, see Gordillo, *Landscapes of Devils*; Hoskins, "Poetic Landscapes of Exclusion."
23. Mitchell, *Colonizing Egypt*.

Chapter One. Hippies on Houseboats

1. Mak, *Amsterdam*, 288; Dalton and Kuechler, *Challenging the Political Order*; Habermas, "New Social Movements."
2. Cotterell, *Amsterdam*; Kennedy, *Building New Babylon*; Mak, *Amsterdam*; Soja, "Stimulus of a Little Confusion."
3. Mak, *Amsterdam*; Pistor, *A City in Progress*; Van Zanden, *Economic History of the Netherlands*.
4. Van Zanden, *Economic History of the Netherlands*.
5. Cotterell, *Amsterdam*; Van Zanden, *Economic History of the Netherlands*.
6. Kloosterman, "Amsterdamned"; Van Zanden, *Economic History of the Netherlands*.
7. Pistor, *A City in Progress*; Pruijt, "The Impact of Citizens' Protest."
8. Fainstein, "The Egalitarian City"; Foundation for Advancement, *Cracking the Movement*; Pruijt, "The Impact of Citizens' Protest"; Smith, *The New Urban Frontier*; Uitermark, "The Co-optation of Squatters" and "Framing Urban Injustices."
9. Dop, "Een relaas."
10. Kloos and De Korte, *Mooring Site Amsterdam*.
11. Dop, "Een relaas."
12. See chapter 4 for more information on housing regulation.
13. Bos, *Amsterdam Afloat*; Koldenhof, "Welstand op het water"; Tagliabue, "Canal Life."
14. BNA, "New Tasks"; Bos, *Amsterdam Afloat*, 5. See also Huijsmans, "Waterwonen nieuwe stijl"; Steutel, "Uitzicht op de gracht"; Tagliabue, "Canal Life"; Wiegman, "Centrum opent de jacht op."
15. Bos, *Amsterdam Afloat*, 74.
16. Spoek, interview.
17. Kloos and De Korte, *Mooring Site Amsterdam*, 70.
18. Dop, "Een relaas."
19. Kloos and de Korte, *Mooring Site Amsterdam*.
20. Dop, "Een relaas"; Kloos and De Korte, *Mooring Site Amsterdam*.
21. Kloos and De Korte, *Mooring Site Amsterdam*, 80; Spoek, interview.
22. Bos, *Amsterdam Afloat*, 46; Spoek, interview.
23. Bos, *Amsterdam Afloat*, 37. See also Dop, "Een relaas"; Huijsmans, "Waterwonen nieuwe stijl."
24. Pistor, *A City in Progress*, 74–77.
25. Smith, *The New Urban Frontier*, 166–70. See also Cortie, Kruit, and Musterd, "Housing Market Change in Amsterdam"; Terhorst, Van de Ven, and Deben, "Amsterdam."
26. Koert, "De pakhuizen en de woonbootfolklore"; Lahaise, "Woonboten bepalen"; Schoonenberg, "Amsterdam, een waterstad" and "Waterplan"; Spaargaren, "Ontsierende woonboten"; Tyrpakova, "De Amsterdamse grachten"; Vermeulen, "Wethouder De Grave"; VVAB, "Waterplan."

27. See chapter 2 and chapter 4 for more on international interest in Amsterdam water and its effect on the local housing market.
28. Escher, "Pleziervaartuigen irriteren woonbootbewoner"; Van der Wall, "Vrede woon- en rondvaartboot."
29. Mak, "Sijtje Boes."
30. Van der Wall, "Vrede woon- en rondvaartboot." See also "Prinsengracht in Amsterdam is vol."
31. Van der Wall, "Vrede woon- en rondvaartboot."
32. Kloos and De Korte, *Mooring Site Amsterdam*, 118.
33. Lahaise, "Woonboten bepalen."
34. Snoeijen, "Ketting dreigt voor uitgeprocedeerde woonboot."
35. Visser, "Bewoners moeten wijken voor aanlegsteiger."
36. Tagliabue, "Canal Life." See also Wiegman, "Centrum opent de jacht op."
37. Couzy, "Ray Selby."
38. Steinmetz, "Extra plaatsen"; Tagliabue, "A Rising Tide"; Van Haastrecht, "Op het KNSM-eiland."
39. C. Vos, "Woonbootbewoner onvindbaar voor post."
40. Tagliabue, "Canal Life."
41. Koldenhof, "Welstand op het water"; Spoek, interview.
42. Bos, *Amsterdam Afloat*, 37.
43. Mak, "Het wateraanzicht van zuipcentra."
44. Van der Wall, "Vrede woon- en rondvaartboot."
45. Huijsmans, "Waterwonen nieuwe stijl."
46. Huijsmans, "Waterwonen nieuwe stijl," emphasis added.
47. Tagliabue, "Canal Life."
48. Tagliabue, "Canal Life."
49. Kloos and De Korte, *Mooring Site Amsterdam*, 94, 118. See also Bos, *Amsterdam Afloat*, 53; Edidin, "Afloat in the Flood Zone"; Overduin, "Als het water."
50. See chapter 6 for more on the architectural movement to build floating cities.
51. Bos, *Amsterdam Afloat*, 38–51.
52. Huijsmans, "Waterwonen nieuwe stijl."
53. Dop, "Een relaas."
54. Spoek, interview.

Chapter Two. Queers on Parade

1. The meaningfulness of this participation is heavily dependent on social factors, such as accessibility and surveillance.
2. I use the term *gay* in official names and direct quotes when my sources also explicitly used this English word. Otherwise, I use the term *queer* when translating the Dutch word *homo* or when writing in my own voice.
3. Three other sizeable public events also contributed to the festival scene between 1990 and 2010 but were not included in this chapter write-up. The *Uitmarkt* festival commemorating the opening of the national cultural season had a turnout comparable with Gay Pride and Queen's Day, and it often opened with an event on the water, but most of the festival occurred on land. Similarly, the Sail exhibition of historic tall ships drew more spectators than these other festivals and had an explicit water theme, but it only

NOTES TO CHAPTER TWO

occurred every five years and took place primarily in the city's harbors rather than the canals. Lastly, the Flower Pageant, one of the most popular festivals in Amsterdam for nearly a half a century, attracted about a million spectators in the early 1990s just before Gay Pride, Queen's Day, and Canal Festival traditions began, but the festival ended in 2007 due to a sharp and persisting drop in attendance.

4. De Baar, interview.
5. Furnee, interview.
6. Furnee, "The Thrill of Frozen Water."
7. Spel, "Een man"; Van Keken, "Varende homo ontbloot voornameliji bovenlijf."
8. Prominent histories of social movements make few references to water. For instance, see Foundation for Advancement, *Cracking the Movement*; Kempton, *Provo*; Pas, *Imaazje*. Confirmed with De Rooy, interview.
9. Escher, "Pleziervaartuigen irriteren woonbootbewoner"; Van Halm, "Watertuinen."
10. Remkes, "Nadruk bij botenparade."
11. Berkhout, "Maar minder gay-toeristen"; Hanuska, "Dutch gays"; Wiegman, "'I amashamed.'"
12. "Europride."
13. "Het bootje van Cohen"; Koele, "Bloot en rood"; ProGay Foundation, "Recordaantal bezoekers Amsterdam Gay Pride"; Sevil, "Plensbuien deren Gay Pride niet"; Van Traa, "Gay Parade."
14. Hemelaar, interview. See also Schipper, "Homo-spektakel eind juni in Amsterdam"; "Varen tegen homohaat."
15. "Canal Parade trekt recordaantal bezoekers"; ProGay Foundation, "Recordaantal bezoekers nieuwe stijl."
16. "Amsterdam Canal Parade 2009." See also "Amsterdam's Floating Gay Pride Parade"; "Gay Pride Parade Set."
17. "Amsterdam Gay Pride wint"; "De 100 meest genoemde"; Hemelaar, interview; TripOut, "2009 TripOut Gay Travel"; Van Dalen, interview.
18. Van Dalen, interview.
19. De Baar, interview; De Rooy, interview. See also C. Janssen, "Bootje varen, biertje drinken."
20. De Baar, interview; Frankfurther in R. Janssen, "Stadsdeel Centrum."
21. Gemeente Amsterdam, "Openbare ruimte, groen en water." See also C. Janssen, "Bootje varen, biertje drinken"; Spaans and Thomassen, "Meeste schippers"; Van Keken, "Zuipschuit zigzag in de gracht."
22. McAllister, "What Is Queen's Day?"
23. Mamadouh, interview no. 2; De Baar, interview; Van Dam, interview.
24. "Nauwelijks gedrang op vrijmarkt"; "Oranjegekte vooral te water"; Sanders, "Met een bootje"; Sevil, "Vogelnest op boot heeft rechten." See also De Baar, interview; De Rooy, interview; Van Dam, interview.
25. Somers, "Vrolijke anarchie op het water." See also Spel, "Een man."
26. Spel, "Een man."
27. IAmsterdam, "Canal Life."
28. Rooijendijk, *The City Is Mine!*, 107; Tyrpakova, "De Amsterdamse grachten." See also Adolf, "Roet en herrie"; Kramer, "Truckers van het water"; "Rondvaart A'dam populairste uitje"; Ter Borg, "Amsterdamse grachtenbussen zitten vol toeristen."
29. This cultural mobilization of water as a literal performance stage does not imply

that water was a passive, neutral backdrop for social activity. For more on this concept, see Pickles, *A History of Spaces*; Massey, *For Space*.

30. Mamadouh, interview no. 2. See also De Baar, interview; Pistor, *A City in Progress*. As a notable exception, the annual Flower Pageant included a small procession of cars and boats.

31. "Europride."

32. Hemelaar, interview; Van Dalen, interview. See also "'Stadschagrijnen' verjagen homotoerist"; "Zonder Gay Pride."

33. Hemelaar, interview; Van Dalen, interview.

34. Hemelaar, interview; Van Dalen, interview.

35. Remkes, "Nadruk bij botenparade."

36. Hemelaar, interview; Van Dalen, interview.

37. Leitner, Sheppard, and Sciarto, "The Spatialities of Contentious Politics."

38. Remkes, "Nadruk bij botenparade."

39. Beusekamp, "Het moet gaan." See also Berkhout, "Gay Pride iets minder homoseksueel"; Koele, "Bloot en rood"; Lahaise, "Bij Clown Parade."

40. Van den Berg, "We gooien."

41. Van den Berg, "We gooien."

42. Van Dam, interview.

43. Van den Berg, "We gooien." See also Verkerk, "Koninginnedag."

44. Van den Berg, "We gooien."

45. Van Dam, interview.

46. This has started to change in recent years, with the decline of multicultural commitments and the rise of xenophobic nationalism. See Buruma, *Murder in Amsterdam*; Dewulf, "In the Jungle of Amsterdam."

47. Pullens, "Amsterdam lokt toerist met water."

48. Somers, "Vrolijke anarchie op het water." See also "Ondanks aanvankelijke."

49. Van den Broek, "Kuisheidsverklaring geist van deelnemers homo-parade."

50. Vugts, "Bloot bij Gay Pride 'functioneel.'"

51. Van den Broek, "Kuisheidsverklaring geist van deelnemers homo-parade."

52. Cheary, "Amsterdam Gay Parade"; Henfling, "Men wil geen relnicht zien."

53. De Fauwe, "Wie doet deze klus"; "Gay Canal Parade vreest"; "Gay Pride wil nu"; Wiegman, "Cohen redt de Gay Parade" and "'I amashamed.'"

54. "Overlast Gay-parade aan banden."

55. "'Stadschagrijnen' verjagen homotoerist"; Wiegman, "Homotrots."

56. "Zomercarnaval is veel bloter."

57. Wiegman, "Cohen redt de Gay Parade."

58. Wiegman, "'I amashamed.'"

59. Wiegman, "'I amashamed.'" See also Houtsma, "Homovertier in Amsterdam."

60. Vermeulen, "Wethouder De Grave"; Spaans and Thomassen, "Meeste schippers."

61. In Van Keken, "Zuipschuit zigzagt in de gracht."

62. "Geachte redactie."

63. BBA, "Jaarverslag en -rekeneing 2006"; "Geachte redactie"; "Inwoners Amsterdam blij met festiviteiten"; Mak, "Het wateraanzicht van zuipcentra"; Spaans and Thomassen, "Meeste schippers"; Van den Broek, "Alle dagen feest"; Van Keken, "Zuipschuit zigzagt in de gracht"; Visser and De Vos, "Vluchten voor de invasie"; Vermeulen, "Wethouder De Grave."

64. "2 minuten"; "Controle pleziervaart betreft"; "Geachte redactie"; Hoedeman, "Amsterdam gaat de crowd managen"; "Regels voor boten op Koninginnedag"; Rombouts, "We pielen en zieken niet."
65. "Geachte redactie."
66. "Alles in vijf weken"; Berkhout, "Maar minder gay-toeristen"; "Canal Parade trekt recordaantal bezoekers"; De Fauwe, "Wie doet deze klus"; Doorduyn, "Minister Plasterk"; "Geld botenparade Gay Pride geregeld"; Koele, "Bloot en rood"; Lahaise, "Bij Clown Parade"; Muller, "De tijd van blote mannen"; Sevil, "Honderd euro is voor Shell"; Wiegman, "'I amashamed.'"
67. "Amsterdam bootvriendelijk"; "Bootvriendelijke pizzeria"; Damen, "Meer steigers" and "Politiek testament Frankfurther"; R. Janssen, "Stadsdeel Centrum"; Visser, "Bewoners moeten wijken voor aanlegsteiger."
68. De Jong, email. See also ATCB, "Amsterdam Water Sensations 2010"; Katstra, "Themajaar"; Metz, "Zelfgemaakt verleden."
69. Oldenburg, *The Great Good Place*.
70. Deben, "Public Space"; Van Melik, "Changing Public Space."

Chapter Three. Heritage Buffs on Canals

1. Many of these documents served the double function of supporting a concurrent application to list Amsterdam's canal belt as a UNESCO World Heritage Site.
2. In the written records documenting this history, the voice of land speculators and real estate developers was absent.
3. Some sources put the count of filled canals slightly higher; e.g., Van Beek, "Er moet weer grachtenwater."
4. Buiter, "Transforming Water Infrastructures"; Frankfurther, "Een voorstel"; Kreling, "Een boterham, parkeerplaats of gracht"; Meurs, "Amsterdam."
5. Mak, "Nostalgia and Modernity," 14.
6. Kreling, "Een boterham, parkeerplaats of gracht."
7. Etty, "Tijd voor burgertrots." See also Brinkgreve, "The Preservation of Historic Buildings."
8. Eggenkamp, "Amsterdam," 201–2, 204–6. See also Krol, "Preserving Amsterdam's Heritage"; Van den Eerenbeemt, "Historie herbouwd." For a critical perspective, see Bosman, "Historische flauwekul of beschermd stadsgezicht?"; Van Gelder and Mak, "Tussen Anton Pieck."
9. Kuipers, "Fragile Structures," 90–93.
10. Kuipers, "Fragile Structures," 92.
11. For a typical favorable assessment, see Deben, Salet, and Van Thoor, "Heritage and the Future," 6. For typical critiques, see Bosman, "Wij zijn blij"; Steinmetz, "Erfgoed mag."
12. "Amsterdam Centre on World Heritage List"; Damen, "Europa's gaafste"; De Fauwe, "Gemeente heeft"; Deben, Salet, and Van Thoor, "Heritage and the Future"; Hageman, "Van zes naar achtien."
13. Van den Eerenbeemt, "Historie herbouwd." See also Krol, "Preserving Amsterdam's Heritage."
14. VVAB, "Welkom."
15. Schoonenberg, "Opengraven grachten."

16. Frankfurther, "Een voorstel."
17. Schoonenberg, "Schriftelijke inspraakbijdrage opengraven grachten."
18. Schoonenberg, "Without Reconstruction, No Inner City" 135–36. See also Apell, "The Power of Power," 124.
19. Frankfurther, "Een voorstel." See also Schoonenberg, "Amsterdam, een waterstad," "Het Waterplan Amsterdam," and "Opengraven grachten."
20. Schoonenberg, "Het Waterplan Amsterdam."
21. Schoonenberg, "Het Waterplan Amsterdam."
22. Schoonenberg, "Het Waterplan Amsterdam" and "Waterplan"; Spaargaren, "Ontsierende woonboten." See also Lahaise, "Woonboten bepalen."
23. Bos, *Amsterdam Afloat*; Bosman, "Historische flauwekul of beschermd stadsgezicht?"; Heijnis, "Prachtige geschiedenissen, maar geen monument"; Van Zelst, "Woonboot wordt weer verjaagd"; Bosman, "Wij zijn blij"; Steinmetz, "Erfgoed mag."
24. For instance, see Sevil, "Meer dan de allure."
25. Frankfurther, "Een voorstel."
26. Deters, "Gedempte grachten in ere hersteld"; Sevil, "Meer dan de allure"; Ten Haaft, "Het water lonkt."
27. Secondary sources characterize late twentieth-century Amsterdam as a second- or perhaps even a third-tier city with a limited international role in global financial and business services and with a limited contribution to national GDP. In the words of one prominent urban sociologist who has studied the city for several decades, "Amsterdam is the social and cultural capital of Netherlands, but not the economic capital" (Deben, interview). See also Angus and Mangoenkarso, "Higher Economic Growth"; Fainstein, *The Just City*; Manshanden and Lambooy, "Innovation in the Amsterdam Region"; O'Loughlin, "Between Stuttgart and Shefield"; Van Leeuwen et al., "Op weg naar 2040."
28. Van Beek, "Er moet weer grachtenwater."
29. Schoonenberg, "Hergraven van grachten."
30. Frankfurther, "Een voorstel."
31. Musterd and Deurloo, "Amsterdam and the Preconditions," 80.
32. Frankfurther, "Een voorstel." See also Pistor, "The Amsterdam Challenge," 270–71. For a critical review, see Lambert, "Making of the Dutch Landscape," 217; Van Gelder, "De schoonheid lag niet." Colonial imperialism was written out of the story. Although this omission is telling, I do not address it here because both canal reconstruction advocates and their opponents ignored it, and so the omission did not become a point of contention in the emerging public debate.
33. Deben, Salet, and Van Thoor, "Heritage and the Future," 4.
34. "Haalbaarheidsonderzoek Opengraven Grachten," 7.
35. Frankfurther, "Een voorstel."
36. Tyrpakova, "De Amsterdamse grachten."
37. Etty, "Tijd voor burgertrots."
38. Van Zanden, *Economic History of the Netherlands*.
39. Genovesi, "Amsterdam moet gracht"; Haagsma and De Haan, "Steden zijn geschapen"; French Heddema, "Eilard Jacobs."
40. Buiter, "Transforming Water Infrastructures"; Deben, Salet, and Van Thoor, "Heritage and the Future"; Kloos and De Korte, *Mooring Site Amsterdam*.
41. Oldenburger, "Actie 'Open de Grachten.'"
42. Kreling, "Een boterham, parkeerplaats of gracht"; Frankfurther summarized in

NOTES TO CHAPTER THREE

Kreling, "Heeft grachtengordel grachten zat?" See also Kreling, "Een boterham, parkeerplaats of gracht."

43. Otten in Genovesi, "Amsterdam moet gracht."
44. Oldenburger, "Actie 'Open de Grachten'"; Schoonenberg, "Hergraven van gedempte grachten," "Hergraven van grachten," and "Burgerinitiatief ElandsGRACHT ingediend"; Wiegman, "Een klein kwartiertje graven."
45. Rooijendijk, "The Narrow-Mindedness of Contemporary Devotees," 298.
46. Schoonenberg, "Schriftelijke inspraakbijdrage opengraven grachten"; Buddingh, "De inrichting"; Schoonenberg, "Eerste stap" and "Opengraven grachten."
47. Buddingh, "De inrichting"; Schoonenberg, "Hergraven van grachten" and "Opengraven grachten"; Ten Haaft, "Het water lonkt."
48. Schoonenberg, "Hergraven van grachten."
49. Michel, "Meer pleinen"; Sevil, "Meer dan de allure."
50. Frankfurther in Damen, "Politiek testament Frankfurther." See also Schoonenberg, "Hergraven van gedempte grachten."
51. "Haalbaarheidsonderzoek Opengraven Grachten"; Kreling, "Een boterham, parkeerplaats of gracht"; Schoonenberg, "Opengraven grachten."
52. Brinkgreve in Sevil, "Meer dan de allure."
53. Otten in Genovesi, "Amsterdam moet"; Kreling, "Een boterham" and "Heeft grachtengordel"; Schoonenberg, interview.
54. Otten in Genovesi, "Amsterdam moet gracht"; Schoonenberg, "Eerste stap."
55. "Haalbaarheidsonderzoek Opengraven Grachten"; Groensmit and Van der Stoel, "Burgerinitiatief opengraven Elandsgracht."
56. Dignum, "Future of Young Senior Citizens"; Huisman, "Ik ben niet"; Smith, *The New Urban Frontier*.
57. Frankfurther, "Een voorstel"; Van Beek, "Er moet weer grachtenwater."
58. Damen, "Politiek testament Frankfurther"; Oldenburger, "Actie 'Open de Grachten'"; Schoonenberg, "Hergraven van grachten."
59. "Haalbaarheidsonderzoek Opengraven Grachten."
60. Gemeente Amsterdam, "Opengraven Grachten"; Greven, "Ontdempen Westerstraat of Elandsgracht"; "Haalbaarheidsonderzoek Opengraven Grachten"; Schoonenberg, interview.
61. Frankfurther in Damen, "Politiek testament Frankfurther."
62. M. Van Rooy, "Ontdemping."
63. Kreling, "Heeft grachtengordel grachten zat?"
64. Kreling, "Heeft grachtengordel grachten zat?"
65. "Geen nieuwe grachten"; Kreling, "Heeft grachtengordel grachten zat?"; Van der Beek, "Comite Geen nattigheid"; M. Van Rooy, "Ontdemping."
66. Kreling, "Een boterham, parkeerplaats of gracht."
67. Kreling, "Een boterham, parkeerplaats of gracht" and "Heeft grachtengordel grachten zat?"; Schoonenberg, interview; Steinmetz, "Driehonderd Jordanezen."
68. Bosman, "Historische flauwekul of beschermd stadsgezicht?"
69. Diederiks, "Gracht is geen geloofsartikel"; Etty, "Tijd voor burgertrots"; "Geen nieuwe grachten"; Kreling, "Een boterham, parkeerplaats of gracht"; Rooijendijk, *The City Is Mine!*; Steinmetz, "Erfgoed mag"; M. Van Rooy, "Ontdemping."
70. Kreling, "Heeft grachtengordel grachten zat?"

71. Bosman, "Historische flauwekul of beschermd stadsgezicht?" See also Steinmetz, "Erfgoed mag."
72. Luttik, "The Value of Trees"; Van Haegen, "Alle zeilen bijzetten"; P. Van Rooy, "Het waterschap."
73. See chapter 4 for more on housing deregulation.
74. "Geen nieuwe grachten"; Kreling, "Heeft grachtengordel grachten zat?"; Van der Beek, "Comite Geen nattigheid."
75. Bosman, "Historische flauwekul."
76. Montag, "Vissen in."
77. Bosman, "Historische flauwekul of beschermd stadsgezicht?" See also Brunink and Scholtes, "Niet nog meer geld"; Kuile in Van Beek, "Er moet weer grachtenwater."
78. Frankfurther in Damen, "Politiek testament Frankfurther." See also "Grachten blijven toch dicht."
79. Schoonenberg, interview.
80. Buddingh, "De inrichting"; Groensmit and Van der Stoel, "Burgerinitiatief opengraven Elandsbracht"; Schuerfeld, "Alleen buitenstaanders willen Jordaangracht"; M. Smit and Nieuwenhuijsen, "Burgerinitiatief."
81. Damen, "Politiek testament Frankfurther"; Groensmit and Van der Stoel, "Burgerinitiatief opengraven Elandsbracht"; Schoonenberg, interview.

Chapter Four. Planners on Harbors

1. The letter combination *IJ*, from an old vowel form in Dutch, is pronounced like the vowel sound in *lay* in Australian or Cockney English (Donaldson, *Colloquial Dutch*, 3).
2. Van der Veer, interview.
3. Dornette and Van Veen, "The Use of Public Ground Lease"; Van der Veer, "Amsterdam Housing Market" and interview; Van der Veer and Schuiling, "The Amsterdam Housing Market."
4. Teune, "Housing in Amsterdam 2009," 2; Van der Veer and Schuiling, "The Amsterdam Housing Market;" Van Leeuwen et al., "Op weg naar 2040."
5. "Rental Housing Points System"; Teune, "Housing in Amsterdam 2009." As a further note, if a property was rated above 142 points, it was not subject to rent controls and could be offered at the going market rate.
6. Drentje, "De rol," 13–14.
7. Much of this owner-occupied housing stock was concentrated in the canal belt area and other old sections of the city, which predated the rise of the land lease system and social housing laws, and which were often built using canal-based water control technology.
8. Dodson, "The 'Roll' of the State"; Stadig, "Maakbare stad?"; Teune, "Housing in Amsterdam 2009"; Van der Veer, "Amsterdam Housing Market" and interview; Van der Veer and Schuiling, "The Amsterdam Housing Market."
9. Musterd and Deurloo, "Amsterdam and the Preconditions"; Vork, "De aantrekkingskracht van Amsterdam."
10. Van Polegeest, "De duurzame metropool," 4.
11. Van Polegeest, "De duurzame metropool," 4.
12. Beaumont and Nicholls, "Between Relationality and Territoriality"; "De opmars

van Noord"; Fainstein, *The Just City*; Van Zanden, *Economic History of the Netherlands*. For upper-income demands for housing see Van der Veer, interview; Terhorst, Van de Ven, and Deben, "Amsterdam."

13. Koper, "Bizar dat een huis."

14. VROM, "Randstad 2040," 49. See also DRO, "Amsterdam, the Place to Be!" 8; Musterd and Deurloo, "Amsterdam and the Preconditions," 92; Stadig, "Maakbare stad?," 22.

15. Van der Veer, interview.

16. "De stad is nog steeds"; Dignum, "Future of Young Senior Citizens," 221; Fainstein, *The Just City*; Stadig, "Maakbare stad?," 26; Van der Veer, "Amsterdam Housing Market" and interview; Van der Veer and Schuiling, "The Amsterdam Housing Market."

17. See chapter 5 for more information on the ecological and infrastructural history of the area.

18. Cotterell, *Amsterdam*; Franssen and Van Soest, *Ontdek het Oostelijk Havengebied*.

19. Ricklefs, *A History of Modern Indonesia*.

20. Combe, "Amsterdam terug aan het IJ," 23; Valk, "Amsterdam voorgoed van IJ gescheiden."

21. M. De Vries, "Havens vol intrigerende woningen"; Van Haastrecht, "Op het KNSM-eiland."

22. Franssen and Van Soest, *Ontdek het Oostelijk Havengebied*, 25.

23. Combe, "Amsterdam terug aan het IJ"; "De opmars van Noord"; Seegers, interview.

24. Steinmetz, "Archipel Amsterdam"; De Vries, "Idyllisch schiereiland op Palen" and "Geheimen van de haven"; H. De Lange, "Het Oostelijk Havengebied."

25. H. De Lange, "Het Oostelijk Havengebied"; M. De Vries, "Geheimen van de haven"; Ellenbroek, "De brug is terug."

26. Mamadouh, interview no. 1; Seegers, interview.

27. Evenhuis, "Het KNSM-Eiland"; Steinmetz, "Archipel."

28. For instance, see Combe, "Amsterdam terug"; M. De Vries, "Geheimen van de haven"; "Plan voor sloop."

29. Blokker, "Dynamische graansilo"; Combe, "Amsterdam terug aan het IJ"; Escher, "Gevecht om graansilo"; Klipp and Vugts, "Broedplaatsen voor artistieke trekvogels"; Koemans, "Het dorpsplein"; "Plan voor sloop."

30. Koper, "Bizar dat een huis."

31. Koper, "Bizar dat een huis."

32. J. De Vries, "Experimenteerde Haussmann dan niet?"; M. De Vries, "Idyllisch schiereiland op palen" and "Dwarsliggers"; Franssen and Van Soest, *Ontdek het Oostelijk Havengebied*; M. Van Rooy, "Een bad dat volloopt."

33. Bosman, "De appartementen"; Bosman and Koemans, "Een uitzicht"; Soeters in Koper, "Bizar dat een huis"; Steinmetz, "Archipel Amsterdam"; M. De Vries, "Geheimen van de haven."

34. For positive comments see M. De Vries, "Dwarsliggers"; P. Van Rooy, "Het waterschap." For negative comments see J. De Vries, "Experimenteerde Haussmann dan niet?"; M. De Vries, "Idyllisch schiereiland op palen"; Mamadouh, interview no. 2; M. Van Rooy, "Een bad dat volloopt" and "Gebouwenduo schnarniert tussen eilanden."

35. Boyer, "Java-eiland." See also M. Van Rooy, "Een bad dat volloopt."

36. M. De Vries, "Een schat aan wetenswaardigheden."

37. Verkerk, "Dromen van arcadische stad."

38. Verkerk, "Dromen van arcadische stad."
39. Beauchemin, "IJburg—Living on the Water"; Klipp, "Eilandtoerisme"; Verkerk, "Dromen van arcadische stad."
40. Steinmetz, "Archipel Amsterdam."
41. Franssen and Van Soest, *Ontdek het Oostelijk Havengebied*. See also Buurman, "Architectuurkaart Oostelijk Havengebied Amsterdam"; Buurman et al., *Eastern Harbour District Amsterdam*; De Korte and Maes, *IJburgh Architectural Map*; M. De Vries, "Een schat aan wetenswaardigheden"; Van Haastrecht, "Op het KNSM"; Koster, *The Eastern Docklands in Amsterdam*.
42. Van Haastrecht, "Op het KNSM." See also M. De Vries, "Geheimen van de haven."
43. "Architectonische hoogstandjes"; Ellenbroek, "De brug is terug"; Haastrecht, "Op het KNSM"; "Plan voor sloop"; Steinmetz, "Archipel Amsterdam."
44. M. De Vries, "Een schat aan wetenswaardigheden"; Kreling, "De pioniers."
45. Combe, "Amsterdam terug aan het IJ," 24; L. De Lange and Milanovic, "De afronding van IJburg"; M. De Vries, "Havens vol intrigerende woningen"; Franssen and Van Soest, *Ontdek het Oostelijk Havengebied*.
46. M. De Vries, "Geheimen van de haven."
47. M. De Vries, "Geheimen van de haven."
48. Ellenbroek, "De brug." See also M. Van Rooy, "Amsterdam krijgt."
49. Steinmetz, "Archipel Amsterdam."
50. According to Schulte ("Bootjes volgens" and "Soeters houdt"), officials later softened their position, closing the canals on the north end but preserving access from the south in the direction of the city center.
51. Steinmetz, "Archipel Amsterdam."
52. H. De Lange, "Het Oostelijk Havengebied." See also M. De Vries, "Geheimen van de haven."
53. H. De Lange, "Het Oostelijk Havengebied." See also M. De Vries, "Geheimen van de haven."
54. Valk, "Amsterdam voorgoed van IJ gescheiden."
55. Combe, "Amsterdam terug aan het IJ," 23.
56. "Amsterdam weer terug."
57. Seegers, interview.
58. Van Brummelen, "Nog steeds Amsterdam."
59. M. De Vries, "Geheimen van de haven."
60. Keulemans, "Een strandpaviljoen van strobalen"; Kloosterman, "Planning for Creativity"; Partners Overhoeks, "Over de partners"; Stadig, "Maakbare stad?," 27.
61. Luttik, "The Value of Trees."
62. Van Haegen, "Alle zeilen bijzetten"; P. Van Rooy, "Het waterschap."
63. Vork, "De aantrekkingskracht van Amsterdam," 25.
64. Van Zanen and Gadet, "Succesvolle vestigingsplekken," 20–22.
65. Franssen and Van Soest, *Ontdek het Oostelijk Havengebied*, 108.
66. Steinmetz, "Archipel Amsterdam"; Zonneveld, untitled article.
67. H. De Lange, "Het Oostelijk Havengebied;" Franssen and Van Soest, *Ontdek het Oostelijk Havengebied*, 112; Bosman, "De appartementen"; Bosman and Koemans, "Een uitzicht."
68. Steinmetz, "Archipel Amsterdam."
69. "De opmars van Noord."

70. Evenhuis, "Het KNSM-Eiland."
71. Science Center NEMO opened in 1997; Muziekgebouw aan 't IJ opened in 2005; Amsterdam Central Public Library opened in 2007.
72. NDSM-Werf became an official cultural "breeding ground" around 2002, and construction of the Overhoeks housing project began in 2007. For more information on municipal policies about the underground art movement, see Combe, "Amsterdam terug aan het IJ"; "Het grootste terrein in Nederland"; "N(D)SM"; Rombouts, "De kop van noord"; Vreeswijk, Van Zane, and Combe, "Stadskennis." For residential development up shore see "De opmars van noord."
73. Rombouts, "De kop van noord."
74. Combe, "Amsterdam terug aan het IJ," 24; M. De Vries, "IJoever stadium van filosoferen voorbij"; Frans Heddema, "Podium wil."
75. Kan, "Kunst bloeit." See also Berkhout and Rosenberg, "Masserend tussen Hells Angels."
76. VROM, "Randstad 2040."
77. Pistor, *A City in Progress*, 197.

Chapter Five. Ecologists on Islands

1. Government agencies often semantically and bureaucratically distinguish large water entities, such as major rivers and bays of national importance, from small waterways, such as inland canals and ponds of local interest.
2. See chapter 3 for more on the twentieth-century push to fill canals in Amsterdam.
3. The project site is located near the intersection of the IJ waterway and IJ Lake, although the visual distinction between these two bodies of water is vague.
4. This ideological polarization, while inaccurate, is common to Western philosophical thinking. For more information, see Castree, "Neoliberalising Nature 1" and "Neoliberalising nature 2"; Williams, *The Country and the City* and "Ideas of Nature."
5. Van der Ben, interview.
6. Hielkema, "De planologen kijken naar ons."
7. A. Vos, *Nederland, een natte geschiedenis*, 20. See also Sellers, "In Man versus Water"; Tienhooven, "Drijvende woonwijk."
8. For a few examples, see Groene Hart, "Groene Hart"; Keessen, "Het is te vroeg"; Neefjes, "De natuur heeft hier gewoonnen" and "Weidse ruimte in de Randstad"; Schreuder, "Alleen op papier"; Van Eijk, "Groene Hart floreert."
9. Neefjes, "De natuur heeft hier gewoonnen." See also Keessen, "Het is te vroeg."
10. Groote, Haartsen, and Van Soest, "Nature in the Netherlands," 314.
11. Groote, Haartsen, and Van Soest, "Nature in the Netherlands," 315, emphasis in original.
12. Pistor, *A City in Progress*.
13. Van der Helm, "Marginale natuur, maar wel veel."
14. "Moeraseiland in Amsterdamse gracht"; Van den Broek, "Moeraseiland"; Van der Helm, "Marginale natuur, maar wel veel"; Van Halm, "Watertuinen."
15. For more information on environmental issues, see Beatley, *Green Urbanism*.
16. Hoeksema, *Designed for Dry Feet*; Nienhuis, *Environmental History*.
17. Van Eijsbergen, Poot, and Van de Geer, "Water Veiligheid."

18. Marijnissen, "Blauwe Hart." See also Van den Akker et al., "Wetlands in het Ijsselmeer."
19. Iedema, "Leegte maakt." See also Van Lieshout, "Water bleef water"; Marijnissen, "Blauwe Hart"; Peters and Oppenhuizen, *50X Naar Buiten!*, 7.
20. Van den Akker et al., "Wetlands in het Ijsselmeer."
21. Breunissen, "Behoud het Blauwe Hart!"; Sijmons, "In IJburg."
22. Briet et al., "Vergroot het IJmeer."
23. Van den Akker et al., "Wetlands in het Ijsselmeer." See also Iedema, "Leegte maakt"; Stichting Wetlands, "Wetlands in het Ijsselmeer."
24. Damen, "Vier nieuwe eilanden bij IJburg"; De Korte and Maes, *IJburgh Architectural Map*; Stadig, "Maakbare stad?" 27; Van Zee et al., "Amsterdam in cijfers 2009."
25. "Vrij, onverveerd." See chapter 3 for additional information on water in Amsterdam's architectural heritage movement.
26. Breunissen, "Behoud het Blauwe Hart!"; Milieudefensie, "Het IJmeer, een waardevol landschap"; "Perspectief voor IJ- en Markermeer"; Ten Haaft, "De slag om de waterkant"; Verbeek, "Ode aan het IJmeer."
27. Sijmons, "In IJburg"; Marijnissen, "Buitendijks bouwen helpt de natuur"; Schreuder, "Sissende zwanen (no. 2)."
28. Nieuwenhuis, "Hoeckelingsdam." See also Peters and Oppenhuizen, *50X Naar Buiten*.
29. Stadig in Nieuwenhuis, "Hoeckelingsdam."
30. Groot in Nieuwenhuis, "Hoeckelingsdam."
31. Daalder in Nieuwenhuis, "Hoeckelingsdam."
32. Daalder in Nieuwenhuis, "Hoeckelingsdam." See also L. De Lange and Milanovic, "De afronding van IJburg."
33. Daalder, interview.
34. Banning, "Middeleeuwse bewakers van water"; M. Van Rooy, "Amsterdam krijgt" and "Door het water ontworpen."
35. Kuiken, "Gemeente vestigt hoop"; Marijnissen, "In het lab"; Smit and Meisner, interview; M. Van Rooy, "Amsterdam krijgt."
36. Kinder, "Planning by Intermediaries."
37. Daalder, interview.
38. Daalder, interview.
39. Smit and Meisner, interview.
40. Daalder, interview.
41. Peters and Oppenhuizen, *50X Naar Buiten*, 8.
42. Daalder, interview.
43. Beauchemin, "IJburg—Living on the Water"; L. De Lange and Milanovic, "De afronding van IJburg"; Steinmetz, untitled article. As a further note, by 2010 the economic recession cast doubt on whether IJburg's phase two would continue as planned, but within a few years the market had improved enough for construction to continue. For more information, see Damen, "Niemand koopt"; Kuiken, "IJburg II."
44. Booneiland, "Woondok"; Huijsmans, "Waterwonen nieuwe stijl"; Schuwer, "Wonen op het water"; "Waterwoningen naar IJburg."
45. Damen, "Benepen en te veel groen"; Steinmetz, untitled article; Kreling, "De pioniers."

46. Beauchemin, "IJburg—Living on the Water"; Ten Haaft, "De slag om de waterkant."
47. Daalder, "IJburg."
48. Daalder in Marijnissen, "Buitendijks bouwen helpt de natuur." See also Kropman, "Natuur gebaat bij komst IJburg."
49. Marijnissen, "In het lab."
50. Breunissen, "Behoud het Blauwe Hart!"; Daalder, interview.; Marijnissen, "Buitendijks bouwen helpt de natuur" and "In het lab."
51. Timar, "De IJburg Principes"; Marijnissen, "Buitendijks bouwen helpt de natuur."
52. Smit and Meisner, interview.
53. Peters and Oppenhuizen, *50X Naar Buiten*.
54. Sijmons, "In IJburg"; Timar, "De IJburg Principes."
55. Breunissen, "Behoud het Blauwe Hart!"
56. Breunissen, "Behoud het Blauwe Hart!"
57. Milieudefensie, "Het IJmeer, een waardevol landschap."
58. Timar, "De IJburg Principes."
59. Breunissen, "Behoud het Blauwe Hart!"; Milieudefensie, "Het IJmeer, een waardevol landschap"; "Perspectief voor IJ- en Markermeer"; Ten Haaft, "De slag om de waterkant."
60. Smits, interview.
61. Schreuder, "Blauwe hart."
62. Groene Noordvleugel, "Nationaal Waterpark IJmeer en Markermeer."
63. Briet et al., "Vergroot het IJmeer."
64. Stegenga, "Snel stappen nemen."
65. For instance, see Briet et al., "Vergroot het IJmeer"; Groene Noordvleugel, "Nationaal Waterpark IJmeer en Markermeer"; NatuurMonumenten, "Dossier Natuur"; Stegenga, "Snel stappen nemen."
66. Schreuder, "Extra natuur creëren."
67. Schreuder, "Strijd om."
68. Groene Noordvleugel, "Nationaal Waterpark IJmeer en Markermeer"; Marijnissen, "Blauwe Hart" and "In het lab"; Stuart, "Markermeer IJmeer."
69. Daalder, interview.
70. Smits, interview.
71. Smits, interview.
72. Smits, interview.
73. Stichting Wetlands, "Wetlands in het Ijsselmeer."
74. Stuart, "Markermeer IJmeer."
75. "Antieke Wierdijk gaat weer water keren"; NatuurMonumenten, "Dossier Natuur"; Stuart, "Markermeer IJmeer."
76. Daalder, interview. See also Stichting Wetlands, "Kengetallen kosten-batenanalyse Wetlands," 14.
77. Stichting Wetlands, "Kengetallen kosten-batenanalyse Wetlands."
78. "Remco Daalder je probeert natuur"; Van Zoest and Timmermans, "Amsterdamse biodiversiteit"; Wedin, "Natural Punk."
79. Daalder, interview; "Remco Daalder je probeert natuur"; "Vijvers van Amsterdam propvol."

80. "Grachtenwater in nieuw aquarium Artis"; Van den Broek and Didde, "'Ajakkes'-beesten in kaart gebracht."

81. Abrahams, "Reiger"; Sevil, "Vogelnest op boot heeft rechten"; Tyrpakova, "De Amsterdamse grachten"; Van Dam, interview; "Zit er nog een beetje leven."

82. Slager, "Hoe groen wordt waterbestuur" and "Invloed van waterschapskiezer"; Van der Ben, interview; Van Zoelen, "Milieupartij wint waterverkiezing"; Water Natuurlijk, "Geef het landschap een stem" and "Over water natuurlijk."

83. These reinterpretations of nature did not overturn problematic nature-society dualisms and instead simply reimagined the relationship between these two artificially polarized spheres. For more information, see Kinder, "Planning by Intermediaries."

Chapter Six. Investors on Floodplains

1. See chapter 5 for more details about Amsterdam's IJburg neighborhood.

2. The Urban Ring (Randstad) is the Netherlands' primary urban economic core, including the metropolitan areas of Amsterdam, Almere, Rotterdam, Utrecht, and The Hague, which form a loose ring around a central green zone reserved for environmental tourism and light agriculture.

3. VROM, "Randstad 2040," 4.

4. VROM, "Randstad 2040," 4. See also DRO, "Metropool Amsterdam"; Stadig, "Maakbare stad?"; Stichting Wetlands, "Wetlands in het Ijsselmeer"; Van Leeuwen et. al., "Op weg naar 2040."

5. Schmit, "Onze doelstelling."

6. For just a few examples, see "Alphen wil Groene Hart sparen"; Didde, "Rivierwater gaat ondergronds"; Hulsman, "Het recht op lelijkheid"; Keessen, "Het is te vroeg"; Pama, "'Stok-en-worst' politiek."

7. NatuurMonumenten "Dossier Natuur." See chapter 5 for more on plans to combine urban expansion and environmental restoration in the IJssel Lake District.

8. Ten Haaft, "De slag om de waterkant"; Salm, "Geen stadsuitbreiding"; Smits, interview.

9. Edidin, "Afloat in the Flood Zone"; Lyall, "At Risk from Floods"; Glancey, "Sink or Swim"; Davies, "Amphibious Houses"; Palca, "Dutch Architects Plan."

10. BNA, "Ideas: New Tasks."

11. BNA, "Water Dwellings: Six Water Houses."

12. BNA, "Water Dwellings: All Hands on Deck."

13. BNA, "Water Dwellings: Aqua Domus and Aqua Villa."

14. Booneiland, "Woondok"; Bouw & Wonen, "Eerste 'floating homes'"; Huijsmans, "Waterwonen nieuwe stijl"; Schuwer, "Wonen op het water"; "Waterwoningen naar IJburg."

15. Dura Vermeer, "De Drijvende Stad" and "Historie Bouwen op Water"; Edidin, "Afloat in the Flood Zone."

16. Dutch Docklands, "Floating City IJmeer."

17. Metz, "Red de wereld"; Tienhooven, "Drijvende woonwijk."

18. Kanter, "As Sea Levels Rise"; RTV, "Rotterdam wil 1300 drijvende woningen."

19. VenW, "15 experimenten."

20. VenW, "De Delta Aanpak."

21. Huizinga, "Lancering van de Watercanon." See also PBL, "Correction Wording Flood Risks."
22. Banning, "Middeleeuwse bewakers van water." See also Van der Helm, "Marginale natuur, maar wel veel."
23. Zonderop, "Help, mijn huis." See also Andersson, "Houden we wel droge"; Heems, "Veilig 'Leven met water'"; Hoovering, "Prins achter critici van cabinet"; Koelewijn and Thie, "De man die Willem-Alexander."
24. Oosterbaan, "Roem, rijkdom en risico's"; Sellers, "Changing Course"; Van Oostrom, *A Key to Dutch History*.
25. Huizinga, "Lancering van de Watercanon" and "Opening Nationaal Landschapscentrum."
26. Sellers, "Changing Course."
27. A. Vos, *Nederland, een natte geschiedenis*, 100. See also Huizinga, "Bestuurlijke conferentie TMO"; "Delta Works: Netherland."
28. A. Vos, *Nederland, een natte geschiedenis*, 30.
29. Lambert, *Making of the Dutch Landscape*, 122.
30. A. Vos, *Nederland, een natte geschiedenis*, 44. See also Borger and Ligtendag, "The Role of Water."
31. Andersson, "Houden we wel droge."
32. Nijburg in Engels, "Te weinig aandacht voor water."
33. VenW, "Flood Protection Policy." See also P. Van Rooy and Sterrenberg, "Het blauwe goud verzilveren"; P. Van Rooy et al., *Het blauwe goud verzilveren*."
34. Van Haegen, "Toespraak [. . .] Politiek Café VVD in Rotterdam"; BNA, "Ideas: New Tasks." See also VenW, "Kabinet," "Nederland leeft met water (no. 1)," and "De Delta Aanpak."
35. VenW, "De Delta Aanpak."
36. Heems, "Veilig 'Leven met water'"; VenW, "Kabinet."
37. VenW, "Nederland leeft met water (no. 1)."
38. VenW, "Nederland leeft met water (no. 1)"; "Nederland leeft met water (no. 3)."
39. Engels, "Te weinig aandacht voor water"; Leven met Water, "Jaarbericht 2009"; "Waterbeheerders bundelen krachten."
40. Huizinga, "De opening van de fototentoonstelling."
41. Huizinga, "Congres 'maak ruimte voor klimaat,'" "De presentatie van het advies," "Symposium 700-jarig bestaan," and "Toespraak bij de Deltatop"; Van Haegen, "Toespraak [. . .] 90 jaar Grontmij in het NAi"; Verbaan, "Water is geen probleem."
42. Huizinga, "De presentatie van het advies."
43. VenW, "Start campagne Nederland" and "Waterwet leidt tot minder regels."
44. Edidin, "Afloat in the Flood Zone."
45. VenW, "15 experimenten."
46. Edidin, "Afloat in the Flood Zone"; Engels, "Te weinig aandacht voor water"; VenW, "15 experimenten"; "Waterbeheerders bundelen krachten."
47. "Gevolgen van herinrichting"; C. Janssen and Van Lieshout, "Biesbosch 'gebaat' bij wateroverlast."
48. "De Blauwe Stad"; Schoof, "Midwolda wordt een badplaats."
49. Metz, "Red de wereld"; Tienhooven, "Drijvende woonwijk"; Waterstudio, "Proeftuin."
50. Aarden, "Compacte stad maakt voeten nat"; Banning and Moerland, "Willen we

dit?"; Schmit, "Onze doelstelling"; Van Dinther, "Revolutie in de polder"; Lokker, "Rust voor de stedeling."

51. Bengevoord, "Twente zoekt ruimte voor waterberging"; Van Haegen, "Congres 'waterveiligheid'"; Huizinga, "Bestuurlijke conferentie Ruimte"; Van der Zwaag, "Tips voor thuis."

52. Bezemer, "Staatsbosbeheer"; M. Moore, "Rethinking Defenses against Sea's Power"; Staal, "Oost-Groningen wil aantrekkelijk worden"; Schreuder, "De natte natuur"; Ten Haaft, "Overspoeld door verandering"; Van Lieshout, "Als het water komt."

53. Lyall, "At Risk from Floods"; VenW, "De Watervisie."

54. Huizinga, "World Water Week High-Level Policy Debate."

55. Huizinga, "World Water Week." See also Huizinga, "Ministerial Roundtable."

56. VenW, "Nederland leeft met water (no. 3)."

57. Huizinga, "Delta Technology Symposium"; Kuijken, "De waterschapsdag."

58. VROM, "Duurzaam bouwen en verbouwen."

59. Rijcken, "Innovatie vertroebelt waterbeheer"; Sekeris, "Huizinga." See also Van Haegen, "Toespraak [. . .] 90 jaar Grontmij."

60. Van Haegen, "Congres waterveiligheid" and "Toespraak [. . .] Politiek Café VVD"; Huizinga, "Bestuurlijke conferentie Ruimte," "De aftrap van de waterschapsverkiezingen," "Delta Technology Symposium," "De presentatie van het advies," and "Symposium 700-jarig bestaan"; VenW, "De Delta Aanpak." See also M. Moore, "Rethinking Defenses against Sea's Power."

61. VenW, "Nederland leeft met water (no. 2)."

62. VenW, "De watercanon."

63. Huizinga, "De opening"; VenW, "De watercanon," "Het Nationaal Waterplan," and "Nederland leeft met water (no. 1)."

64. Huizinga, "De opening van de fototentoonstelling."

65. Huizinga, "De aftrap van de waterschapsverkiezingen."

66. Huizinga, "Lancering van de Watercanon."

67. Aarden, "Compacte stad maakt voeten nat."

68. Van Haegen, "Congres waterveiligheid" and "Speech by Melanie Schultz van Haegen."

69. Oosterbaan, "Roem, rijkdom en risico's."

70. Huizinga, "Delivering Big" and "World Water Week High-Level Policy Debate." See also Van Haegen, "Opening of Aquaterra."

71. For more on uses of history, see Lowenthal, *The Heritage Crusade*; Mason, *Once and Future New York*.

72. For more on this concept of territory, see D. Moore, *Suffering for Territory*, 210–13.

73. BNA, "Ideas: New Tasks"; Hale, "Climate Changes"; Huizinga, "De presentatie van het advies."

74. Van Lieshout, "Tegen de Zeeuwse natuur." See also BNA, "Ideas: New Tasks."

75. Van Haegen, "Toespraak [. . .] 90 jaar Grontmij."

76. Van Haegen, "Toespraak [. . .] 90 jaar Grontmij."

77. Hulsman, "Het recht op lelijkheid"; Schreuder, "Sissende zwanen (no. 1)"; Tagliabue, "Low Country Seeks Higher Ground."

78. Huizinga, "Ondertekening Nationaal Bestuursakkoord Water"; VenW, "De Watervisie" and "Water in Beeld."

79. M. Moore, "Rethinking Defenses against Sea's Power."

80. Huizinga, "Natura 2000-beheerplan." See also Faiola and Eilperin, "Dutch Defense against Climate Change"; Huizinga, "De conferentie van UNICEF," "50-jarig bestaan," and "Ministerial Roundtable"; VenW, "De Watervisie" and "Nederland en Vietnam werken samen."
81. VenW, "Nederland leeft met water (no. 1)"; Van Haegen, "Toespraak [. . .] Politiek Café VVD."
82. Kuijken, "De waterschapsdag."

Conclusion. The Everyday Politics of Urban Water

1. Reisner, *Cadillac Desert*; Kaika, *City of Flows*; O'Neill, *Rivers by Design*; Swyngedouw, "Modernity and Hybridity"; White, *The Organic Machine*.
2. Baviskar, *Waterscapes*; Swyngedouw, *Social Power*. See also Brechin, *Imperial San Francisco*, chapter 2; Gandy, *Concrete and Clay*, chapter 1.
3. Baviskar, *Waterscapes*; Carney, "Gender Conflict"; White, *The Organic Machine*.
4. For local history of land reclamation, see Hoeksema, *Designed for Dry Feet*; Lambert, *Making of the Dutch Landscape*; Nienhuis, *Environmental History*; Steenbergen, *The Polder Atlas*. For the polder model, see Margry, "Ethnology and Folklore"; Schama, *The Embarrassment of Riches*. For clean drinking water, see Bijlard, "Water in kaart," 2; Van Zanden and Riel, *Strictures of Inheritance*; Waternet, "Nota Grondwater Amsterdam." For governing water boards see Bijlard, "Water in kaart," 2; Van Zanden and Riel, *Strictures of Inheritance*; Waternet, "Nota Grondwater Amsterdam." For landscape painting, see De Kroon and Willems, *Hollands Licht*; Metz and Van den Heuvel, *Sweet & Salt*.
5. Baviskar, *Waterscapes*; Bunce and Desfor, "Introduction to 'Political Ecologies'"; Gibbs, "Bottles, bores, and Boats"; Raffles, *In Amazonia*; Mitchell, "Can the Mosquito Speak?"; Linton, *What Is Water?*

Bibliography

Aarden, Marieke. "Compacte stad maakt voeten nat" [Compact city makes feet wet]. *De Volkskrant*, October 28, 1999: sec. Wetenschap, 5.
Abrahams, Fritz. "Reiger" [Heron]. *NRC Handelsblad*, October 1, 1999: sec. Achterpagina, 20.
Adolf, Steven. "Roet en herrie in de gracht" [Soot and racket in the canal]. *NRC Handelsblad*, June 14, 1993, 3.
"Alles in vijf weken" [All in five weeks]. *Het Parool*, August 7, 2006: sec. Binnenland, 11.
"Alphen wil Groene Hart sparen" [Alphen wants to save the Green Heart]. *Trouw*, November 28, 1995.
"Amsterdam bootvriendelijk" [Boat friendly Amsterdam]. *Grachtenjournaal*, October 20, 2007. Accessed July 20, 2009. http://www.grachtenjournaal.nl/ (no longer accessible).
"Amsterdam Canal Parade 2009." *PR-inside.com: News and Free PR*. Accessed July 19, 2009. http://www.pr-inside.com/amsterdam-canal-parade-r1346239.htm.
"Amsterdam Centre on World Heritage List." *Radio Netherlands Worldwide*, June 21, 2010.
"Amsterdam Gay Pride wint Welcome Award" [Amsterdam Gay Pride wins Welcome Award]. *Gay Krant*, September 24, 2008. Accessed June 9, 2009. http://www.progay.nl/nieuws.html?id=71.
"Amsterdam's Floating Gay Pride Parade Draws 300,000 People." *Agence France Presse*, August 2, 2003.
"Amsterdam weer terug aan het IJ" [Amsterdam returns again to the IJ]. *Stadsdeel Nieuws* 13, no. 2 (March 27, 2006): 1.
Andersson, Lars. "Houden we wel droge voeten in onze delta?" [Are we really keeping feet dry in our delta?]. *De Volkskrant*, August 1, 2009: sec. Forum, 12.
Angus, Edgar, and Paul Mangoenkarso. "Higher Economic Growth in Big Cities." *Statistics Netherlands Web Magazine*, April 25, 2005. Accessed November 6, 2009. http://www.cbs.nl/en-GB/menu/themas/macro-economie/publicaties/artikelen/archief/2005/2005-1694-wm.htm.
"Antieke Wierdijk gaat weer water keren" [Ancient dike allows water to flow again]. *Noordhollands Dagblad*, October 27, 2007: sec. Region, 205.
Apell, Robert. "The Power of Power: The Role of the Government as Real Estate Manager in the Preservation of the City of Amsterdam as a Heritage Site." In Deben, Salet, and Van Thoor, *Cultural Heritage and the Future*, 121–32.

"Architectonische hoogstandjes" [Architectural tour de force]. *De Telegraaf*, July 8, 2009: sec. Woonkrant, 26.
ATCB. "Amsterdam Water Sensations 2010." Amsterdam: Amsterdam Tourism & Convention Board, promotional flier, 2010.
Banning, Cees. "Middeleeuwse bewakers van water" [Medieval water guards]. *NRC Handelsblad*, October 11, 2003, 49.
Banning, Cees, and Rene Moerland. "Willen we dit? De toekomst van de landbouw in Nederland" [Do we want this? The future of agriculture in the Netherlands]. *NRC Handelsblad*, March 31, 2001: sec. Wetenschap & Onderwijs, 55.
Baviskar, Amita, ed. *Waterscapes: The Cultural Politics of a Natural Resource*. Delhi: Permanent Black, 2007.
BBA. "Jaarverslag en -rekening 2006" [Annual report and accounts, 2006]. Amsterdam: Gemeente Amsterdam Dienst Binnenwaterbeheer, 2007.
Beatley, Timothy. *Green Urbanism: Learning from European Cities*. Washington, D.C.: Island Press, 2000.
Beauchemin, Eric. "Ijburg—Living on the Water." *Radio Netherlands Worldwide*, May 21, 2009. Accessed November 29, 2009. http://www.rnw.nl/english.
Beaumont, Justin, and Walter Nicholls. "Between Relationality and Territoriality: Investigating the Geographies of Justice Movements in the Netherlands and the United States." *Environment and Planning A* 39, no. 11 (2007): 2554–75.
Bengevoord, Joris. "Twente zoekt ruimte voor waterberging" [Twente searches for water storage area]. *Dagblad Tubantia*, October 10, 2008, 31.
Berkhout, Karel. "Gay Pride iets minder homoseksueel" [Gay Pride a little less homosexual]. *NRC Handelsblad*, August 3, 2009: sec. Binnenland, 3.
———. "Maar minder gay-toeristen" [But fewer gay tourists]. *NRC Next*, August 1, 2008: sec. Cover, 4.
Berkhout, Karel, and Esther Rosenberg. "Masserend tussen Hells Angels en vastgoedbaronnen" [Massage between Hells Angels and real estate barons]. *NRC Handelsblad*, July, 29, 2009: sec. Binnenland, 2.
Beusekamp, Willem. "Het moet gaan om seks, drugs en feesten" [It should be about sex, drugs, and parties]. *De Volkskrant*, August 2, 2008: sec. Binnenland, 3.
Bezemer, Maaike. "Staatsbosbeheer: Werleg de dijken" [National Forestry Service: Shift the dikes]. *Trouw*, April 23, 2005: sec. Nederland, 7.
Bijlard, R. "Water in kaart: De legger-rechten en plichten voor veilig leven en werken temidden van het water" [Water mapped: Rights and obligations for safe living and working amidst water]. Hoogheemraadschap Amstel Gooi en Vecht, report, May 2008.
Blokker, Bas. "Dynamische graansilo houdt Schaefer in ere" [Dynamic grain silo honors Schaefer]. *NRC Handelsblad*, September 4, 1995: sec. Binnenland, 3.
BNA. "Ideas: New Tasks." *H₂olland: Architecture with Wet Feet*. Bond van Nederlandse Architecten, n.d. Accessed March 28, 2014. http://www.h2olland.nl/popupthema.asp?id=1.
———. "Water Dwellings: All Hands on Deck; 47 Dwellings." *H₂olland: Architecture with Wet Feet*. Bond van Nederlandse Architecten, 2001. Accessed March 28, 2014. http://www.h2olland.nl/projectdetails.asp?id=226.
———. "Water Dwellings: Aqua Domus and Aqua Villa. *H₂olland: Architecture with Wet

Feet. Bond van Nederlandse Architecten, 2001. Accessed March 28, 2014. http://www.h2olland.nl/projectdetails.asp?id=228.

———. "Water Dwellings: Six Water Houses." *H₂olland: Architecture with Wet Feet.* Bond van Nederlandse Architecten, 2001. Accessed March 28, 2014. http://www.h2olland.nl/project.asp?id=223.

Booneiland. "Woondok: Wonen op water in Almere" [House Dock: Living on water in Almere]. Booneiland, n.d. Accessed December 16, 2010. http://www.booneiland.nl/home.aspx (no longer accessible).

"Bootvriendelijke pizzeria" [Boat friendly pizzeria]. *Grachtenjournaal,* April 15, 2007. Accessed May 20, 2010. http://www.grachtenjournaal.nl/ (no longer accessible).

Borger, Guus J., and Willem A Ligtendag. "The Role of Water in the Development of the Netherlands: A Historical Perspective." *Journal of Coastal Conservation* 4, no. 2 (1998): 109–14.

Bos, Frank. *Amsterdam Afloat: 350 Years of Houseboats.* Amsterdam: Leijten, 2007.

Bosman, Frans. "De appartementen—koop en huur—vliegen weg, en niet alleen die aan het water" [The apartments—for sale and rent—fly off the market, and not only those on the water]. *Het Parool,* October 3, 1997, 1.

———. "Historische flauwekul of beschermd stadsgezicht?" [Historical rubbish or protected cityscape?]. *Het Parool,* October 27, 2005: sec. Amsterdam, 16.

———. "Wij zijn blij als de politiek onze suggesties oppikt" [We're happy if politics pick up our suggestions]. *Het Parool,* October 27, 2005: sec. Amsterdam, 16.

Bosman, Frans, and Martin Koemans. "Een uitzicht om in katzwijm te vallen" [A view to faint from]. *Het Parool,* April 23, 1994, 26.

Bouw & Wonen. "Eerste 'floating homes' van Europa in Zuiderburen" [Europe's first 'floating homes' in Zuiderburen]. Bouw & Wonen. Accessed March 13, 2014. http://www.bouwenwonen.net/nieuwbouw/read.asp?id=5336.

Boyer, Maurice. "Java-eiland" [Java Island]. *NRC Handelsblad,* April 5, 1997: sec. Economie, 15.

Brechin, Gray. *Imperial San Francisco: Urban Power, Earthy Ruin.* Berkeley: University of California Press, 2006.

Breunissen, Klaas. "Behoud het Blauwe Hart!" [Protect the Blue Heart!]. Milieudefensie, press release, December 12, 2007.

Briet, Ernest, Vera Dam, Jupijn Haffmans, Frank Köhler, and Mirjam de Rijk. "Vergroot het IJmeer" [Enlarge IJ Lake]. Milieudefensie, press release, June 26, 2009.

Brinkgreve, Geurt. "The Preservation of Historic Buildings in Amsterdam." In Deben, Salet, and Van Thoor, *Cultural Heritage and the Future,* 101–20.

Brunink, Gerrit, and Alexander Scholtes. "Niet nog meer geld voor welzijn" [Not still more money for welfare]. *Het Parool,* October 29, 2009: sec. Meningen, 26.

Buddingh, Marianne. "De inrichting van de Elandsdgracht in het Plan van Aanpak Jordaan" [The design of the Elands Canal in the Jordaan approach plan]. Gemeente Amsterdam Stadsdeel Centruum, public letter, January 26, 2006.

Buiter, Hans. "Transforming Water Infrastructures in Amsterdam and Utrecht, 1860–2000: Power Relations, Social Functions and Urban Identities." Paper presented at the 6th International Summer Academy on Technology Studies, Deutschlandsberg, Austria, 2004. Accessed July 18, 2014. http://www.ifz.tugraz.at/Archiv/International-Summer-Academy-on-Technology-Studies-Archiv/Proceedings-2004.

Bunce, Susannah, and Gene Desfor. "Introduction to 'Political Ecologies of Urban Waterfront Transformations.'" *Cities* 24, no. 4 (2007): 251–58.

Buruma, Ian. *Murder in Amsterdam: Liberal Europe, Islam, and the Limits of Tolerance*. New York: Penguin Press, 2006.

Buurman, Marlles. "Architectuurkaart Oostelijk Havengebied Amsterdam" [Architectural map Eastern Docklands Amsterdam]. Amsterdam: Nai Uitgevers, 2002.

Buurman, Marlles, Bernard Hulsman, Hans Ibelings, Allard Jolles, Ed Melet, and Ton Schaap. *Eastern Harbour District Amsterdam: Urbanism and Architecture*. Amsterdam: Nai Uitgevers, 2007.

"Canal Parade trekt recordaantal bezoekers" [Canal Parade draws a record number of visitors]. *Radio Nederland Wereldomroep*, August 1, 2009.

Carney, Judith. "Gender Conflict in the Gambian Wetlands." In *Liberation Ecologies: Environment, Development and Social Movements*, edited by Richard Peet and Michael Watts, 165–87. New York: Routledge, 2004.

Carter, Paul. "Elysiums for Gentlemen." *The Road to Botany Bay: An Exploration of Landscape and History*. New York: Alfred A. Knopf, 1967.

Castree, Noel. "Neoliberalising Nature 1: The Logics of Deregulation and Reregulation." *Environment and Planning A* 40, no. 1 (2008): 131–52.

———. "Neoliberalising Nature 2: Processes, Outcomes and Effects." *Environment and Planning A* 40, no. 1 (2008): 153–73.

Cheary, Melanie. "Amsterdam Gay Parade Wants More Naked Bottoms." Reuters, August 1, 2003.

Combe, Caroline. "Amsterdam terug aan het IJ" [Amsterdam returns to the IJ]. *PlanAmsterdam*, Gemeente Amsterdam Dienst Ruimtelijke Ordening, no. 2, 2008.

"Controle pleziervaart betreft 'boten waar de dronkenschap van afdruipt'" [Pleasure boat checks concern 'boats where the drunkenness trickles out']. *Het Parool*, April 23, 2009: sec. Amsterdam, 11.

Cortie, Cees, Bert Kruit, and Sako Musterd. "Housing Market Change in Amsterdam: Some Trends." *Journal of Housing and the Built Environment* 4, no. 3 (1989): 217–33.

Cotterell, Geoffrey. *Amsterdam: The Life of a City*. Boston: Little, Brown, 1972.

Couzy, Michiel. "Ray Selby." *Het Parool*, December 24, 2009: sec. PS, 22.

Daalder, Remco (city ecologist, Gemeente Amsterdam Dienst Ruimtelijke Ordening). Interview by the author, June 8, 2010.

———. "IJburg: Te gast in de natuur" [IJburg: A guest in nature]. *Groen* 66, no. 5 (2010): 39–46.

Dalton, Russell J., and Manfred Kuechler, eds. *Challenging the Political Order: New Social and Political Movements in Western Democracies*. New York: Oxford University Press, 1990.

Damen, Tom. "Benepen en te veel groen" [Timid and too much green]. *Het Parool*, June 20, 2002: sec. Voorpagina, 1.

———. "Europa's gaafste oude stad niet beschermd" [Europe's most intact old city not protected]. *Het Parool*, March 11, 2008: sec. Amsterdam, 99.

———. "Meer steigers in de grachten, minder drukte op de wal" [More risers in the canals, less commotion on the wall]. *Het Parool*, January 26, 2008: sec. Amsterdam, 26.

———. "Niemand koopt, verkoopt of verhuist en een opleving is niet in zicht" [No one buys, sells, or rents, and a revival is not in sight]. *Het Parool*, January 16, 2010: sec. Amsterdam, 18.

———. "Politiek testament Frankfurther" [Frankfurt's political testament]. *Het Parool*, February 16, 2007: sec. Amsterdam, 15.

———. "Vier nieuwe eilanden bij IJburg" [Four new islands in IJburg]. *Het Parool*, November 19, 2008: sec. Amsterdam, 99.

Davies, Gareth, trans. "Amphibious Houses: Dutch Answer to Flooding: Build Houses That Swim." *Der Spiegel Online International*, September 26, 2005. Accessed January 9, 2011. http://www.spiegel.de/international/spiegel/0,1518,377050,00.html.

De Baar, Peter P. (chief editor, *Ons Amsterdam*). Interview by the author, April 28, 2009.

Deben, Leon (emeritus professor of urban sociology, University of Amsterdam). Interview by the author, April 27, 2009.

———. "Public Space and the Homeless in Amsterdam." In *Amsterdam Human Capital*, edited by Sako Musterd and Willliam Salet, 229–46. Amsterdam: Amsterdam University Press, 2003.

Deben, Leon, William Salet, and Marie Therese van Thoor, eds. *Cultural Heritage and the Future of the Historic Inner City of Amsterdam*. Amsterdam: Aksant, 2004.

Deben, Leon, William Salet, and Marie Therese van Thoor. "Heritage and the Future of the City: Fitting the Monumental Shape of Amsterdam with its Social Dynamics." In Deben, Salet, and Van Thoor, *Cultural Heritage and the Future*, 3–12.

"De Blauwe Stad drijft op water" [Blue City floats on water]. *Trouw*, May 12, 2005: sec. Nederland, 6.

De Fauwe, Loes. "Gemeente heeft aanvraag na jaren gedoe klaar" [City council finishes application after several years of fuss]. *Het Parool*, September 13, 2008: sec. Amsterdam, 16.

———. "Wie doet deze klus in 2007?" [Who will do this task in 2007?]. *Het Parool*, August 7, 2006: sec. Amsterdam, 99.

De Jong, Beatrijs (Amsterdam Tourism and Convention Board). Email message to author, August 13, 2009.

De Korte, Yvonne, and Lieselore Maes. *IJburgh Architectural Map*. Amsterdam: ARCAM, 2009.

De Kroon, Maarten, and Gerrit Willems. *Hollands Licht* [Dutch Light]. Directed by Pieter-Rim De Kroon. Amsterdam, Wissenraet & Associes BV, 2003. DVD.

De Lange, Henny. "Het Oostelijk Havengebied: Van rafelrand tot festivalterrein" [The Eastern Docklands: From fringe to festival grounds]. *De Trouw*, August 23, 2007: sec. De gids, 8–9.

De Lange, Lia, and Mirjana Milanovic. "De afronding van IJburg" [Rounding off IJburg]. *PlanAmsterdam, Gemeente Amsterdam Dienst Ruimtelijke Ordening*, no. 2, 2009.

Deleuze, Gilles, and Felix Guattari. "Becoming-Intense, Becoming-Animal, Becoming-Imperceptible." *A Thousand Plateaus: Capitalism and Schizophrenia*, 232–309. Minneapolis: University of Minnesota Press, 1978.

"Delta Works: Netherland." *Awesome Planet*. January 27, 2009. Accessed March 4, 2010. http://www.awesomeplanet.org/great-wonders/modern-wonders/delta-works-netherland/ (no longer accessible).

"De 100 meest genoemde tradities in 2008" [The hundred most mentioned traditions of 2008]. Amsterdam: Het Nederlands Centrum voor Volkscultuur, 2008.

"De opmars van noord" [The march north]. *De Telegraaf*, August 7, 2009: sec. Metropool, 4.

De Rooy, Piet (professor of Dutch history, University of Amsterdam). Interview by the author, April 27, 2009.

Desfor, Gene, and Roger Keil. *Nature and the City: Making Environmental Policy in Toronto and Los Angeles*. Tucson: University of Arizona Press, 2004.

Desfor, Gene, Jennefer Laidley, Quentin Stevens, and Dirk Schubert. *Transforming Urban Waterfronts: Fixity and Flow*. Abingdon, UK: Routledge, 2011.

"De stad is nog steeds bezeten van het geld" [The city is still obsessed with money]. *Het Parool*, March 10, 2000: sec. Amsterdam, 6.

Deters, Sigrid. "Gedempte grachten in ere hersteld" [Filled canals recovered in honor]. *Radio Netherlands World Service*, November 14, 2006.

Deverell, William. "Remembering a River." *Whitewashed Adobe: The Rise of Los Angeles and the Remaking of Its Mexican Past*, 91–128. Berkeley: University of California Press, 2005.

De Vries, Jeroen. "Experimenteerde Haussmann dan niet?" [Didn't Haussmann experiment?]. *Het Parool*, May 12, 2007: sec. Meningen, 31.

De Vries, Marina. "Dwarsliggers" [Trouble makers]. *Het Parool*, August 25, 2000: sec. Amsterdam, 17.

———. "Een schat aan wetenswaardigheden" [A wealth of information]. *Het Parool*, December 17, 1998, 21.

———. "Geheimen van de haven" [Secrets of the Harbor]. *De Volkskrant*, March 12, 2007: sec. Kunst, 14–15.

———. "Havens vol intrigerende woningen" [Harbors full of intriguing housing]. *Het Parool*, March 31, 1994, 11.

———. "Idyllisch schiereiland op palen" [Idyllic peninsula on poles]. *Het Parool*, April 23, 1994, 25.

———. "IJoever stadium van filosoferen voorbij" [IJ-shore past philosophizing stage]. *Het Parool*, December 12, 1997, 3.

Dewulf, Jeroen. "In the Jungle of Amsterdam: On the Re-invention of Dutch Identity." Berkeley: University of California, 2008. Accessed April 11, 2009. http://digitalassets.lib.berkeley.edu/morrisonlectures/ucb/text/51163759.pdf.

Didde, Rene. "Rivierwater gaat ondergronds" [River water goes underground]. *De Volkskrant*, February 25, 1995.

Diederiks, Daan. "Gracht is geen geloofsartikel" [Canals are not sacred]. *Het Parool*, September 9, 2004: sec. Meningen, 11.

Dignum, Kees. "The Future of Young Senior Citizens in Old Amsterdam." In Deben, Salet, and Van Thoor, *Cultural Heritage and the Future*, 211–27.

Dodson, Jago R. "The 'Roll' of the State: Government, Neoliberalism and Housing Assistance in Four Advanced Economies." *Housing, Theory and Society* 23, no. 4 (2006): 224–43.

Donaldson, Bruce. *Colloquial Dutch*. New York: Routledge, 1996.

Doorduyn, Yvonne. "Minister Plasterk toegejuicht op Gay Pride" [Minister Plasterk welcomed at Gay Pride]. *De Volkskrant*, August 4, 2008, 4.

Dop, Jan Maarten Fiedeldij, "Een relaas van 20 jaar actie" [An account of 20 years of activism]. *Amsterdams Boten Comité*, 1992. Accessed March 4, 2014. http://www.amsterdamsbotencomite.nl/ges_20jaaractie.htm.

Dornette, Johanna, and Iris van Veen. "The Use of Public Ground Lease in European Cities." City of Amsterdam Development Corporation, n.d., ca. mid-2000s. Accessed March 19, 2014. http://www.amsterdam.nl/publish/pages/418782/use_of_public_ground_lease_in_european_cities.pdf.

Dovey, Kim. *Fluid City: Transforming Melbourne's Urban Waterfront*. Sydney: University of New South Wales, 2005.

Drentje, Anko. "De rol van het Woningwaarderingsstelsel in het huidige woonbeleid" [The role of the Residential Assessment System in current housing policy]. Master's thesis, Delft University of Technology, 2011. Accessed July 18, 2014. http://repository.tudelft.nl/view/ir/uuid%3A0f77a819-ba42-4554-aade-e40c64869d36/.

DRO. "Amsterdam, the Place to Be! De aantrekkelijkheid van Amsterdam als vestigingsplaats voor kenniswerkers en mensen werkzaam in de creatieve sectoren" [The attraction of Amsterdam as a living location for knowledge workers and creative sector employees]. Amsterdam: Diesnt Ruimtelijke Ordening, 2006.

———. "Metropool Amsterdam" [Amsterdam Metropolis]. Gemeente Amsterdam Diesnt Ruimtelijke Ordening, April 6, 2010. Accessed July 22, 2010. http://www.dro.amsterdam.nl/over_dro/dro_werkt_aan/metropoolstrategie.

Dura Vermeer. "De Drijvende Stad" [The floating city]. Dura Vermeer Business Development, n.d. Accessed December 10, 2010. http://infra.duravermeer.nl/default.aspx.

———. "Historie Bouwen op Water" [History of building on water]. Dura Vermeer. Accessed September 20, 2010. http://infra.duravermeer.nl/default.aspx.

Dutch Docklands. "Floating City IJmeer." Company press release, February 2, 2007. Accessed July 18, 2014. http://www.dutchdocklands.com.

Edidin, Peter. "Afloat in the Flood Zone." *New York Times*, October 27, 2005, 1.

Eggenkamp, Wim. "Amsterdam: A Unique Example of Public/Private Partnership in Restoring a City." In Deben, Salet, and Van Thoor, *Cultural Heritage and the Future*, 197–210.

Ellenbroek, Willem. "De brug is terug" [The bridge is back]. *De Volkskrant*, July 12, 2001: sec. Kunst Katern, 4.

Engels, Joep. "Te weinig aandacht voor water" [Too little attention to water]. *Trouw*, July 31, 2009: sec. Nederland.

Escher, Emilie. "Gevecht om graansilo kan lang duren" [Fighting over grain silo can could go on]. *Het Parool*, December 4, 1996, 9.

———. "Pleziervaartuigen irriteren woonbootbewoner" [Pleasure boaters irritate house boat resident]. *Het Parool*, August 24, 1992, 5.

Etty, Elsbeth. "Tijd voor burgertrots" [Time for Citizen Pride]. *NRC Handelsblad*, April 7, 2000: sec. Boeken, 32.

"Europride: Roze golf spoelt door hoofdstad" [EuroPride: Pink wave washes through capital]. *Het Parool*, March 28, 1994, 11.

Evenhuis, Arend. "Het KNSM-Eiland is ingenomen en meteen vol" [KNSM-Island is charmingly and immediately full]. *Trouw*, April 14, 1994, KK 01.

Fainstein, Susan S. "The Egalitarian City." *International Planning Studies* 2, no. 3 (1997): 295–314.

———. *The Just City*. Ithaca: Cornell University Press, 2010.

Faiola, Anthony, and Juliet Eilperin. "Dutch Defense against Climate Change: Adapt." *Washington Post*, December 6, 2009, A01.
Foucault, Michel. *The Essential Foucault*. Edited by Paul Rabinow and Nicolas Rose. New York: New Press, 1994.
Foundation for Advancement of Illegal Knowledge. *Cracking the Movement: Squatting beyond the Media*. New York: Autonomedia, 1994.
Franck, Karen, and Quentin Stevens, eds. *Loose Space: Possibility and Diversity in Urban Life*. Abingdon, UK: Routledge, 2007.
Frankfurther, Guido. "Een voorstel voor het hergraven van gedempte grachten" [A proposal for the excavation of filled canals]. D66 Werkgroep Stadsontwikkeling Gemeenteblad, no. 466, June 27, 2000.
Franssen, Bart, and Ruud van Soest. *Ontdek het Oostelijk Havengebied* [Discover the Eastern Docklands]. Amsterdam: Stokerkade, 2009.
Furnee, Jan H. (professor of cultural history, University of Amsterdam). Interview by the author, April 27, 2009.
———. "The Thrill of Frozen Water: Class, Gender and Ice-Skating in the Netherlands, 1600–1900." In *Water, Leisure and Culture: European Historical Perspectives*, edited by Susan C. Anderson and Bruce Tabb, 53–69. New York: Berg, 2002.
Gandy, Matthew. *Concrete and Clay: Reworking Nature in New York City*. Cambridge, Mass.: MIT Press, 2002.
"Gay Canal Parade vreest stille omgang te moeten worden" [Gay Canal Parade dreads having to proceed quietly]. *Het Parool*, July 19, 2000: sec. Amsterdam, 5.
"Gay Pride Parade Set to Paint Amsterdam Pink." *Reuters News*, August 2, 2002.
"Gay Pride wil nu toch uitwijken" [Gay pride will now emigrate]. *Het Parool*, August 7, 2000: sec. Amsterdam, 5.
"Geachte redactie: Koninginnedag" [Dear editor: Queen's Day]. *De Volkskrant*, April 28, 2009: sec. Forum, 11.
"Geen nieuwe grachten" [No new canals]. *NRC Handelsblad*, July 2, 2004: sec. Opinie, 7.
"Geld botenparade Gay Pride geregeld" [Money ruled the Gay Pride boat parade]. *Het Parool*, July 4, 2006: sec. Amsterdam, 4.
Gemeente Amsterdam. "Openbare ruimte, groen en water" [Public space, green and water]. Gemeente Amsterdam Stadsdeel Centrum, n.d. Accessed October 26, 2009. http://www.centrum.amsterdam.nl.
———. "Opengraven Grachten: Nieuwsbrief" [Opening canals: Newsletter]. Gemeente Amsterdam Stadsdeel Centruum, September 2004.
Genovesi, Inaki O. "Amsterdam moet gracht in ere herstellen" [Amsterdam must recover canal honor]. *De Volkskrant*, August 4, 2000: sec. Binnenland, 7.
"Gevolgen van herinrichting voor bewoners nog niet bekend" [Consequences of redesign for residents not yet known]. *De Volkskrant*, May 7, 2008: sec. Binnenland, 2.
Gibbs, Leah M. "Bottles, Bores, and Boats: Agency of Water Assemblages in Post/colonial Inland Australia." *Environment and Planning A* 45, no. 2 (2013): 467–84.
Glancey, Jonathon. "Sink or Swim: In Times of Flood, These Houses Rise to the Occasion." *Guardian*, May 24, 2004.
Gordillo, Gaston. *Landscapes of Devils: Tensions of Place and Memory in the Argentinean Chaco*. Durham, N.C.: Duke University Press, 2004.

"Grachten blijven toch dicht" [Canals still remain closed]. *NRC Handelsblad*, October 5, 2004: sec. Binnenland, 2.

"Grachtenwater in nieuw aquarium Artis" [Canal water in new Artis aquarium]. *De Volkskrant*, December 11, 1995, 7.

Greven, Jessica. "Ontdempen Westerstraat of Elandsgracht" [Excavate Wester Street or Elands Canal]. *Gemeente Amsterdam Dienst Onderzoek en Statistiek*, project report 4053-24, February 2004.

Groene Hart. "Groene Hart" [Green Heart]. Stuurgroep Groene Hart website, n.d., ca. 2009. Accessed February 25, 2010. http://stuurgroepgroenehart.nl/.

Groene Noordvleugel. "Nationaal Waterpark IJmeer en Markermeer" [National Water Park IJ Lake and Marker Lake]. Groene Noordvleugel, promotional flier, September 2009.

Groensmit, Hanneke, and Anne Lize E. C. Van der Stoel. "Burgerinitiatief opengraven Elandsgracht" [Excavate Elands Canal citizen initiative]. Gemeente Amsterdam Stadsdeel Centruum, public letter number 05-11723/OR, January 2006.

Groote, Peter, Tialda Haartsen, and Francien van Soest. "Nature in the Netherlands." *Tijdschrift voor Economische en Sociale Geografie* 97, no. 3 (2006): 314-20.

Haagsma, Ids, and Hilde de Haan. "Steden zijn geschapen voor ritme van water" [Cities are created from the rhythm of water]. *De Volkskrant*, January 6, 1995.

"Haalbaarheidsonderzoek Opengraven Grachten" [Opening canals feasibility report]. Amsterdam: Gemeente Amsterdam Stadsdeel Centruum, 2004.

Habermas, Jürgen. "New Social Movements." *Telos*, no. 49 (1981): 33-37.

Hageman, Esther. "Van zes naar achtien" [From six to eighteen]. *Trouw*, July 29, 2006, 1.

Hale, Ellen. "Climate Changes Could Devastate the Netherlands." *USA Today*, November 22, 2000, 27.

Hannigan, John. *Fantasy City: Pleasure and Profit in the Postmodern Metropolis*. London: Routledge, 1998.

Hanuska, Karl E. "Dutch Gays Celebrate Pride, See Rising Homophobia." Reuters, August 6, 2004.

Harvey, David. "From Managerialism to Entrepreneurialism: The Transformation in Urban Governance in Late Capitalism." *Geograpfiska Annaler* 71, no. 1 (1989): 3-17.

Heddema, Frans. "Podium wil debat over IJ-oevers leven inblazen" [Podium wants to breath life into debate over IJ-shores]. *Het Parool*, November 15, 1994, 13.

Heddema, French. "Eilard Jacobs of the Water and Sewerage Service: 'New Canal Is Good for Disposal of Water.'" *Binnenstad*, De Vereniging Vrienden van de Amsterdamse Binnenstad, no. 207, 2004.

Heems, G. C. "Veilig 'Leven met water' is een gevaarlijke illusie" [Safely 'Living with water' is a dangerous illusion]. *NRC Handelsblad*, January 28, 2006: sec. Opinie, 15.

Heijnis, Jesse. "Prachtige geschiedenissen, maar geen monument" [Beautiful histories, but no monument]. *Het Parool*, February 9, 2009: sec. Amsterdam, 18.

Hemelaar, Irene (secretary, ProGay Foundation). Interview, with Frank van Dalen (president, ProGay Foundation), by the author, September 9, 2009.

Henfling, Marijn. "Men wil geen relnicht zien" [People don't want to see poofs]. *Het Parool*, August 1, 2003: sec. Amsterdam, 5.

"Het bootje van Cohen" [Cohen's boat]. *NRC Next*, August 3, 2009, 3.

"Het grootste terrein in Nederland" [The biggest terrain in the Netherlands]. *Het Parool*, June 19, 2004: sec. Amsterdam, 18.

Heynen, Nik, James McCarthy, Scott Prudham, and Paul Robbins. "Introduction: False Promises." In *Neoliberal Environments: False Promises and Unnatural Consequences*, edited by Nik Heynen, James McCarthy, Scott Prudham, and Paul Robbins. Abingdon, UK: Routledge, 2007.

Hielkema, Haro. "De planologen kijken naar ons" [The planners are looking to us]. *Trouw*, October 15, 1998: sec. Kerk, 10.

Hoedeman, Jan. "Amsterdam gaat de crowd managen" [Amsterdam manages the crowd]. *De Volkskrant*, April 27, 2009: sec. Binnenland, 3.

Hoeksema, Robert J. *Designed for Dry Feet*. Reston, Va.: American Society of Civil Engineers, 2006.

Hoovering, Sane T. "Prins achter critici van cabinet" [Prince behind criticisms of cabinet]. *De Volkskrant*, October 23, 2006: sec. Binnenland, 3.

Hoskins, Gareth. "Poetic Landscapes of Exclusion: Chinese Immigration at Angel Island." In *Landscape and Race in the United States*, edited by Richard Schein. New York: Routledge, 2006.

Houtsma, Jella. "Homovertier in Amsterdam al jaren in het slop" [Queer entertainment in Amsterdam already years in the doldrums]. *Het Parool*, August 9, 2002: sec. Meningen, 4.

Huijsmans, Linda. "Waterwonen nieuwe stijl" [New style water housing]. *Het Financieele Dagblad*, December 1, 2007: sec. Omslagartikel, 6.

Huisman, Jaap. "Ik ben niet voor niets gebleven" [I didn't stay for nothing]. *De Volkskrant*, September 25, 1997: sec. Voorkant, 6.

Huizinga, Tineke. "Bestuurlijke conferentie Ruimte voor de Rivier" [Room for the River administration conference]. Ministrie van Verkeer en Waterstaat, speech transcript, October 28, 2009.

———. "Bestuurlijke conferentie TMO" [TMO administrative conference]. Ministrie van Verkeer en Waterstaat, speech transcript, May 25, 2007.

———. "Congres 'maak ruimte voor klimaat'" ["Make room for climate" conference]. Ministrie van Verkeer en Waterstaat, speech transcript, November 27, 2007.

———. "De aftrap van de waterschapsverkiezingen" [The kick-off of the water elections]. Ministrie van Verkeer en Waterstaat, speech transcript, November 13, 2008.

———. "De conferentie van UNICEF, NWP en Aqua for all in het kader van Wereldwaterdag" [UNICEF conference, NWP and Aqua for everyone in the World Water Day framework]. Ministrie van Verkeer en Waterstaat, speech transcript, March 26, 2009.

———. "Delivering Big: Translating Knowledge into Action through Internet Action." Ministrie van Verkeer en Waterstaat, speech transcript, August 21, 2008.

———. "Delta Technology Symposium." Ministrie van Verkeer en Waterstaat, speech transcript, June 26, 2008.

———. "De opening van de fototentoonstelling 'Document Nederland: Het Wassende Water'" [Opening of the photography exhibition 'Document the Netherlands: Rising Water']. Ministrie van Verkeer en Waterstaat, speech transcript, November 28, 2008.

———. "De presentatie van het advies van de deltacommissie" [Presentation of Delta

Commission's Advice]. Ministrie van Verkeer en Waterstaat, speech transcript, September 3, 2008.
———. "50-jarig bestaan van UNESCO-IHE" [UNESCO-IHE's 50-year anniversary]. Ministrie van Verkeer en Waterstaat, speech transcript, June 13, 2007.
———. "Lancering van de Watercanon" [Water canon launch]. Ministrie van Verkeer en Waterstaat, speech transcript, December 16, 2008.
———. "Ministerial Roundtable on Bridging the Water and Climate Agenda." Ministrie van Verkeer en Waterstaat, speech transcript, March 21, 2009.
———. "Natura 2000-beheerplan" [Natura 2000 management plan]. Ministrie van Verkeer en Waterstaat, speech transcript, March 2, 2009.
———. "Ondertekening Nationaal Bestuursakkoord Water" [National Water Administration Agreement]. Ministrie van Verkeer en Waterstaat, speech transcript, June 25, 2008.
———. "Opening Nationaal Landschapscentrum" [National Landscape Center opening]. Ministrie van Verkeer en Waterstaat, speech transcript, June 20, 2008.
———. "Symposium 700-jarig bestaan waterschap Groot-Salland" [Symposium 700-year anniversary of Groot-Salland water board]. Ministrie van Verkeer en Waterstaat, speech transcript, June 4, 2008.
———. "Toespraak bij de Deltatop 2008" [Speech at Deltatop 2008]. Ministrie van Verkeer en Waterstaat, speech transcript, November 3, 2008.
———. "World Water Week." Ministrie van Verkeer en Waterstaat, speech transcript, August 20, 2009.
———. "World Water Week High-Level Policy Debate." Ministrie van Verkeer en Waterstaat, speech transcript, August 21, 2008.
Hulsman, Bernard. "Het recht op lelijkheid" [The right to ugliness]. *NRC Handelsblad*, February 10, 1995, 2.
IAmsterdam. "Canal Life." Amsterdam Partners tourism promotional webpage. Accessed August 18, 2009. http://www.iamsterdam.com.
Iedema, Wouter. "Leegte maakt IJsselmeer nog niet nutteloos" [Emptiness doesn't make IJssel Lake fruitless]. *De Volkskrant*, December 4, 1996: sec. Forum, 11.
Illich, Ivan. *H$_2$O and the Waters of Forgetfulness*. Dallas: Dallas Institute of Humanities and Culture, 1985.
"Inwoners Amsterdam blij met festiviteiten" [Amsterdam residents happy with festivities]. *Het Parool*, August 11, 2000: sec. Kunst, 2.
Janssen, Caspar. "Bootje varen, biertje drinken" [Sail boat, drink beer]. *De Volkskrant*, April 28, 2007: sec. De Verleiding, 4–5.
Janssen, Caspar, and Marcel van Lieshout. "Biesbosch 'gebaat' bij wateroverlast" [Biesbosch "profits" from flooding]. *De Volkskrant*, May 7, 2008: sec. Binnenland, 2.
Janssen, Remco. "Stadsdeel Centrum wil passagiersvervoer over water stimuleren" [Center Borough wants to stimulate passenger transport over water]. *Het Parool*, December 6, 2005: sec. Amsterdam, 13.
Kaika, Maria. *City of Flows: Modernity, Nature, and the City*. New York: Routledge, 2005.
Kan, Willemijn R. "Kunst bloeit op tussen staal en beton" [Art blossoms between steel and concrete]. *Trouw*, July 3, 2008: sec. De gids, 12.
Kanter, James. "As Sea Levels Rise, Dutch See Floating Cities." *New York Times*, October 27, 2009. Accessed October 28, 2009. http://green.blogs.nytimes.com/2009/10/27/as-sea-levels-rise-dutch-see-floating-cities/.

Katstra, Judith. "Themajaar 'Amsterdam, stad aan het water' begonnen" [Theme year "Amsterdam, city on the water" begun]. *Algemeen Nederlands Persbureau*, March 1, 2005: sec. Binnenland.

Katz, Cindi. "Whose Nature, Whose Culture?" In *Remaking Reality: Nature at the Millennium*, edited by Bruce Braun and Noel Castree, 46–63. New York: Routledge, 1998.

Keessen, Jurjen. "Het is te vroeg om het Groene Hart af te schrijven" [It is too early to write off the Green Heart]. *De Volkskrant*, January 28, 1995.

Kempton, Richard. *Provo: Amsterdam's Anarchist Revolt*. New York: Autonomedia, 2007.

Kennedy, James C. "Building New Babylon: Cultural Change in the Netherlands during the 1960s." PhD diss., University of Iowa, 1995.

Keulemans, Chris. "Een strandpaviljoen van strobalen" [A straw bale beach pavilion]. *De Volkskrant*, March 22, 2001: sec. Kunst en Cultuur, 25.

Kinder, Kimbereley. "Planning by Intermediaries: Making Cities Make Nature in Amsterdam." *Environment and Planning A* 43, no. 10, (2011): 2435–51.

Klipp, Mijntje. "Eilandtoerisme" [Island Tourism]. *Het Parool*, June 1, 2002, 8–13.

Klipp, Mijntje, and Paul Vugts. "Broedplaatsen voor artistieke trekvogels" [Breeding grounds for artistic birds of passage]. *Het Parool*, January 7, 2000: sec. Amsterdam, 4.

Kloos, Maarten, and Yvonne de Korte, eds. *Mooring Site Amsterdam: Life on Water*. Amsterdam: ARCAM, 2007.

Kloosterman, Robert. "Amsterdamned: The Rise of Unemployment in Amsterdam in the 1980s." *Urban Studies* 31, no. 8 (1994): 1325–44.

———. "Planning for Creativity: The Transformation of the Amsterdam Eastern Docklands." In *New Urbanism: Life, Work, and Space in the New Downtown*, edited by Ilse Helbrecht and Peter Dirksmeier, 61–85. Surrey, UK: Ashgate, 2012.

Koele, Theo. "Bloot en rood op de paradeboot" [Naked and pink on the parade boat]. *De Volkskrant*, August 3, 2009: sec. Binnenland, 3.

Koelewijn, Jannetje, and Merel Thie. "De man die Willem-Alexander als koning aflevert" [The man Willem-Alexander delivers as king]. *NRC Handelsblad*, April 28, 2008: sec. Binnenland, 2.

Koemans, Martin. "Het dorpsplein van de oostelijke havens" [The village square of the Eastern Docklands]. *Het Parool*, May 16, 1994, 9.

Koert, Dea. "De pakhuizen en de woonbootfolklore" [Warehouses and houseboat folklore]. *NRC Handelsblad*, October 20, 1994: sec. Opinie, 9.

Koldenhof, Erik. "Welstand op het water" [Well-being on the water]. Amsterdam: Gemeente Amsterdam Stadsdeel Centrum, report, 2009.

Koper, Arnold. "Bizar dat een huis niet op een huis mag lijken" [Bizarre that one house cannot look like another house]. *De Volkskrant*, June 29, 2002, 15.

Koster, Egbert. *The Eastern Docklands in Amsterdam*. Amsterdam: ARCAM, 1995.

Kramer, Tijn. "Truckers van het water" [Truckers of the water]. *NRC Handelsblad*, June 15, 2000: sec. Agenda, 23.

Kreling, Tom. "De pioniers zijn de werkelijkheid tegengekomen" [The pioneers met reality]. *NRC Handelsblad*, February 23, 2007: sec. Binnenland, 3.

———. "Een boterham, parkeerplaats of gracht" [A sandwich, parking space or canal]. *NRC Handelsblad*, July 1, 2004: sec. Binnenland 3.

———. "Heeft grachtengordel grachten zat?" [Does the canal belt have enough canals?]. *NRC Handelsblad*, September 30, 2004: sec. Binnenland, 7.

Krol, Bertine. "Preserving Amsterdam's Heritage." Dutch Horizons radio program. *Radio Nederland Wereldomroep*. September 12, 2006. Accessed October 12, 2009. http://www.rnw.nl.

Kropman, Rosanne. "Natuur gebaat bij komst IJburg" [Nature profits from IJburg arrival]. *Het Parool*, October 30 2009: sec. Amsterdam, 11.

Kuijken, Wim. "De waterschapsdag" [District water board day]. Ministrie van Verkeer en Waterstaat. Speech transcript, October 8, 2007.

Kuiken, Alwin. "Gemeente vestigt hoop op revolutionaire ideeën van de Amerikaan William McDonough" [City Council focuses on revolutionary ideas from American William McDonough]. *Het Parool*, February 5, 2010: sec. Amsterdam, 13.

———. "IJburg II kan er toch snel komen" [IJburg II may still come quickly]. *Het Parool*, February 5, 2010. Accessed March 26, 2014. http://www.parool.nl/parool/nl/4/AMSTERDAM/article/detail/278240/2010/02/05/IJburg-II-kan-er-toch-snel-komen.dhtml.

Kuipers, Marieke. "Fragile Structures: The City as Cultural Heritage." In Deben, Salet, and Van Thoor, *Cultural Heritage and the Future*, 84–100.

Lahaise, Joop. "Bij Clown Parade was het even druk geweest" [It was just as busy as the Clown Parade]. *Het Parool*, August 5, 2009: sec. Meningen, 99.

———. "Woonboten bepalen het gezicht van Amsterdam" [Houseboats determine Amsterdam's face]. *NRC Handelsblad*, October 20, 1994: sec. Opinie, 9.

Lambert, Audrey. *The Making of the Dutch Landscape: An Historical Geography of the Netherlands*. London: Academic Press, 1985.

Latour, Bruno. *Reassembling the Social: An Introduction to Actor-Network-Theory*. Oxford: Oxford University Press, 2007.

Lave, Rebecca. *Fields and Streams: Stream Restoration, Neoliberalism, and the Future of Environmental Science*. Athens: University of Georgia Press, 2012.

Leitner, Helga, Eric Sheppard, and Kristin Sciarto. "The Spatialities of Contentious Politics." *Transactions of the Institute of British Geographers* 33, no. 2 (2008): 157–72.

Leven met Water. "Jaarbericht 2009" [Annual report 2009]. Stichting Leven met Water, report project number K20108. Accessed July 18, 2014. http://www.levenmetwater.nl.home.

Levine, Marc V. "Downtown Redevelopment as an Urban Growth Strategy: A Critical Appraisal of the Baltimore Renaissance." *Journal of Urban Affairs* 9, no. 2 (1987): 103–23.

———. "'A Third-World City in the First World': Social Exclusion, Racial Inequality, and Sustainable Development in Baltimore." In *The Social Sustainability of Cities: Diversity and the Management of Change*, edited by Mario Polese and Richard Stren, 123–56. Toronto: University of Toronto Press, 2000.

Linton, Jamie. *What Is Water? The History of a Modern Abstraction*. Vancouver: University of British Columbia Press, 2010.

Lokker, Jan P. "Rust voor de stedeling, brood voor de boer" [Peace for the urbanites, bread for the farmer]. *Trouw*, April 13, 2006: sec. Podium, 11.

Lowenthal, David. *The Heritage Crusade and the Spoils of History*. Cambridge: Cambridge University Press, 1998.

Luttik, Joke. "The Value of Trees, Water, and Open Space as Reflected by House Prices in the Netherlands." *Landscape and Urban Planning* 48, no. 3–4 (2000): 161–67.

Lyall, Sarah. "At Risk from Floods, but Looking Ahead with Floating Houses." *New York Times*, April 3, 2007, F5.
Mak, Geert. *Amsterdam: A Brief Life of the City*. Amsterdam: Uitgeverij Atlas, 1995.
———. "Het wateraanzicht van zuipcentra" [The water view from booze central]. *NRC Handelsblad*, December 13, 1994, 9.
———. "Nostalgia and Modernity." In Deben, Salet, and Van Thoor, *Cultural Heritage and the Future*, 13–22.
———. "Sijtje Boes tegen wil en dank" [Reluctant Sijtje Boes]. *NRC Handelsblad*, July 27, 1992, 13–14.
Mamadouh, Virginie (associate professor, University of Amsterdam). Interview by the author, August 22, 2008, and April 28, 2009.
Manshanden, Walter, and Jan Lambooy. "Innovation in the Amsterdam Region." In *Innovative Cities*, edited by James Simmie, 129–53. New York: Routledge, 2001.
Margry, Peter J. "Ethnology and Folklore in the Netherlands." Meertens Instituut. Entry for *World Encyclopedia on Folklore*, 2005. Accessed October 13, 2009. http://www.meertens.knaw.nl/meertensnet/file/peterjanm/20050203/The_Netherlands_in_World_Encyclopedia_on_Folklore.pdf.
Marijnissen, Hans. "Blauwe Hart wordt wegrestaurant voor vogels" [Blue Heart is wayside restaurant for birds]. *Trouw*, September 8, 2009: sec. Nederland, 6.
———. "Buitendijks bouwen helpt de natuur" [Building outside dikes helps nature]. *Trouw*, October 28, 2009.
———. "In het lab van IJburg is bijna alles mogelijk" [In the IJburg lab almost everything is possible]. *Trouw*, October 28, 2009.
Mason, Randall. *The Once and Future New York: Historic Preservation and the Modern City*. Minneapolis: University of Minnesota Press, 2009.
Massey, Doreen B. *For Space*. London: Sage, 2005.
Matless, David. *Landscape and Englishness*. London: Reaktion Books, 1998.
McAllister, Shannon. "What Is Queen's Day? The Story behind the Biggest Holiday in the Netherlands." About.com., n.d. Accessed June 12, 2009. http://goamsterdam.about.com/od/eventsfestivalsholidays/a/queensday.htm.
Mele, Christopher. *Selling the Lower East Side: Culture, Real Estate, and Resistance in New York City*. Minneapolis: University of Minnesota Press, 2000.
Merrifield, Andy. *Dialectical Urbanism*. New York: Monthly Review Press, 2002.
Metz, Tracy. "Red de wereld en bouw op water" [Save the world and build on water]. *NRC Next*, December 22, 2009.
———. "Zelfgemaakt verleden" [Self-made past]. *NRC Handelsblad*, December 6, 2002: 21.
Metz, Tracy, and Maartje van den Heuvel. *Sweet & Salt: Water and the Dutch*. Rotterdam: NAi, 2012.
Meurs, Paul. "Amsterdam: A Modern Historical City." In Deben, Salet, and Van Thoor, *Cultural Heritage and the Future*, 73–83.
Michel, Han. "*Meer pleinen*" [More squares]. *NRC Handelsblad*, June 15, 1991, 6.
Milieudefensie. "Het IJmeer, een waardevol landschap" [IJ Lake, a valuable landscape]. Milieudefensie, n.d., ca. 2010. Accessed February 25, 2010. http://milieudefensie.nl/weguitbreidingen/ijmeer.
Mitchell, Timothy. "Can the Mosquito Speak?" *Rule of Experts: Egypt, Techno-Politics, Modernity*, 19–54. Berkeley: University of California Press, 2002.

———. *Colonizing Egypt*. Berkeley: University of California Press, 1991.
"Moeraseiland in Amsterdamse gracht" [Marsh island in Amsterdam canal]. *Trouw*, February 28, 1995.
Montag, Sarah. "Vissen in de Elandsgracht" [Fish in the Elands Canal]. *NRC Handelsblad*, September 25, 2004: sec. Zaterdags Bijvoegsel, 19.
Moore, Donald S. *Suffering for Territory: Race, Place, and Power in Zimbabwe*. Durham, N.C.: Duke University Press, 2005.
Moore, Molly. "Rethinking Defenses against Sea's Power: Flood Experts See Lessons in New Orleans." *Washington Post*, September 8, 2005: A22.
Mukerji, Chandra. *Territorial Ambitions and the Gardens of Versailles*. Cambridge: Cambridge University Press, 1997.
Muller, Jaus. "De tijd van blote mannen is voorbij" [The time for naked men has passed]. *NRC Handelsblad*, July 31, 2009: sec. Binnenland, 3.
Musterd, Sako, and Rinus Deurloo. "Amsterdam and the Preconditions for a Creative Knowledge City." *Tijdschrift voor Economische en Sociale Geografie* 97, no. 1 (2006): 80–94.
NatuurMonumenten. "Dossier Natuur in IJmeer en Markermeer" [Report on nature in IJ Lake and Marker Lake]. N.d. Accessed May 21, 2010. http://www.natuurmonumenten.nl.
"Nauwelijks gedrang op vrijmarkt" [Barely jostling on street market]. *Het Parool*, May 2, 1994, 9.
"N(D)SM." *Het Parool*, August 19, 2000, 61.
Neefjes, Jan. "De natuur heeft hier gewonnen" [Nature won here]. *Trouw*, August 29, 2002: sec. Verdieping, 13.
———. "Weidse ruimte in de Randstad" [Grand space in the Urban Ring]. *Trouw*, August 8, 2002, 11.
Nienhuis, Piet H. *Environmental History of the Rhine-Meuse Delta*. Houten, Netherlands: Springer, 2010.
Nieuwenhuis, Marijn. "Hoeckelingsdam: Ruimte voor nieuwe natuur rond IJburg" [Hoeckelings Dam: Space for new nature around IJburg]. Amsterdam: Gemeente Amsterdam Projectbureau IJburg, ca. 2005.
Oldenburg, Ray. *The Great Good Place: Cafes, Coffee Shops, Bookstores, Bars, Hair Salons, and Other Handouts at the Heart of a Community*. New York: Marlowe, 1989.
Oldenburger, Juliet. "Actie 'Open de Grachten' van start gegaan" ["Open the Canals" campaign takes off]. *Binnenstad*, De Vereniging Vrienden van de Amsterdamse Binnenstad, no. 205, 2004.
Oliver, Stuart. "The Thames Embankment and the Disciplining of Nature in Modernity." *Geographical Journal* 166, no. 3 (2000): 227–38.
O'Loughlin, James. "Between Stuttgart and Shefield." In *Understanding Amsterdam: Essays on Economic Vitality, City Life, and Urban Form*, edited by Leon Deben, Willem Heinemeijer, and Dick van der Vaart, 27–68. Amsterdam: Het Spinhuis, 2001.
"Ondanks aanvankelijke scepsis al twintig jaar fietsen door de gracht" [Despite original skepticism, already twenty years cycling through the canals]. *Het Parool*, May 29, 2004: sec. Economie, 35.
O'Neill, Karen. *Rivers by Design: State Power and the Origins of U.S. Flood Control*. Durham, N.C.: Duke University Press, 2006.

Oosterbaan, Warna. "Roem, rijkdom en risico's" [Glory, wealth, and risks]. *NRC Handelsblad*, November 29, 2008: sec. Thema, 2–3.

"Oranjegekte vooral te water" [Orange insanity especially on water]. *Het Parool*, May 1, 1998, 1.

Osman, Suleiman. *The Invention of Brownstone Brooklyn: Gentrification and the Search for Authenticity in Postwar New York*. Oxford: Oxford University Press, 2011.

Overduin, Irene. "Als het water stijgt floreert de arkenbouw" [Houseboat construction thrives if water rises]. *Leeuwarder Courant*, April 22, 2003.

"Overlast Gay-parade aan banden" [Gay Parade to curb nuisance]. *Het Parool*, June 21, 2001: sec. Amsterdam, 5.

Palca, Joe. "Dutch Architects Plan for a Floating Future." *All Things Considered*, National Public Radio, January 28, 2008. Accessed December 10, 2010. http://www.npr.org.

Pama, Gretha. "'Stok-en-worst' politiek in Groene Hart" ["Stick-and-sausage" politics in the Green Heart]. *NRC Handelsblad*, November 1, 1995: sec. Binnenland, 6.

Partners Overhoeks. "Over de partners" [Over the Partners]. N.d., ca. late 2000s. Accessed November 24, 2009. http://www.overhoeks.nl.

Pas, Niek. *Imaazje: De verbeelding van Provo, 1965–1967*. Amsterdam: Wereldbibliotheek, 2003.

PBL Netherlands Environmental Assessment Agency. "Correction Wording Flood Risks for the Netherlands in IPCC Report." Report correction, February 2010. Accessed December 17, 2010. http://www.pbl.nl/en/dossiers/Climatechange/content/correction-wording-flood-risks.html.

"Perspectief voor IJ- en Markermeer" [Prospect for IJ and Marker Lake]. *Noordhollands Dagblad*, July 8, 2008: sec. Region.

Peters, Leonie, and Rita Oppenhuizen. *50X Naar Buiten! Ontdek de natuur rondom IJburg* [50x Outside! Discover the nature around IJburg]. Amsterdam: Gemeente Amsterdam Projectbureau IJburg, promotional booklet, 2009.

Pickles, John. *A History of Spaces: Cartographic Reason, Mapping, and the Geo-Coded World*. New York: Routledge, 2004.

Pistor, Rob. "The Amsterdam Challenge: Can a Historic Inner City Survive as a Modern Metropolis?" In Deben, Salet, and Van Thoor, *Cultural Heritage and the Future*, 270–83.

———, ed. *A City in Progress*. Translated by Harold Alexander. Amsterdam: Dienst Ruimtijke Ordering, 1994.

"Plan voor sloop pand 'Einde van de Wereld'" [Plans to demolish "End of the World" building]. *Het Parool*, May 5, 1994, 15.

"Prinsengracht in Amsterdam is vol" [Prince's Canal in Amsterdam is full]. *Het Parool*, August 21, 2010. Accessed November 7, 2010. http://www.parool.nl/parool/nl/23/MUZIEK/article/detail/1003939/2010/08/21/Deel-Prinsengracht-in-Amsterdam-is-vol.dhtml.

ProGay Foundation. "Recordaantal bezoekers Amsterdam Gay Pride" [Record number of guests at Amsterdam Gay pride]. ProGay Foundation press release, August 1, 2009. Accessed July 18, 2014. http://www.progay.nl/nieuws.html?id=120.

Pruijt, Hans. "The Impact of Citizens' Protest on City Planning in Amsterdam." In Deben, Salet, and Van Thoor, *Cultural Heritage and the Future*, 228–40.

Pullens, Rick. "Amsterdam lokt toerist met water" [Amsterdam lures tourists with water]. *De Telegraaf*, August 13, 2004, 31.

Raffles, Hugh. *In Amazonia: A Natural History*. Princeton: Princeton University Press, 2002.
"Regels voor boten op Koninginnedag" [Rules for boats on Queen's Day]. *Radio+TV Noord-Holland*, June 12, 2009. Accessed July 10, 2014. http://www.rtvnh.nl /nieuws/35046/Regels+voor+boten+op+Koninginnedag.
Reisner, Marc. *Cadillac Desert: The American West and Its Disappearing Water*. New York: Penguin, 1993.
"Remco Daalder je probeert natuur in stad te proppen" [Remco Daalder you try to cram nature into the city]. *Metro NL*, November 11, 2009: sec. Amsterdam.
Remkes, Xander. "Nadruk bij botenparade ligt op saamhorigheid van homo's en hetero's" [Boat parade emphasis on queer and straight unity]. *De Volkskrant*, August 4, 1997, 12.
"Rental Housing Points System." Rijksoverheid. Accessed March 29, 2014. http://www .rijksoverheid.nl/onderwerpen/huurwoning/puntensysteem-huurwoning.
Ricklefs, M. C. *A History of Modern Indonesia since c. 1300*. Stanford: Stanford University Press, 1993.
Rijcken, Ties. "Innovatie vertroebelt waterbeheer" [Innovation obscures water management]. *De Volkskrant*, February 12, 2008: sec. Forum, 12.
Rombouts, Ron. "De kop van noord" [The northern head]. *Het Parool*, November 6, 2003: sec. PS, 5.
———. "We pielen en zieken niet, zegt Cohen" [We don't piddle and puke, says Cohen]. *Het Parool*, April 29, 2009: sec. Amsterdam, 2.
"Rondvaart A'dam populairste uitje" [Boat tour through A'Dam most popular outing]. *NRC Handelsblad*, May 22, 2007: sec. Binnenland, 7.
Rooijendijk, Cordula. *The City Is Mine! Urban Ideal Images in Public Debates and City Plans, Amsterdam and Rotterdam, 1945–1995*. Amsterdam: Amsterdam University Press, 2005.
———. "The Narrow-Mindedness of Contemporary Devotees of Cultural Heritage: Cultural Urban Heritage in Images of Amsterdam in the 1950s and 1990s." In Deben, Salet, and Van Thoor, *Cultural Heritage and the Future*, 298–310.
RTV. "Rotterdam wil 1300 drijvende woningen" [Rotterdam wants 1,300 floating homes]. *Radio and Television Rijnmond*, May 21, 2010. Accessed December 17, 2010. http://www.rijnmond.nl/Homepage/Nieuws?view=/News%2FDefault%2F2010 %2Fmei%2FDrijvende%20bollen%200p%20de%20Maas.
Salm, Nico P. "Geen stadsuitbreiding in het Blauwe Hart" [No urban expansion in the Blue Heart]. *Het Parool*, March 4, 1994: 21.
Sanders, Martijn. "Met een bootje de Nederlandse grachten op" [In a boat on the Netherlands' canals]. *De Volkskrant*, October 20, 2001: sec. Economie, E2.
Schama, Simon. *The Embarrassment of Riches: An Interpretation of Dutch Culture in the Golden Age*. New York: Vintage Books, 1987.
Schipper, Aldert. "Homo-spektakel eind juni in Amsterdam" [Queer spectacle in end June Amsterdam]. *Trouw*, June 11, 1994, 9.
Schmit, Hans. "Onze doelstelling is verdubbeling van de natuur om 35 jaar verlies goed te maken" [Our goal is to double nature to correct 35 years of loss]. *Trouw*, August 11, 1995.
Schoof, Rob. "Midwolda wordt een badplaats" [Midwolda becomes a bathtub]. *NRC Handelsblad*, May 6, 2005: sec. Binnenland, 2.

Schoonenberg, Walter (chairman, De Vereniging Vrienden van de Amsterdamse Binnenstad). Interview by the author, August 22, 2008.

———. "Amsterdam, een waterstad" [Amsterdam, a water city]. Walter Schoonenberg, website. Accessed March 31, 2010. http://www.onderdekeizerskroon.nl /wschoonenberg/water2.html (no longer accessible).

———. "Burgerinitiatief ElandsGRACHT ingediend" [Elands Canal citizen initiative submitted]. Amsterdam: De Vereniging Vrienden van de Amsterdamse Binnenstad, press release, December 16, 2005.

———. "Eerste stap gezet op weg naar een referendum over het opengraven van een gracht" [First step put on road to a referendum over the excavation of a canal]. *Binnenstad*, De Vereniging Vrienden van de Amsterdamse Binnenstad, no. 215, 2006.

———. "Hergraven van gedempte grachten: Deelraad besluit tot haalbaarheidsonderzoek" [Excavating filled canals: District council rounds off feasibility study]. *Binnenstad*, De Vereniging Vrienden van de Amsterdamse Binnenstad, no. 203, 2003.

———. "Hergraven van grachten: Nu is het College aan zet" [Canal excavation: Now it is the Board's move]. De Vereniging Vrienden van de Amsterdamse Binnenstad, press release, February 28, 2002.

———. "Het Waterplan Amsterdam" [Amsterdam Water Plan]. *Binnenstad*, De Vereniging Vrienden van de Amsterdamse Binnenstad, no. 181, 2000.

———. "Opengraven grachten: Belangrijke feiten op een rijtje" [Excavate canals: Important facts straightened out]. *Binnenstad*, De Vereniging Vrienden van de Amsterdamse Binnenstad, no. 206, 2004.

———. "Schriftelijke inspraakbijdrage opengraven grachten" [Excavate canals written contribution]. De Vereniging Vrienden van de Amsterdamse Binnenstad, open letter, September 29, 2004.

———. "Waterplan: De waterscheidingen worden eindelijk doorbroken" [Water Plan: The water impasse is finally broken]. De Vereniging Vrienden van de Amsterdamse Binnenstad, open letter, September 3, 2001.

———. "Without Reconstruction, No Inner City." In Deben, Salet, and Van Thoor, *Cultural Heritage and the Future*, 133–48.

Schreuder, Arjen. "Alleen op papier is het Groene Hart nog heilig" [Only on paper is the Green Heart still holy]. *NRC Handelsblad*, March 16, 2007: sec. Binnenland, 2.

Schubert, Dick. "Waterfront Revitalizations: From a Local to a Regional Perspective in London, Barcelona, Rotterdam, and Hamburg." In *Transforming Urban Waterfronts: Fixity and Flow*, edited by Gene Desfor, Jennefer Laidley, Quentin Stevens, and Dirk Schubert, 74–97. New York: Routledge, 2011.

Schuerfeld, Arno. "Alleen buitenstaanders willen Jordaangracht" [Only outsiders want Jordaan canal]. *NRC Handelsblad*, October 7, 2004: sec. Opinie, 8.

———. "'Blauwe hart' moet het nationale belang dienen" ["Blue Heart" must serve national interest]. *NRC Handelsblad*, September 10, 2008: sec. Binnenland, 2.

———. "De natte natuur is niet welkom" [Wet nature is not welcome]. *NRC Handelsblad*, December 12, 2009: sec. Weekbad Reportage.

———. "Extra natuur creëren, om die later weer te kunnen aantasten" [Create extra nature to harm later]. *NRC Handelsblad*, May 29, 2008: sec. Binnenland, 6.

———. "Sissende zwanen (no. 1)" [Hissing Swans]. *NRC Handelsblad*, January 31, 2009: sec. Zaterdags Bijvoegsel, 11.

———. "Sissende zwanen (no. 2)" [Hissing swans]. *NRC Handelsblad*, February 5, 2009. Accessed April 11, 2010. http://vorige.nrc.nl/achtergrond/article2137619.ece.

———. "Strijd om 't blauwe hart van Nederland" [Battle over the blue heart of the Netherlands]. *NRC Handelsblad*, March 15, 2008: sec. Binnenland, 3.

Schulte, Addie. "Bootjes volgens stadsdeel Zeeburg bron van lawaai, schade en gevaar" [Boats according Zeeburg source of noise, damage and danger]. *Het Parool*, March 18, 2009: sec. Amsterdam, 1.

———. "Soeters houdt grachtje liever open, maar ach" [Soeters prefer to keep canal open, but oh well]. *Het Parool*, March 26, 2009: sec. Amsterdam, 15.

Schuwer, Dries. "Wonen op het water: Succes- en faalfactoren" [Living on the water: success—and failure—factors]. Wageningen University, 2007. Accessed February 25, 2010. http://waterarchitect.nl/download/Rapport_Wonen_op_het_water_-_succes_en_faalfactoren.pdf.

Seegers, Co (head of the Economic History and New Social Movements archives, International Institute for Social History). Interview by the author, August 25, 2008.

Sekeris, Rinder. "Huizinga: Binnenvaart heeft veel toekomst" [Huizinga: Inland navigation has much future]. *Nederlands Dagblad*, June 15, 2007, 3.

Sellers, Frances S. "Changing Course to Go with the Flow." *Washington Post*, September 11, 2005, B02.

———. "In Man versus Water, a Shift in Tactics." *Washington Post*, December 24, 2000, B02.

Sevil, Malika. "Honderd euro is voor Shell niet echt een problem" [A hundred euro is really not a problem for Shell]. *Het Parool*, August 4, 2006: sec. Amsterdam, 14.

———. "Meer dan de allure van een greppel" [More than the air of a ditch]. *Het Parool*, April 8, 1999: sec. Amsterdam, 4.

———. "Plensbuien deren Gay Pride niet" [Downpour doesn't bother Gay Pride]. *Het Parool*, August 8, 2005: sec. Amsterdam, 5.

———. "Vogelnest op boot heeft rechten" [Bird nests on boats have rights]. *Het Parool*, April 30, 2009: sec. Amsterdam, 13.

Shaw, Kate. "The Place of Alternative Culture and the Politics of Its Protection in Berlin, Amsterdam and Melbourne." *Planning Theory & Practice* 6, no. 2 (2005): 149–69.

Sijmons, Dirk. "In IJburg valt voor mens en natuur veel te beleven" [In IJburg there's something for people and nature]. *NRC Handelsblad*, March 7, 1997, 7.

Slager, Seije. "Hoe groen wordt waterbestuur?" [How green is water management?]. *Trouw*, December 1, 2008: sec. Nederland, 4–5.

———. "Invloed van waterschapskiezer onzichtbaar in nieuwe besturen" [Influence of water voters unclear in new administration]. *Trouw*, January 16, 2009: sec. Nederland, 4–5.

Smit, Marieke, and Pieter Nieuwenhuijsen. "Burgerinitiatief over opengraven Elandsgracht misbruikt door teleurgestelde buitenstaanders" [Citizens initiative over Elands Canal excavation abused by disappointed outsiders]. *Het Parool*, January 12, 2006: sec. Menningen, 19.

Smit, Tamara (project manager, Projectbureau IJburg), and Edwin Meisner (project manager of engineering, Projectbureau IJburg). Interview by the author, June 9, 2010.

Smith, Neil. *The New Urban Frontier: Gentrification and the Revanchist City*. London: Routledge, 1996.

Smits, Geertjan (Natuurmonumenten). Interview by the author, June 10, 2010.
Snoeijen, Monique. "Ketting dreigt voor uitgeprocedeerde woonboot" [Arrest threatens houseboater exhausted of all legal procedures]. *NRC Handelsblad*, December 29, 1997: sec. Binnenland, 2.
Soja, Edward. "The Stimulus of a Little Confusion: A Contemporary Comparison of Amsterdam and Los Angeles." In *After Modernism: Global Restructuring and the Changing Boundaries of City Life*, edited by Michael P. Smith, 17–38. New Brunswick, N.J.: Transaction, 1992.
Somers, Maartje. "Vrolijke anarchie op het water" [Festive anarchy on the water]. *Het Parool*, June 9, 1998: sec. Festivals, 20.
Spaans, Vera, and Joris Thomassen. "Meeste schippers kennen de regels niet" [Most skippers don't know the rules]. *Het Parool*, July 21, 2005: sec. Amsterdam, 18.
Spaargaren, Ruut. "Ontsierende woonboten" [Houseboat eyesores]. *Het Parool*, May 20, 2009: sec. Meningen, 31.
Spel, Mischa. "Een man met een piano krijgt de hele gracht stil" [One man with one piano holds the whole canal still]. *NRC Handelsblad*, August 20, 2001: sec. Kunst, 8.
Spoek, Paul (Amsterdams Boten Comité). Interview by the author, June 7, 2010.
Staal, Herman. "Oost-Groningen wil aantrekkelijk worden" [East-Groningen wants to become attractive]. *NRC Handelsblad*, January 23, 1996, 3.
Stadig, Duco. "Maakbare stad?" [Making the City?]. *PlanAmsterdam*, Gemeente Amsterdam Dienst Ruimtelijke Ordening, no. 2, 2005.
"'Stadschagrijnen' verjagen homotoerist" ["City chagrin" chases away queer tourists]. *De Volkskrant*, August 3, 2002: sec. Binnenland, 3.
Steenbergen, Clemens M. *The Polder Atlas of the Netherlands*. Loughboroug, UK: THOTH, 2009.
Stegenga, Herre. "Snel stappen nemen om het 'blauwe hart van de Randstad' te creeren" [Take quick steps to create the 'Blue Heart of the Urban Ring']. *Dagblad Flevoland*, September 9, 2009, 21.
Steinmetz, Bert. "Archipel Amsterdam" [Amsterdam Archipeligo]. *Het Parool*, May 18, 2002, 8–15.
———. "Driehonderd Jordanezen en andere binnenstadsbewoners discussieren over grachten open of dicht" [Three hundred Jordaanese and other inner city residents discuss open or closed canals]. *Het Parool*, September 30, 2004: sec. Amsterdam, 13.
———. "Erfgoed mag van stad geen museum maken" [Inheritance mustn't make a museum from a city]. *Het Parool*, December 23, 2002: sec. Amsterdam, 5.
———. "Extra plaatsen, maar ook extra regels" [Extra spaces, but also extra rules]. *Het Parool*, May 26, 2005: sec. Amsterdam, 15.
———. Untitled article. *Het Parool*, October 30, 2009. sec. PS, 18.
Steutel, Willemijn. "Uitzicht op de gracht levert flink geld op" [Canal views deliver cash]. *De Volkskrant*, July 15, 2004: sec. Binnenland, 3.
Stevens, Quentin. "The German 'City Beach' as a New Approach to Waterfront Development." In *Transforming Urban Waterfronts: Fixity and Flow*, edited by Gene Desfor, Jennefer Laidley, Quentin Stevens, and Dirk Schubert, 235–56. Abingdon: Routledge, 2011.
Stichting Wetlands. "Kengetallen kosten-batenanalyse Wetlands in het Ijsselmeer" [Key figures of cost-benefit analysis of wetlands in the IJssel Lake]. Stichting Wetlands in het Ijsselmeer, report, 2007.

———. "Wetlands in het IJsselmeer, thema Economie: Tussenrapport "Maatschappelijke functies wetlands" [Wetlands in IJssel Lake, Economy theme: Interim report "Wetland social functions"]. Stichting Wetlands in het Ijsselmeer, report, 2006.

Stuart, Barbara, ed. "Markermeer IJmeer; LelyNatuur en Waterpark" [Marker Lake IJ Lake: LelyNature and Waterpark]. NatuurMonumenten, report, 2008. Accessed May 21, 2010. https://www.natuurmonumenten.nl/sites/default/files/LelyNatuur_en_Waterpark.pdf.

Swyngedouw, Erik. "Modernity and Hybridity: Nature, Regeneracionismo, and the Production of the Spanish Waterscape, 1890–1930." *Annals of the Association of American Geographers* 89, no. 3 (1999): 443–65.

———. *Social Power and the Urbanization of Water: Flows of Power.* New York: Oxford University Press, 2004.

Tagliabue, John. "Canal Life: Too Rich for Hans Brinker, and for Hippies." *New York Times*, August 14, 2007, 4.

———. "A Low Country Seeks Higher Ground." *New York Times*, November 7, 2008, 15.

———. "A Rising Tide of Gentrification Rocks Dutch Houseboats." *New York Times*, August 14, 2007. Accessed May 11, 2008. http://www.nytimes.com/2007/08/14/world/europe/14houseboat.html.

Ten Haaft, Gonny. "De slag om de waterkant" [The battle over the waterfront]. *Trouw*, February 10, 2000: sec. De Verdieping, 13.

———. "Het water lonkt" [Water beckons]. *Trouw*, August 27, 2001: sec. De Verdieping, 13.

———. "Overspoeld door verandering" [Overrun with change]. *Trouw*, April 26, 2001: sec. De Verdieping, 13.

Ter Borg, Lucette. "Amsterdamse grachtenbussen zitten vol toeristen" [Amsterdam canal busses are full of tourists]. *NRC Handelsblad*, September 2, 1993, 4.

Terhorst, Pieter, Jacques van de Ven, and Leon Deben. "Amsterdam: It's All in the Mix." In *Cities and Visitors: Regulating People, Markets, and City Space*, edited by Lilly Hoffman, Susan Fainstein, and Dennis Judd, 75–91. Malden, Mass.: Blackwell, 2003.

Teune, Willem. "Housing in Amsterdam 2009: Eerste resultaten" [Initial results]. Gemeente Amsterdam Dienst Wonen, December 2009. Accessed March 29, 2014. http://www.afwc.nl/templates/afwc/images/files/wia_2013_factsheet_eerste_resultaten.pdf.

Tienhooven, Gudo. "Drijvende woonwijk in onder water gezette polder" [Floating neighborhood in polder set under water]. *Algemeen Dagblad*, June 20, 2008: sec. Bibuo8, 9.

Timar, Endre, ed. "De IJburg Principes: Voor een duurzame Amsterdamse wijk" [The IJburg principles: For a sustainable Amsterdam neighborhood]. Amsterdam: Gemeente Amsterdam Projectbureau IJburg. Promotional brochure, June 10, 2010.

TripOut. "2009 TripOut Gay Travel." TripOut Gay Travel, n.d., ca. 2009. Accessed November 12, 2009. http://www.tripoutgaytravel.com.

"2 minuten" [2 minutes]. *Algemeen Dagblad*, April 23, 2009: sec. Achter, 36.

Tyrpakova, Darina, ed. "De Amsterdamse grachten" [The Amsterdam Canals]. Amsterdam Guide, n.d. Accessed June 12, 2009. http://www.amsterdam.info/nl/grachten/.

Uitermark, Justus. "The Co-optation of Squatters in Amsterdam and the Emergence of a Movement Meritocracy." *International Journal of Urban and Regional Research*, 28 no. 3 (2004): 687–98.

———. "Framing Urban Injustices." *Space and Polity* 8, no. 2 (2004): 227–44.

Valk, M. "Amsterdam voorgoed van IJ gescheiden" [Amsterdam divorced from the IJ for good]. *Het Parool*, January 30, 2010: sec. Meningen, 50.

Van Beek, Thea. "Er moet weer grachtenwater gaan stromen" [Canal water must stream again]. Dagblad van het Noorden, September 28, 2000.

Van Brummelen, Peter. "Nog steeds Amsterdam" [Still Amsterdam]. *Het Parool*, March 28, 2009: sec. ps van de week, 18.

Van Dalen, Frank (president, ProGay Foundation). Interview, with Irene Hemelaar (secretary, ProGay Foundation), by the author, September 9, 2009.

Van Dam, Petra (chair of water history, Vrije Universiteit). Interview by the author, April 27, 2009.

Van den Akker, Janne, Hein Sas, Frans Klijn, Mariken Betsema, and Marc Beets. "Wetlands in het Ijsselmeer, thema geo-ecologie" [Wetlands in IJssel Lake Geo-ecology Theme]. Stichting Wetlands in het Ijsselmeer, interim report, March 2006.

Van den Berg, Peter. "We gooien dat gewoon allemaal overboard" [We just throw it all overboard]. *De Volkskrant*, April 29, 1995, 17.

Van den Broek, Marc. "Alle dagen feest" [Every day a party]. *De Volkskrant*, August 22, 2000, 11.

———. "Kuisheidsverklaring geeist van deelnemers homo-parade" [Chastity declaration required from queer-parade participants]. *De Volkskrant*, July 24, 1996, 19.

———. "Moeraseiland brengt zuurstof en natuur in grachten van Amsterdam" [Marsh island brings oxygyn and nature to Amsterdam]. *De Volkskrant*, February 28, 1995.

Van den Broek, Marc, and Rene Didde. "'Ajakkes' beesten in kaart gebracht" ['Ajax'-animals mapped]. *De Volkskrant*, November 13, 1998: sec. Buitenland, 5.

Van den Eerenbeemt, Marc. "Historie herbouwd" [History rebuilt]. *De Volkskrant*, August 31, 2005: sec. Voorkant, 213.

Van der Beek, Hans. "Comite Geen nattigheid" [No wetness committee]. *Het Parool*, December 31, 2004: sec. ps van de week, 44.

Van der Ben, Jan (secretary of Water Natuurlijk, chairman of the Amsterdam chapter of Natuur Monumenten). Interview by the author, June 8, 2010.

Van der Helm, Frans. "Marginale natuur, maar wel veel" [Marginal nature, but lots of it]. *NRC Handelsblad*, September 22, 1994: sec. Wetenschap en onderwijs, 1.

Van der Veer, Jeroen. "Amsterdam Housing Market and the Role of Housing Associations." Paper presented at the Free University Real Estate Economics meeting, Amsterdam, May 12, 2009.

Van der Veer, Jeroen (policy advisor, Amsterdamse federatie van woningcorporaties). Interview by the author, September 8, 2009.

Van der Veer, Jeroen, and Dick Schuiling, "The Amsterdam Housing Market and the Role of Housing Associations." *Journal of Housing and the Built Environment* 20, no. 2 (2005): 167–81.

Van der Wall, Sake. "Vrede woon- en rondvaartboot" [House and tour boat Peace]. *Het Parool*, April 5, 2005: sec. Amsterdam, 15.

Van der Zwaag, Jelle. "Tips voor thuis" [Tips for at home]. *Het Parool*, January 26, 2009: sec. Amsterdam, 12.

Van Dinther, Mac. "Revolutie in de polder" [Revolution on the polder]. *De Volkskrant*, February 21, 2001: sec. Forum, 9.

Van Eijk, Pim. "Groene Hart floreert dankzij het water" [Green Heart flourishes thanks to water]. *Rijn en Gouwe*, April 24, 2004: sec. Zaterdag en Zondag, 70.

Van Eijsbergen, Evelien, Kees Poot, and Isabel van de Geer. "Water Veiligheid" [Water Safety]. Ministerie van Verkeer en Waterstaat, report, 2007.

Van Gelder, Roelof. "De schoonheid lag niet in de grachten" [Beauty doesn't lie in the canals]. *NRC Handelsblad*, January 28, 2010: sec. Boeken, B02.

Van Gelder, Roelof, and Geert Mak. "Tussen Anton Pieck en de bulldozer" [Between Anton Pieck and the Bulldozer]. *NRC Handelsblad*, February 5, 1993, 1, 3.

Van Haastrecht, Ruud. "Op het KNSM-eiland geschieden cultureel opmerkelijke dingen" [On KNSM Island culturally remarkable things are occurring]. *Trouw*, October 14, 1995.

Van Haegen, Melanie S. "Alle zeilen bijzetten, kansen voor regionale ruimtelijke regie in water en ruimtelijke kwaliteit" [Go ahead full, opportunities for regional spatial state control in water and spatial quality]. Ministrie van Verkeer en Waterstaat, speech transcript, August 19, 2005.

———. "Congres 'waterveiligheid in de 21e eeuw'" [Conference "Water safety in the 21st century"]. Ministrie van Verkeer en Waterstaat, speech transcript, July 3, 2006.

———. "Opening of Aquaterra." Ministrie van Verkeer en Waterstaat, speech transcript, February 7, 2007.

———. "Speech by Melanie Schultz van Haegen, Vice Cabinet Minister for Transport, Public Works and Water Management at the World Water Forum in Mexico City at the opening session on Risk Management." Speech transcript, March 21, 2006.

———. "Toespraak van de staatssecretaris van Verkeer en Waterstaat, Melanie Schultz van Haegen, tijdens bijeenkomst 90 jaar Grontmij in het NAi in Rotterdam" [State Secretary Melanie Schultz van Haegen Speech at the Grontmij 90 Years Assembly in NAi in Rotterdam]. Ministrie van Verkeer en Waterstaat, speech transcript, September 5, 2005.

———. "Toespraak van de staatssecretaris van Verkeer en Waterstaat, Melanie Schultz van Haegen, tijdens bijeenkomst Politiek Café VVD in Rotterdam" [Speech by State Secretary Melanie Schultz van Haegen from the Ministry of Transport, Public Works, and Water Management during the Political Café VVD conference in Rotterdam]. Ministrie van Verkeer en Waterstaat, speech transcript, November 7, 2005.

Van Halm, Henk. "Watertuinen in Amsterdamse grachten onder vuur" [Water gardens in Amsterdam canals under fire]. *Trouw*, July 13, 1996.

Van Keken, Kim, "Varende homo ontbloot voornamelijk bovenlijf" [Sailing queers mostly bare-chested]. *De Volkskrant*, August 4, 2003: sec. Binnenland, 3.

———. "Zuipschuit zigzagt in de gracht" [Booze barge zigzags in the canal]. *De Volkskrant*, August 12, 2003: sec. Binnenland, 2.

Van Leeuwen, Bas, Karen Buschman, Koos van Zanen, and Susan Jeurissen. "Op weg naar 2040" [En route to 2040]. *PlanAmsterdam*, Gemeente Amsterdam Dienst Ruimtelijke Ordening, no. 6, 2009.

Van Lieshout, Marcel. "Als het water komt" [When the water comes]. *De Volkskrant*, May 26, 2005: sec. Voorkant, 215.

———. "Tegen de Zeeuwse natuur" [Against Zeeuw's Nature]. *De Volkskrant*, April 21, 2006: sec. Voorkant, 13.

———. "Water bleef water" [Water remains water]. *De Volkskrant*, September 22, 2006: sec. Voorkant, 13.

Van Melik, Rianne G. "Changing Public Space: The Recent Redevelopment of Dutch City Squares." Doctoral thesis, Utrecht University, 2008.

Van Oostrom, Frits. *A Key to Dutch History: Report by the Committee for the Development of the Dutch Canon*. Amsterdam: Amsterdam University Press, 2007.

Van Polegeest, Maarten. "De duurzame metropool" [The sustainable metropolis]. *PlanAmsterdam*, Gemeente Amsterdam Dienst Ruimtelijke Ordening, no. 8, 2007.

Van Rooy, Max. "Amsterdam krijgt nieuwe, lange brug" [Amsterdam receives a new, long bridge]. *NRC Handelsblad*. February 4, 1997, 7.

———. "Door het water ontworpen" [Designed through water]. *NRC Handelsblad*, March 14, 1997, 4.

———. "Een bad dat volloopt" [A filled bath]. *NRC Handelsblad*, June 23, 2000: sec. CS, 31.

———. "Gebouwenduo scharniert tussen eilanden" [Building pair hinges between islands]. *NRC Handelsblad*, January 19, 2002: sec. Kunst, 11.

———. "Ontdemping" [Excavation]. *NRC Handelsblad*, October 8, 2004: sec. CS, 18.

Van Rooy, Peter. "Het waterschap als overheid is uit de tijd" [District water board as government is outdated]. *NRC Handelsblad*, April 9, 2002: sec. Opinie, 8.

Van Rooy, Peter, and Lydia Sterrenberg, eds. "Het blauwe goud verzilveren: Een actualisering" [Capitalizing on Blue Gold: An Update]. Den Haag: Rathenau Institute, 2001.

Van Rooy, Peter, Petrus T. J. C. Rooy, and Lydia Sterrenberg, eds. "Het blauwe goud verzilveren: Integraal waterbeheer en het belang van omdenken" [Capitalizing on Blue Gold: Integrated water management and the importance of a change in thinking]. Den Haag: Rathenau Institute, 2000.

Van Traa, Julie. "Gay Parade: Kijken, keuren en een berouwvolle varende 'paus'" [Gay Parade: look, assess, and a contrite sailing "pope"]. *Het Parool*, August 7, 2000: sec. Economie, 6.

Van Zanden, Jan L. *The Economic History of the Netherlands, 1914–1995: A Small Open Economy in the "Long" Twentieth Century*. New York: Routledge, 1998.

Van Zanden, Jan L., and Arthur van Riel. *Strictures of Inheritance: The Dutch Economy in the Nineteenth Century*. Princeton: Princeton University Press, 2000.

Van Zanen, Koos, and Jos Gadet. "Succesvolle vestigingsplekken" [Successful Business and Living Locations]. *PlanAmsterdam*, Gemeente Amsterdam Dienst Ruimtelijke Ordening, no. 3, 2006.

Van Zee, Wim, Cor Hylkema, Els de Boer, and Jeroen Slot, eds. "Amsterdam in cijfers 2009" [Amsterdam in Figures 2009]. Gemeente Amsterdam Dienst Onderzoek en Statistiek, report, 2009.

Van Zelst, Giel. "Woonboot wordt weer verjaagd" [House boaters are chased away again]. *Het Parool*, May 11, 2009: sec. Meningen, 23.

Van Zoelen, Bart. "Milieupartij wint waterverkiezing" [Environmental party wins water elections]. *Het Parool*, December 1, 2008: sec. Binnenland, 7.

Van Zoest, Johan, and Geert Timmermans. "Amsterdamse biodiversiteit" [Amsterdam's biodiversity]. *PlanAmsterdam*, Gemeente Amsterdam Dienst Ruimtelijke Ordening, no. 8, 2009.

"Varen tegen homohaat" [Sail against queer hate]. *NRC Handelsblad*, August 1, 2008: sec. Opinie, 7.

VenW. "De Delta Aanpak" [The Delta Approach]. Ministerie van Verker en Waterstaat, video, June 27, 2008.

———. "De watercanon: De Nederlandse watergeschiedenis in 25 vensters" [The water canon: The Netherlands' water history in 25 windows]. Ministerie van Verker en Waterstaat, press release, December 16, 2008.

———. "De Watervisie 'Nederland veroveren op de toekomst'" [Water vision, "the Netherlands conquers the future"]. Ministerie van Verker en Waterstaat, report, 2007.

———. "15 experimenten met bouwen in het rivierbed" [15 experiments building in riverbeds]. Ministerie van Verker en Waterstaat, report, 2005.

———. "Flood Protection Policy." Ministerie van Verker en Waterstaat, n.d. Accessed November 5, 2009. http://www.verkeerenwaterstaat.nl/english/topics/water/water_and_safety/ (no longer accessible).

———. "Het Nationaal Waterplan: Een veilige leefbare Delta, nu en in de toekomst" [The National Water Plan: A safe, livable delta, now and in the future]. Ministerie van Verker en Waterstaat, video, December 18, 2008.

———. "Kabinet: 2,8 miljard extra voor anders omgaan met water" [Cabinet: 2.8 billion extra for a different approach to water]. Ministerie van Verker en Waterstaat, press release, December 18, 2000.

———. "Nederland en Vietnam werken samen aan veilige Mekong Delta" [The Netherlands and Vietnam work together on a safe Mekon Delta]. Ministerie van Verker en Waterstaat, press release, October 5, 2009.

———. "Nederland leeft met water (no. 1)" [The Netherlands lives with water]. Ministerie van Verker en Waterstaat, press release, April 25, 2002.

———. "Nederland leeft met water (no. 2)" [The Netherlands lives with water]. Ministerie van Verker en Waterstaat, video, April 14, 2008.

———. "Nederland leeft met water (no. 3): Meer ruimte voor water noodzakelijk" ["The Netherlands lives with water": More space needed for water]. Ministerie van Verker en Waterstaat, press release, February 11, 2003.

———. "Start campagne Nederland leeft met Water: Nederland 'onder constructie'" [Campaign the Netherlands lives with Water begins: The Netherlands "under construction"]. Ministerie van Verker en Waterstaat, press release, April 20, 2009.

———. "Water in Beeld: Voortgangsrapportage over het waterbeheer in Nederland" [Water in pictures: Progress report on water management in the Netherlands]. Ministerie van Verker en Waterstaat, report, 2009.

———. "Waterwet leidt tot minder regels en minder lasten" [Water law leads to fewer rules and less bother]. Ministerie van Verker en Waterstaat, press release, December 22, 2009.

Verbaan, Willem. "Water is geen probleem maar een goudmijn" [Water is not a problem but rather a goldmine]. *Het Financieele Dagblad*, October 3, 2003.

Verbeek, Simon. "Ode aan het IJmeer" [Ode to IJ Lake]. Milieudefensie, 2009. Accessed January 6, 2010. https://www.milieudefensie.nl/weguitbreidingen/ijmeer/ode-aan-het-ijmeer.

Verkerk, Corrie. "Dromen van arcadische stad" [Dreams of an Arcadian city]. *Het Parool*, August 30, 1999: sec. Binnenland, 5.

———. "Koninginnedag is nu een zuipfeest voor provincialen" [Queen's Day is now a booze party for provincials]. *Het Parool*, April 30, 1998, 5.

Vermeulen, Fred. "Wethouder De Grave in de boot genomen" [Alderman De Grave fooled]. *Het Parool*, October 24, 1994: sec. Meningen, 7.

"Vijvers van Amsterdam propvol met nieuw leven" [Amsterdam ponds jam-packed with new life]. *Metro*, April 17, 2013. Accessed March 16, 2014. http://www.metronieuws.nl/regionaal/vijvers-van-amsterdam-propvol-met-nieuw-leven/SrZmdp!Rc4HfooynIAKc/.

Visser, Marlou. "Bewoners moeten wijken voor aanlegsteiger" [Residents must give way for landing stage]. *Het Parool*, May 6, 2009: sec. Amsterdam, 14.

Visser, Marlou, and Eva De Vos. "Vluchten voor de invasie der boeren" [Flee before the invasion of farmers]. *Het Parool*, April 30, 2009: sec. Amsterdam, 66.

Vork, Jacques. "De aantrekkingskracht van Amsterdam" [Amsterdam's gravitational force]. In Holland University of Applied Sciences, report, 2007. Accessed October 12, 2009. http://www.inholland.nl/NR/rdonlyres/B761C520-0A0A-43A1-8095-9FA3F6453DBC/0/DeaantrekkingskrachtvanAmsterdamnovember2007Print.pdf.

Vos, Art. *Nederland, een natte geschiedenis [The Netherlands, a wet history]*. Schiedam: Scriptum, 2006.

Vos, Carlijn. "Woonbootbewoner onvindbaar voor post" [Houseboat resident unfindable by mail service]. *De Volkskrant*, September 12, 2007: sec. Beurs, 8.

Vreeswijk, Elvira, Koos van Zanen, and Caroline Combe. "Stadskennis: Planologie Nieuwe Stijl" [Urban expertise: New-style planning]. *PlanAmsterdam*, Gemeente Amsterdam Dienst Ruimtelijke Ordening, no. 2, 2007.

"Vrij, onverveerd" [Free, fearless]. *Het Parool*, March 18, 1997: sec. Meningen, 7.

VROM. "Duurzaam bouwen en verbouwen" [Sustainable building and cultivation]. Ministerie van Volkshuisvesting, Ruimtelijke Ordening en Milieubeheer. Accessed May 17, 2010. http://www.vrom.nl/pagina.html?id=42908 (no longer accessible).

———. "Randstad 2040: Summary of the Structural Vision." Ministerie van Volkshuisvesting, Ruimtelijke Ordening en Milieubeheer, report, 2006.

Vugts, Paul. "Bloot bij Gay Pride 'functioneel'" [Nakedness in Gay Pride "functional"]. *Het Parool*, August 6, 1999: sec. Amsterdam, 2.

VVAB, "Waterplan: Water—het Blauwe Goud van Amsterdam" [Water Plan: Water, Amsterdam's Blue Gold]. Vereniging Vrienden van de Amsterdamse Binnenstad, 2001. Accessed July 12, 2009. http://www.sba2000.dds.nl/main6b.html.

———. "Welkom" [Welcome]. Vereniging Vrienden van de Amsterdamse Binnenstad, n.d., ca. 2007. Accessed November 18, 2009. http://www.amsterdamsebinnenstad.nl/.

"Waterbeheerders bundelen krachten" [Water managers bundle strength]. *Algemeen Nederlands Persbureau*, May 27, 2004: sec. Binnenland.

Water Natuurlijk. "Geef het landschap een stem" [Give the landscape a voice]. Promotional flyer, n.d., ca. 2010.

———. "Over water natuurlijk" [About Natural Water]. N.d., ca. 2010. Accessed April 18, 2010. http://www.waternatuurlijk.nl/.

Waternet. "Nota Grondwater Amsterdam" [Amsterdam groundwater memorandum]. Report, 2007.

Waterstudio. "Proeftuin: Het Nieuwe Water" [Laboratory: New water]. Waterstudio, n.d., ca. 2010. Accessed December 16, 2010. http://www.waterstudio.nl/en/198-new-water-waterkader-haaglanden.

"Waterwoningen naar IJburg" [Water houses to IJburg]. Gemeente Amsterdam Project-

bureau IJburg. Accessed December 16, 2010. http://www.ijburg.nl/main.php?obj_id=705526834 (no longer accessible).
Wedin, Mark. "Natural Punk." *Amsterdam Weekly*, July/August (2008): 7.
White, Richard. *The Organic Machine*. New York: Hill and Wang, 1995.
Wiegman, Marcel. "Centrum opent de jacht op" [City center begins search]. *Het Parool*, July 22, 2006: sec. Amsterdam, 6.
———. "Cohen redt de Gay Parade" [Cohen rescues Gay Parade]. *Het Parool*, June 15, 2005: sec. Voorpagina, 1.
———. "Een klein kwartiertje graven voor de fotograaf" [A small quarter-hour dig for the photograph]. *Het Parool*, March 1, 2002: sec. Amsterdam, 5.
———. "Homotrots" [Queer pride]. *Het Parool*, August 3, 2002, 16–21.
———. "'I amashamed' verwijst duidelijk naar 'I Amsterdam'" ['I amashamed' clearly refers to 'I amsterdam']. *Het Parool*, August 4, 2007: sec. Amsterdam, 6.
Williams, Raymond. *The Country and the City*. New York: Oxford University Press, 1975.
———. "Ideas of Nature." *Problems of Materialism and Culture: Selected Essays*, 67–85. New York: Verso, 1972.
Winichakul, Thongchai. *Siam Mapped: A History of the Geo-Body of a Nation*. Honolulu: University of Hawaii Press, 1997.
Winner, Langdon. *The Whale and the Reactor: A Search for Limits in an Age of High Technology*. Chicago: University of Chicago Press, 1986.
"Zit er nog een beetje leven in de Amsterdamse grachten?" [Is there still a little life in the Amsterdam canals?]. *Trouw*, May 1, 2006: sec. De Gids, 10.
"Zomercarnaval is veel bloter, echt waar" [Summer carnival is much more naked, it's true]. *De Volkskrant*, August 5, 2002: sec. Binnenland, 3.
"Zonder Gay Pride verdwijnt homoseksualiteit uit 't zicht" [Without Gay Pride queer sexuality disappears from sight]. *De Volkskrant*, August 19, 2000, 17.
Zonderop, Yvonne. "Help, mijn huis staat onder water" [Help, my house is under water]. *De Volkskrant*, February 12, 2007: sec. Binnenland, 6–7.
Zonneveld, Joost. Untitled article. *Het Parool*, April 3, 2010: sec. Specials, 8.
Zukin, Sharon. *Naked City: The Death and Life of Authentic Urban Places*. New York: Oxford University Press, 2010.

Index

accessibility, of urban water, 3–4, 5–7, 21, 81, 146
Almere, 121, 123, 124
Amstel River, 58, 66, 90
authenticity: cultural landscape, 47, 64, 85; houseboats, 38, 61, 72; reconstruction, 71–72, 119

big water, 94, 95, 97, 117, 121
brownfield, 1, 2, 9; limits of, 94; ports, 75, 81

canal belt, 63; flooding, 131; heritage movement, 55–56, 58–59, 63–64, 84; land ownership, 78; music festivals, 43; squatting, 20
Canal Festival, 37, 42–43, 47, 61
canal heritage recognition, 59, 62, 134
canal infill, 5, 64, 70, 94
canal reconstruction: in central city, 66–69; as heritage project, 62, 63–66; national context, 62; opposition to, 70–72; in postindustrial harbor, 83–84, 90–91
central city: counterculture, 17, 20–21, 24, 40–43; property ownership, 28, 78; Rokin, 66–67; urban renewal, 19–20, 21, 55. *See also* canal belt; gentrification
city ecologist, 104, 105, 108–9, 114
climate change, 118, 132; adaptation, 122, 128–30, 131, 132; urban development, 135–37
colonization, 80, 86–87; decolonization, 19
creative class, 79, 90, 92
cultural landscape, 7, 12–13, 36–37, 56, 141–42; human-environment connections, 98–102, 116
cultural movement, 2, 10–11, 38, 76, 141
cultural symbolism, 13, 47, 84, 92

deindustrialization, 1, 9, 24, 81
Department of Inland Waterway Management, 22, 39–40. *See also* regulatory authority
depoliticization, 13, 45–47, 118, 132–35, 141
de-reclamation, 119, 128–31, 132, 136; Biesbosch, 130; Blue City, 130; Waterstudio, 125, 130–31
Dura Vermeer, 122, 124, 130

Eastern Docklands, 76–77, 82–91; history, 80–82. *See also* port redevelopment
ecology, 95, 96; avian rookery, 101–2, 104–5; Dutch environmental thought, 98–99; preservation through development, 103–4, 112, 113; urban development, 99–100; water, 100, 112–13, 106–7, 108–10. *See also* political ecology
environment. *See* ecology; nature
EuroPride, 40–41, 44
everyday practice, 2–6, 140–47

floating architecture, 118, 122–26; floating city, 124–25; floating homes, 31–32, 123
floating events, 36, 37–38, 40–42; complaints, 28, 46, 49–50; co-optation, 36, 51–52
flood risks, 126, 127, 131, 134–35, 136–37
Friends of the Earth Netherlands, 103–4, 111

Gay Pride Parade, 37, 40–41, 45–46; regulations, 48–51
gentrification, 8–9; in central city, 27, 54, 68, 70–72; controversy about houseboats, 23, 26, 30, 33
golden age, 63–64, 70, 83–84, 93

hegemonic landscapes, 5, 7–8, 12, 140–43, 146–47

INDEX

heritage: counternarratives, 70–72; as economic driver, 54–56, 83; nautical, 76, 82–83, 86, 89; preservation movement, 56–59, 64, 82–83; preservation through development, 65, 83, 86. *See also* canal reconstruction

houseboats, 16–18, 25; building codes, 30–31, 33; classifications, 25, 33, 61; displacement and exclusion, 29, 61, 88; self-built, 24–26, 32, 33

housing affordability: in central city, 20, 24, 30, 84; housing shortage, 18–19; in neoliberal era, 76, 79, 92

identity, 42, 46–47, 60, 89; Amsterdam as water city, 2, 47, 60, 64, 134. *See also* heritage

IJburg, 76, 95–100, 108, 113–14; floating homes, 123, 124; influence on urban growth, 109–10, 112, 113–15, 121; nature development, 105–7, 108–12, 125; referendum, 103–4

IJssel Lake District, 101–3; IJ Lake, 95, 101, 103, 105, 110–11

industrial urban form, 3–4, 58, 64, 70, 80–81

Jordaan, 56, 67–71

mayor, 19, 25, 41, 50–51, 134
Ministry of Education and Culture, 83
Ministry of Housing, Spatial Planning, and the Environment, 120–21
Ministry of Transport, Public Works, and Water Management, 112, 118, 126, 128–30, 133–34
mobilization: cultural, 7, 14, 139–40; landscape, 47, 146–47. *See also* selective mobilization

nature, 4, 90, 99, 121, 136; consciousness, 95–100, 102–3, 107; IJburg nature development, 105–7, 108–12, 125; makeable, 105–6, 108–10, 112–13; reconstruction, 114–15, 130. *See also* ecology

Nature Monuments, 103–4, 112–13
new social movements, 17–18, 20, 39

physical planning department: economic development, 79; environmental movement, 99–100, 103–4, 108, 114; heritage preservation, 84–86; houseboats, 21–22, 30–31; public open space, 22, 39, 46

pleasure boats, 42, 50, 52; conflict with houseboats, 27–28, 29; as national hobby, 42, 46, 47; restrictions, 66, 70, 83, 114

political ecology, 11, 144; assemblages, 3, 12–13, 96–97, 138–40, 146; material agency, 10–11, 96, 145

port activity, 19, 80, 81

port redevelopment: Amsterdam, 76, 82–83; international context, 4–5, 7, 9–10, 74

postindustrial waterfront redevelopment, 5, 35, 56, 91–92, 94. *See also* port redevelopment

profit imperatives: disaster capitalism, 104, 118, 132; festivals, 51, 53; heritage, 65, 83, 96; houseboats, 32, 36; shoreline redevelopment 4, 9. *See also* gentrification

protected cityscape, 59, 60–61, 72

provisional use, 1, 5–7, 10, 142–43. *See also* regulatory authority

public space, 27; de facto, 35, 36–37, 52–53; regulations, 21, 22–23, 39–40, 50–51, 53; shorelines, 38–39, 42, 97

Queen's Day, 37, 42, 46; regulations, 50–51, 114

real estate: cultural explanations, 8–10, 146; limits on development, 4–6; market liberalization, 77, 79–80, 81; waterfront development as economic driver, 29, 74–75, 90, 120–21, 135–37; waterfront premiums, 71, 76, 78–79, 90–91, 108. *See also* gentrification

regulations, environmental, 102, 110–11, 121–22, 125

regulatory authority: land versus water, 21–22, 26, 33, 39–40; loopholes and exceptions, 17, 24–26, 33

regulatory frameworks, 21, 28

regulatory reform: houseboats, 29, 30–31; public space, 48–53

rent gap, 1–2, 8–10; in Amsterdam, 36, 55, 76, 92

Rotterdam, 19, 81, 125

selective mobilization, 141–45; heritage, 55, 66, 70, 97; real estate development, 8–9, 13

spectacle, 35–39, 41, 85, 112
squatting movement, 16, 20, 25, 26, 83
squatting skippers, 16–17, 20, 21–24

technology, 5–6, 97, 122, 124, 126–28
territories of profit, 17, 32, 142
tourism: canal festivals, 43, 47; canal reconstruction, 65, 69, 71; central city canals, 2; houseboats, 23, 27, 28, 33; nature, 98–99, 107, 113; port redevelopment, 75, 84–85, 88; queer, 40–41; water theme years, 51

UNESCO, 55, 59, 62
United Friends of the Amsterdam Inner City: canal reconstruction, 57, 60–65, 67–70, 72; houseboats, 61–62

urban renewal, 19–20, 21, 55
Urban Ring, 118, 120, 126, 131, 135; nature, 111
Utrecht, 62, 68, 124

water: national identity symbol, 35–36, 47, 53, 85, 133–34; reflectivity, 61–62; romance, 23–26, 31–33, 85, 123, 137; stage, 44–45, 47; transportation space, 22, 39–40, 68; vista, 80, 88, 91
waterfront redevelopment, 1–4, 13, 139. *See also* postindustrial waterfront redevelopment

zoning. *See* regulatory authority; regulatory frameworks; regulatory reform